The Theatre of Friedrich Dürrenmatt

A Study in the Possibility of Freedom

by

KENNETH S. WHITTON

OSWALD WOLFF
London

HUMANITIES PRESS
New Jersey

Published by
Oswald Wolff (Publishers) Ltd., London
and
Humanities Press Inc., Atlantic Highlands, N.J.

British Library Cataloguing in Publication Data

Whitton, Kenneth Stuart
    The theatre of Friedrich Dürrenmatt.
    1. Dürrenmatt, Friedrich — Criticism and
    Interpretation.
    I. Title
    832'.9'14   PT2607.U4932/   79-90271
    ISBN UK 0-85496-072-4
        US 0-391-01694-6

Set by Reproproof Ltd., 7 Soho Square, London W1M 5DD
Reproduced from copy supplied
printed and bound in Great Britain
by Billing and Sons Limited
Guildford, London, Oxford, Worcester

for

MARJORY, KIRSTY and KENNETH

CONTENTS

Acknowledgements

I should like to express my gratitude, firstly, to the many colleagues in Britain and abroad who have allowed me to discuss my work on Dürrenmatt with them. They will recognize their contributions in the following pages, I am certain.

The Librarians and staff of the following establishments are due my sincere thanks for tracing out-of-the-way material for me:

The University of Bradford

The University of Leeds

The University of Berne

The University of Hamburg (Germanistisches Seminar)

The Schweizerische Landesbibliothek, Bern

Herr Peter Schifferli and the Verlag der Arche, Zürich

Theaterverlag Reiss, Basel.

I am beholden to Dr Paul Stauffer and Dr Birrer, formerly of the Swiss Embassy in London, and to Dr Peter Zeindler of the Stiftung Pro Helvetia in Zürich, for the organization of my meeting with Friedrich Dürrenmatt, and I should like to thank the author for his generous hospitality and stimulating conversation.

My thanks are due also to Professor H. Morgan Waidson of the University College of Swansea for his kind interest in, and help with my work, and to Mr Geoffrey Axworthy of the Sherman Theatre, University College of Swansea and the Welsh Arts Council. *German Life and Letters, Forum for Modern Language Studies* and *New German Studies*, through their editors, have kindly allowed me to use material which first appeared in their pages.

I owe a long-standing debt of gratitude to three gentlemen without whose encouragement I should never have been in a position to write this book: Professor Walter Bruford of the Universities of Edinburgh and Cambridge, the late Professor Eudo Mason of the University of Edinburgh, my first "Doktorvater", and the late Dr Hans Eggeling of the University of Edinburgh who first opened up to me the worlds of German literature and *Lieder*.

Finally, I must thank Mrs Ilse Wolff for her enthusiastic encouragement and, as always, my wife, "dass sie da war".

Kenneth S. Whitton
Leeds
1979

Foreword

To want to be an author nowadays means
banging one's head against a brick wall.
Ladies and gentlemen, I love doing that,
and it is my opinion that brick walls were
invented for that very purpose.

Finger Exercises for the present Day (1952)

This study of Friedrich Dürrenmatt attempts to put the author firmly in the framework of the comic tradition in the theatre. Its purpose is to remind readers that Dürrenmatt is, above all, a man of the theatre who always writes with the possibilities of the theatre in mind and who uses comic techniques and devices that have stood the test of time.

At the same time, the study will attempt to show that Dürrenmatt uses this comic tradition to castigate those ills of modern society that offend him, and that his *Komödie*, light-hearted and even trivial though it may sometimes appear, is meant to realize that possibility "to which I cling" — the possibility that the individual will gain his freedom from those that oppress him.

Kenneth S. Whitton

Chapter One

DÜRRENMATT AND SWITZERLAND

There would be a good deal of justification for the claim that Friedrich Dürrenmatt is the best-known of the dramatists at present writing in the German language. It would also be true to say that, by dint of the extent of his dramatic output and the importance of his critical writings on the theatre, he now holds the place once occupied by Bertolt Brecht (1898-1956), although the latter's plays still receive more performances on German and foreign stages than those of any other German-speaking dramatist.

Like his predecessor Brecht, Dürrenmatt has never been found "easy", either by audiences or by critics. Where Brecht was termed an "annoyance" ("ein Ärgernis"), Dürrenmatt has been called "uncomfortable ("unbequem").[1] It is true that many of Dürrenmatt's sternest critics are to be found in his native Switzerland, but much the greater burden of anti-Dürrenmatt criticism emanates from West Germany, or from Germans living abroad. Where, in the case of Brecht, critical attacks were directed mainly against his ideological left-wing convictions and their expression in his new "epic theatre", in Dürrenmatt's case they are directed as often as not against the lack of seriousness or "profundity", or against the prevalence of stylistic gaffes in his writings. Dürrenmatt parries all attacks with good humour — or with coruscating wit. He writes: "The obstinate idea, mainly from Germans, that the message is all-important has already bedevilled the performance of many plays in the theatre".[2] *

To be taken seriously is one thing, he maintains; to be taken *deadly* seriously, quite another. It is for this reason that Dürrenmatt, like Brecht before him, detests the label "Dichter" (poet) — he is no "poet-writer", but rather a down-to-earth "Stückeschreiber" (a playwright), a "Theatermann", (a man of the theatre). (In the Foreword to his 1971 play *Portrait of a Planet*, he is still telling us that, for him, the stage is a

---

*Since some of the published translations of Dürrenmatt's plays are incomplete "acting versions" and others are not quite accurate, I have elected to use my own translations throughout this study (KSW).

"theatrical medium", not a "literary podium"). Any study of the writer
which fails to stress that point is bound to present a false image.
Although Dürrenmatt would lay no claim to being a "professional"
philosopher, philosophy has always attracted him and he told Heinz
Ludwig Arnold in March 1975 that he was once again very interested
in philosophical problems.[3] He certainly vehemently rejects any suggestion that his works lack intellectual substance: "It is against my
principles," he once wrote, "to write plays for blockheads".

Dürrenmatt's battles with West German critics remind us continually
to bear in mind that he is Swiss. It is not always realized in other
countries that a child in German-speaking Switzerland will speak his
own local dialect (his form of "Schwyzerdütsch", Swiss German), until
he goes to school where he will begin the study of his first "foreign"
language, "Hochdeutsch" (High German), the language of educated
Germans. Some Germans, of course, will try to make the point that a
Swiss is thus speaking or writing a foreign language, which allows them
to criticize the Swiss author's stylistic peculiarities.

Friedrich Dürrenmatt was born in the Emmental village of Konolfingen on 5 January, 1921. Konolfingen lies in the canton of Berne, not
far from the Swiss Federal capital, Berne, and on the road to the Bernese
Oberland. Dürrenmatt remembers the village as "ugly", but as a place
to which he still feels attracted. The Dürrenmatts (the name means
"through the meadow", he told me) came from this predominantly
agricultural environment. Friedrich was born after twelve years of
childlessness to a Protestant parson, Reinhold, and his wife Hulda
(née Zimmermann), just after they had adopted a little girl. (Their own
daughter, Vroni, was born three years later.)

The father occupied the manse in Konolfingen from 1921 to 1934,
when the family moved to the Salemspital in Berne where young
"Fritz" attended the Grammar School till 1941. Dürrenmatt's descriptions of his isolated childhood betray a sense of unhappiness and some
frustration. He obviously disliked formal education and strict parental
discipline and found an outlet for his imagination not only in a study of
the stars and planets, references to which abound in his later works, but
also in sketching and painting which, he told Dieter Fringeli in 1977, is
still his "greatest and most intensive experience", one for which, he
often thinks, he would gladly give up writing.[4] Interestingly enough, in
view of some of the themes of his plays, he says that he enjoyed drawing scenes of catastrophes most of all!

Although it would be quite wrong to underestimate the strongly
religious content of Dürrenmatt's early works and to deny the influence
of the Calvinist teachings of his father, the writer's later development,

his constant battles with "Authority" and the overtly political nature of his later works seem to me to point to a much more powerful influence on the boy — that of his grandfather, Ulrich Dürrenmatt (1849-1908). In his essay *Vom Anfang her (From the Beginning*, 1957), Dürrenmatt freely admits that he learned from his grandfather's career that "writing can be a way of doing battle . . ."

The grandfather lived through that period of religious and political strife known as the "Kulturkampf" (the struggle between State and Church). The modern political battles, radicals versus conservatives, were merged with age-old religious hatreds, Catholics against Protestants. From the 1870's on, Ulrich Dürrenmatt fought the "system" of the radical parties, firstly as a writer of occasional satirical verse, then as the polemical editor of the *Berner Volkszeitung* (from 1882), and finally as a politician and member of the Swiss National Council (Nationalrat) from 1902.

Ulrich Dürrenmatt claimed that he took over the editorship of the *BVZ*, "so that no one would be able to frighten him or deflect him in his battle against a rotten radical system". For twenty years or more, each number of the paper began with a biting satirical poem (the grandson still knows many of these by heart), directed against what he believed to be the ills of the day. Howald, Ulrich's biographer, listed a few of his aversions. ". . . illicitly-gained doctorates, pompous dignitaries, swollen clichés, vain sabre-rattling, hypocritical speeches, backstairs diplomacy and trickery . . . foreign fashions and the cult of nudity . . .", and behind these attacks, Howald adds, was the desire to *educate*.[5] This very Swiss didacticism reappears constantly in the grandson's work. Like his grandson, "Ueli" Dürrenmatt was, and remained, an outsider; he attacked evils and ills wherever he saw them and was frightened of and by no one.

Such peasant aggressiveness and political awareness has remained a feature of the Dürrenmatt clan; Ueli's son was a member of the Berne Council, while his son, Peter, became Chief Editor of the *Berner Nachrichten*. Friedrich Dürrenmatt himself distrusts organized political parties and mass referenda, yet one cannot deny the political content of many of his plays, and his ownership of the Zürich *Sonntags Journal* for a time from 1969 enabled him to enter the lists of political and cultural debates at will.

Like his grandfather before him, Dürrenmatt has remained a countryman at heart. He has a strong sense of "belonging" to his origins, both human and geographical; his slow, heavily-accentuated Bernese speech and his equally slow physical movements, exaggerated in his case by his not inconsiderable bulk, betray these rural origins.[6] (Although he has suffered grievously from diabetes for the last 25 years, he is a connoisseur and an unashamed lover of good food and wine to which a vast wine-cellar bears visible witness. These sensual pleasures spill over into many of his works, as will be seen). Yet slow physical movements do not necessarily denote slow mental processes; indeed, Dürrenmatt's outstanding characteristic as a conversationalist, a public speaker and a writer of stage dialogue, is the speed of his witty repartee.

Professor Elisabeth Brock-Sulzer, a friend, and author of books on Dürrenmatt, has described him most accurately:

> . . . he is heavy and quick at the same time. Heavy masses can general-
> ly be moved only but slowly. In Dürrenmatt's case, however, they
> move as quickly as lighter objects. That makes his art dangerous for
> him and for us. Its energy is more difficult to control; its impact is
> more severe. Peasant energy is united here with the quickness of the
> intellectual — and not always amicably. The intellectual in him often
> wants to impress the peasant, and the peasant in him takes revenge
> later on the intellectual. Where, however, they come together in
> agreement, something very special is created, something very Swiss.[7]

★   ★   ★

Since I agree with the Swiss critic, Hans Bänziger, who maintains of both Dürrenmatt and his older Swiss colleague, Max Frisch, that "their work is firmly anchored in their Swiss-ness",[8] we might now briefly consider the position of Switzerland in the post-war world to establish the background against which both writers were working.

Fritz Ernst's book *Helvetia Mediatrix* (Zürich, 1945 edition) gives a very typical view of traditional Switzerland, the "natural bulwark of neutrality", as Ranke had called it; a country famed for its milk and chocolate, its alpenhorns and ski-pistes, the home of "democracy". It was Orson Welles, however, in the rôle of the black marketeer, Harry Lime, in Carol Reed's celebrated post-war film *The Third Man*, who succinctly summed up a cynical, more modern (and, incidentally, inaccurate!) view of democracy when he said to Holly Martin: "Demo- cracy? Switzerland has had 500 years of democracy and peace — and what did that produce? The cuckoo clock!"

For this idyllic country has known disharmony. Not all of its famous citizens or writers have been content with the Swiss way of life. The dissonances noted in the lives of writers as diverse as Albrecht Haller (1708-1777), Gottfried Keller (1819-1890) or Conrad Ferdinand Meyer

(1825-1898), were often either overlooked or explained away. Such underlying dissonances, dissatisfaction with the physical smallness of the country, with the solid bourgeois parochialism of many of its inhabitants and with the unworthy status accorded the writer, drove many creative spirits abroad. Haller, Rousseau, Keller, Meyer, Carl Spitteler and Robert Walser all lived for some time away from Switzerland, perhaps because of what the French-Swiss writer, C.F. Ramuz, called "le besoin de grandeur". (Dürrenmatt has given his own view, of course. He wrote that "the artists in Switzerland are still regarded as dubious characters, unfitted for Life and in constant need of handouts".)[9]

These dissonances and dissatisfactions became even more apparent after 1945 when, with the advent of the Cold War, Switzerland took fright at the "reds under the beds" and had to abandon its traditional neutral rôle as the "Guardian of the Middle Way" ("Hüter der Mitte") and align itself with the West against the threat of a Communist invasion. The resultant anti-Communist movement aroused discontent among the younger generation generally and the artistic colony in particular, Professor J.R. von Salis wrote in the troubled "year of revolts", 1968, about the young Swiss then: "Our young people no longer want to know. They are rebelling against tradition, against bourgeois morality, against conventional dress, against our conforming society".[10] These were perhaps conventional remarks to make about the youth of large western cities — but they certainly did not conform to the average foreigner's idea of the youth of idyllic Switzerland, of Davos, Wengen and St Moritz. Yet a visit to Zürich's Niederdorf district or Berne's Gerechtigkeitsgasse would confirm the existence of what Max Wehrli has called the "Swiss malaise", expressed at one time in the highest suicide rate and the most wide-spread juvenile delinquency figures in Western Europe, as well as in the concern of the Swiss Federal Council about the excessive number of divorces in their land.[11]

It was their peculiar ability to put into words what many of the younger generation were feeling and thinking after 1945 that gave Dürrenmatt and Max Frisch (born 1911) their acknowledged status as leaders of the Swiss literary community and, indeed, of the German-speaking literary world. Although they are often bracketed together (like Goethe and Schiller), I agree with Frau Brock-Sulzer when she writes that the "similarity is very small when compared with the differences". The fact that both writers belong to a nation not hitherto distinguished for producing internationally-known literary figures was probably as much responsible for this pairing as was the title of Hans Bänziger's book *Frisch und Dürrenmatt* (see *Note* 8).

There is indeed a world of difference between the two men; Frisch is ten years older than Dürrenmatt, had a pre-war literary career and experienced the Second World War as an adult. His excellent *Tagebuch 1946-1949 (Diary 1946-1949)* is superlative source material for Switzerland's attitude to the war. Secondly, Frisch hails from urban Zürich, Dürrenmatt from the rural Emmental. Thirdly, Frisch is a qualified architect, distinguished enough to have designed Zürich's open-air swimming-pool in the Letzigraben (1947-1949), whereas Dürrenmatt has had no profession other than that of writer. Fourthly, Frisch is a much-travelled "jet-age" writer, as much at home in New York as in Zürich who, at one stage indeed, went to live in Rome. Dürrenmatt seems to me to be unhappy outside Switzerland, and his only concession to increasing affluence has been to move from Berne to his present twin-house domicile high above the Bielersee in Neuchâtel in French-speaking Switzerland (which, however, he likes to call by its German name of Neuenburg!).

Add to these factors Dürrenmatt's pre-eminence as a dramatist and Frisch's as a novelist, and it will be seen that the similarities are indeed small compared with the differences, and that they really have only their "Swiss-ness" in common.

Therese Giehse, the veteran German actress who was, as will be seen, one of the artistic links binding Dürrenmatt to Brecht, once said of them: "In Germany, Frisch is thought of as a German, Dürrenmatt as a Swiss", to which Dürrenmatt added: "Frisch is more attractive to Germans than I am".[12] It is certainly true that Dürrenmatt's earliest artistic roots are buried deep in the soil of Swiss, rather than German, theatrical tradition. The Swiss "Laientheater" (amateur theatres), presenting plays in "Schwyzerdütsch", on the one hand, and the earthy folk-bound cabaret tradition, on the other, both claimed Dürrenmatt's early allegiance.

It is often overlooked that the zany "Dada" movement was born in bourgeois Switzerland. It was in the Cabaret Voltaire in No.1 Spiegelgasse (opposite the house occupied by the revolutionary Lenin) in Zürich in 1916 that Tristan Tzara, Hugo Ball, Richard Huelsenbeck and Hans (or Jean) Arp gave birth to that seminal movement which Martin Esslin among others sees as the *fons et origo* of the modern "Theatre of the Absurd". We know that "Dadaism" (the arbitrarily-chosen term derives from the French "le dada", a child's word for a hobby-horse) can trace its origins back to the "mimus" of classical antiquity — and I shall be showing Dürrenmatt's own links with the classical tradition shortly.

The cabaret tradition, strongly satirical and indeed destructive, since the aim of Dadaism was the destruction of the conventional art-forms of the bourgeois which (in their opinion) were indicative of the attitude of mind which had produced the horrors of the First World War, re-appeared in the Cabaret Cornichon in the immediate pre-1939 period in Zürich. (In 1948, Dürrenmatt was engaged by the Cabaret to write three sketches and a song for a monthly honorarium of 500 francs. These sketches bear the hallmarks of his future comic style: in one, a professor enters a party carrying a miniature atom-bomb. The "fate of the world" lies literally in his hands – but the bomb ends up in a lady's generous *décoletté*. The song he wrote told of the cleansing of the dung of Noah's Ark.) Dürrenmatt eventually found the ephemeral nature of the work too undemanding, but the experience gained with the Cabaret was greatly to influence his later dramatic technique, as will be seen.

★   ★   ★

When the Second World War ended, Dürrenmatt was twenty-four. According to his *Monstervortrag über Gerechtigkeit und Recht* (*Gigantic Lecture on Justice and the Law*) (1969), ten Semester (i.e. five years) of desultory literary and philosophical studies at the Universities of Berne and Zürich lay behind him (p.9). He had read Aristophanes, Kierkegaard and many of the famous German Expressionists such as Trakl and Heym. He had begun to write. There is an as yet unpublished play, entitled simply *Komödie*, written in 1943 with a chapter dedicated to Kafka, and some Kafkaesque short stories, now collected in the 1952 volume *Die Stadt* (The City).[13]

Hans Mayer claims that Dürrenmatt knew that he would make nothing of his university studies, which is why he abandoned them. Dürrenmatt told me that he wanted to marry Lotti Geissler, a stage and film actress – which he did at the end of 1946. Frau Dürrenmatt recalls that she tried to persuade him not to give up his studies. She also recalls how horrified she was at their first meeting in Berne when Dürrenmatt tried to amuse her by relating one of his short stories called "The Sausage". A man had murdered his wife, butchered her, made up sausages from the remains and sold them. During the subsequent trial, one of the sausages lay on a plate in front of the President of the Court – who absent-mindedly consumed the "evidence". Lotti told her brother not to bother bringing this bloodthirsty young writer back to their room – but the pair were soon on the bus to the Berne Registry Office to get married. But even here, Dürrenmatt managed to be unconventional, leaping off the bus to go back for the wedding ring.[14]

The Dürrenmatts lived in penury in one room of an 18-roomed schoolhouse. Frau Dürrenmatt tells how her husband decorated the walls "with grotesque pictures". Had he not become a successful dramatist, he could certainly have made a good living at that time as a cartoonist, since he continues to draw in the same sharp satirical style as his friends, the Britisher Ronald Searle, and the German Flora of *Die Zeit*. So, there is something of the intellectual *manqué* mixed with the buffoon in the Dürrenmatt make-up; he certainly had had the intention of writing a doctoral dissertation on *Kierkegaard and the Tragic*, and we shall see that his interest in the Danish philosopher of *Angst* has never waned.

But Dürrenmatt had finished his first play *Es steht geschrieben* (*It is written*) in March 1946, and a chance meeting with the Zürich actor-manager, Kurt Horwitz, was to change his life and family fortune. Horwitz had read the manuscript with great enthusiasm and persuaded Oskar Wälterlin and Kurt Hirschfeld to put the play on in the celebrated Zürich Schauspielhaus on 19 April, 1947.

The story of Dürrenmatt's *succès de scandale* will be related later; suffice here to report that it made Dürrenmatt's name as a playwright who could be relied upon to shock, scandalize and provoke his audiences. Twenty-three years later enraged audiences were still shouting "Down with Dürrenmatt!" as they watched his version of *Titus Andronicus*. We shall see that it took Dürrenmatt some time to realize where his artistic potential lay, but when he did discover that he possessed that rare talent to make people laugh in the theatre, he began to examine the nature of comedy and the comic in the twentieth century. Here the intellectual *manqué* and the didactic joined hands; a stream of theoretical writings issued forth, some of which have been accepted as authoritative statements on the theatre of our times. No Dürrenmatt play now appears without its *Anmerkungen* (Notes) or suggestions for performance. The author has spoken and written at length on his attitude to theatre, to the comic and tragic modes and to many other cultural and political phenomena of our age, and these comments will be discussed as we follow his career throughout this study.[15]

★   ★   ★

Dürrenmatt's attitude towards the world and his fellow-men could rightly be termed "Aristophanic". Like the fifth-century Greek writer, the Swiss playwright sees his world through the distorting mirror of the comic. Like Aristophanes, Dürrenmatt seeks to "distance" his audiences by his use of satire, parody, irony and grotesque obscenities. It is surely no coincidence, nor can it be without significance, that Dürrenmatt has chosen to call most of his stage-works *Komödien*.[16] Comedy is realistic, it is interested more in men than in ideas, it concerns itself with the weaknesses and foibles of Man rather than with his strengths and idealisms. Above all, it is didactic; like Dürrenmatt's grandfather, Ueli, "it wants to educate". I believe that this is how Dürrenmatt should be studied; not (as some have chosen to do) as a Calvinistic "philosopher" primarily concerned with theological problems of "Grace", but rather as a practical man of the theatre striving to inculcate in his audiences a critical approach to the theatre in particular, but also to Art in general. Like Brecht, Dürrenmatt wants a theatre which asks questions rather than one which attempts to provide answers. Dürrenmatt's later appointments to practical posts at the theatres of Basel and Zürich prove the point, I believe. His plays are written for production, not for the scholar's study.[17] For this reason, they exist like Brecht's *Versuche* (Experiments) in many different versions. If scholars want a "definitive" version, then, as Dürrenmatt remarked to me with a chuckle, "they'll have to wait until I am dead".

Although Dürrenmatt knows better than most that the theatre cannot "change the world", there is nevertheless something very Swiss in the didactic nature of his work. He writes to teach as well as to entertain — but he wants his theatre to remain *theatre*, not a theoretical dissertation. "The theatre cannot be anything else but theatre", he writes. "That it is aware of this fact makes it a critical theatre". In his *Anatomy of Satire* (Princeton 1962), Gilbert Highet called Aristophanes a "moral and political reformer" and quoted Werner Jaeger's remark that Aristophanes' plays were "critics of culture with a strong educational mission" (p.27). Could the same not be said of Friedrich Dürrenmatt, whom Siegfried Melchinger has called the "Helvetic Aristophanes"?

NOTES TO CHAPTER ONE

1. See *Das Ärgernis Brecht* (edited by Willi Jäggi and Hans Oesch), Basilius Press, Basel and Stuttgart, 1959, and *Der unbequeme Dürrenmatt* (edited R. Grimm, W. Jäggi and H. Oesch), Basilius Press, Basel and Stuttgart, 1962. See too the report of his face-to-face encounter with his critics at Stuttgart's treffpunkt foyer on 16.4.71: *Den Uranarchisten ertragen* (Stuttgarter Abendblatt, 19.4.71).
2. In *Standortbestimmung zu Frank V* (*Locational Guide to Frank V*) in *Theaterschriften und Reden*, q.v. pp.184-189, here p.187.

3. In *Gespräch mit Heinz Ludwig Arnold*, Arche Verlag, Zürich, 1976 (= *GHLA*)
   pp. 19-20. He certainly "philosophizes" in a Kierkegaardian manner in the
   Epilogue to the Epilogue in his commentary on his play *Der Mitmacher (The
   Man who never said: No!)* (1973). See *Der Mitmacher: Ein Komplex*, Arche
   1976 (= *DMMK*), particularly pp. 193-198. See too his autobiographical
   sketch *Dokument* in *Theater-Schriften und Reden*, pp. 30-37, and my
   article on my conversations with him in his home at Neuchâtel: *An afternoon conversation with an uncomfortable person*, New German Studies,
   Vol.II, No. 1, Spring 1974, pp. 14-30.
4. D. Fringeli: *Nachdenken mit und über Friedrich Dürrenmatt* (Reflections
   with and on Friedrich Dürrenmatt), Verlag Jeger-Moll, Breitenbach-Schweiz,
   September 1977. The pages are unnumbered. I shall refer later to the scurrilous cartoons drawn for his three children: *Die Heimat im Plakat: Ein Buch
   für Schweizer Kinder (The Homeland in Posters: A Book for Swiss Children)*
   Diogenes, Zürich 1963 and to his illustrations to his own works, particularly
   to *Hercules and the Augean Stables*, 1963.
5. J. Howald: *Ulrich Dürrenmatt und seine Gedichte*, Loepthien Verlag, Meiringen, 1927. 2 Vols, here Vol.1., p.237.
6. His Bernese accent can be heard perhaps to best advantage on the DGG
   recording of his radio play *Herkules und der Stall des Augias (Hercules and
   the Augean Stables)*, DGG No.43013, 1957.
7. In E. Brock-Sulzer's review of *Ein Engel kommt nach Babylon (An Angel
   comes to Babylon)* in Die Tat, 2.2.65. See too Dürrenmatt's self-portrait in
   his short story *Der Tunnel (The Tunnel)* in the volume *Die Stadt (The City)*,
   Arche 1952, pp.165-183. It is of a fat, 24-year-old student travelling to the
   University of Zürich where he is "occupied with nebulous studies". Jan
   Knopf writes that Dürrenmatt's first publication was a story *Der Alte (The
   Old Man)* in the Berner Tageszeitung of 25.3.45. (J. Knopf: *Friedrich Dürrenmatt*), Autorenbücher, München, 1976, pp.15-16.
8. H. Bänziger: *Frisch und Dürrenmatt*, Francke Verlag, Bern-München, 1960
   (7th edn. 1976), p.11.
9. In *Schriftsteller als Beruf (Writing as a profession)*, revised 1965 in *Theater-
   Schriften und Reden*, pp.50-55, here p.51. See too Paul Nizon's *Diskussion
   in der Enge: Aufsätze zur Schweizer Kunst (Discussion in Narrowness)*, Bern
   1970 ("Swiss art history is a tragic history").
10. J.R. von Salis: *Die Unrast der Jugend und die Zukunft einer menschlichen
    Gesellschaft (The unrest of our young people and the future of a human
    society)* in *Schwierige Schweiz*, Orell Füssli Verlag, Zürich 1968, pp.288-313
    here p.288. See too the translations of some of Professor von Salis' writings
    in *Switzerland and Europe*, Oswald Wolff, London, 1971.
11. See H.F. Garten: *Dürrenmatt's Tragic Comedies*, Drama, Spring 1971,
    pp.30-33, and W.Sorell: *The Swiss*, Oswald Wolff, London, 1972, particular-
    ly pp.265-280. Also K.Marti: *Die Schweiz und ihre Schriftsteller – die
    Schriftsteller und ihre Schweiz (Switzerland and its writers – the writers
    and their Switzerland)* EVZ Verlag, Zürich 1966.
12. In P. Wyrsch: *Die Dürrenmatt-Story* in the periodical *Schweizer Illustrierte*.
    The quotation is from the second of five articles, on 25.3.63, pp.23-25. The
    others appeared on March 18, April 1, 7, 15 and 22. Although the style
    tends more to the journalistic than the scholarly, these articles are neverthe-
    less valuable source material for the early part of Dürrenmatt's life and career.
13. There has been much scholarly debate on the Kafkaesque provenance of
    these stories, but Dürrenmatt told me (and repeated himself to Fringeli
    in 1977) that he read Kafka only much later. He said that the source was
    Plato's "caves" rather than Kafka. Timo Tiusanen in his *Dürrenmatt: A
    Study in Plays, Prose, Theory* (Princeton 1977) states that Dürrenmatt began
    as a "heavyweight Kafkaist", not as a realist. This seems more than a little
    exaggerated. (See p.34).

14. The story reminds us of Dürrenmatt's abiding interest in grotesque fantasies (cf. *GHLA* p.15) and of its reappearance in his treatment of Shakespeare's *Titus Andronicus* (1970). It is now in *Lesebuch* (Arche 1978) pp. 21-23.

15. The most important of these have been collected in *Theater-Schriften und Reden* (*Writings and Speeches on the Theatre*), Arche Verlag, Zürich: Vol. I (1966), Vol. II (*Dramaturgisches und Kritisches*) (1972). I shall refer to them as *TSR1* and *TSR2*. See too *Friedrich Dürrenmatt: Writings on Theatre and Drama*, translated by H.M. Waidson, Cape 1976, a selection from the above.

16. These are now gathered in three volumes: *Komödien I* (1957) (7th edn. 1965) (= *KI*); *Komödien II and Frühe Stücke* (1964) (= *KII*) and *Komödien III* (1972) (= *KIII*) all published by Arche Verlag, Zürich. Peter Schifferli, the owner of the Arche Verlag has often expressed his gratitude to "Dürri" for making his firm famous.

17. He has stressed this throughout his career, latterly in his "fragment" *Aspekte des dramaturgischen Denkens* (*Aspects of dramaturgical thinking*): "The dramatist has no longer absolute command of his material. He is limited by the stage". (in *TSR* 2, pp.206-231, here p.208.)

Chapter Two

THE KOMÖDIE

(i) THE MEANING OF *KOMÖDIE*

Since, as we have already noted, the three volumes of Dürrenmatt's collected plays are titled *Komödien I, II and III,* and 12 of his seventeen stage-works (including his latest work *Die Frist*, (*The Waiting Period*), of 1977) bear the sub-title *Komödie*, of one sort or another, it is worthwhile considering what the term *Komödie* has come to mean in German literature.

The *Reallexikon der deutschen Literatur* in its 1958 article on the native German term for "comedy", *Lustspiel*, asserted:

> Nowadays, the term *Lustspiel* covers the most hilarious extemporized pieces as well as those serious plays, overcast with tragedy, where often only the end is happy. For a general overall term, it is more practicable to employ the word *Lustspiel* as being synonymous with the foreign word *Komödie*.

Yet the authors, as will be seen, change their ground later.[1]

It would seem, moreover, that what Professor Walter Bruford called the "didactic and realistic" trait in German literature has been responsible for the fact that German Literature has for long been able to muster only three genuine "comedies": Lessing's *Minna von Barnhelm* (1767), Kleist's *Der zerbrochene Krug* (1808) and Grillparzer's *Weh' dem, der lügt* (1838). (Dürrenmatt himself refers to the "old myth . . . that there are only three comedies (*Lustspiele*) in German".)[2]

Many reasons might be advanced to account for this fact: Germany's turbulent and unhappy political history, the many tragic invasions of her territory, perhaps even the clichéd "Teutonic earnestness". Yet, if German literature lacks the "social comedy" so familiar in France, it does not lack the type of comedy which the early nineteenth-century German Romantic Novalis had in mind when he wrote: "Only *Komödien* can be written after a war has been lost"; it is not uninteresting that misquoters of the German original: "Nach einem verlorenen Krieg müssen Komödien geschrieben werden", often write *Lustspiele* for *Komödien. Is* there a difference?[3]

A.W. Schlegel broached the problem in his famous Vienna lectures in 1801 when he was describing the "New Comedy" which arose in Greece ·after Athens had lost her political independence with the defeat by the Macedonians in Chaeronea in 338 BC. The "New Comedy" of Menander (342-291 BC) with its emphasis on love, intrigue and marriage and its introduction of "comic types" became the model for the Latin comedies of Plautus and Terence, and, with Terence's "re-emergence" in the Renaissance, for most European "social comedies".

Schlegel (in Lectures XI - XIII) spoke of this "New Comedy", "which we may call *Komödie* or *Lustspiel*". The terms seemed to be synonymous. Yet, in differentiating the "New" from the "Old" Comedy, he did make the suggestion that *Komödie* would be the better term for those biting, satirical comedies of Aristophanes (c.445-c.386/380 BC), derived from the classical "mimus".[4]

Paul Kluckhohn has suggested that

they (the *Lustspiele*) arise mainly from an attitude to life for which humour is an essential, while the true *Komödie* certainly contains comedy and a good deal of wit, but does not need the deeper sense of humour.

He goes on to quote Dr Rogge's comment that, in the *Komödie*, "the comic elements dominate and the emphasis is placed on a ridiculed frailty. . ."[5]

Such a "ridiculed frailty" was the major element of those theories of the comic which postulated that, as Thomas Hobbes put it, "men laugh at the infirmities of others by comparison wherewith their own abilities are set off and illustrated". This view lies close to Theodor Lipps' that the "ridiculed frailty" was to be found in the ludicrous degradation of a dignified person: "Something great shrinks to something small".[6]

In modern times, theorists have taken these views further, and the *Komödie* now does seem to have become the term applied to a more serious type of comedy, inclined to the satirical and to the expression of human frailty and impotence. Otto Rommel presented this modern view well in 1943:

A play is a *Lustspiel* when it succeeds in illuminating one of life's problem areas in a more cheerful and relaxed way, or when, through the fiction of a dramatic plot, it succeeds in creating such a feeling. The *Komödie*, on the other hand, is dominated by the "comic figure" which is viewed in the light of a derogatory contrast; in this figure, and through all the merriment, one usually senses the sharpness of satirical anger or the bitterness of impotence . . .[7]

"Bitterness of impotence" has a modern ring about it.

Thus it would seem that the *Komödie*, originally the foreign word used almost synonymously with *Lustspiel*, is now understood to be a genre of its own. Certainly the *Reallexikon* shifts its ground towards the end of the article already quoted and says:

> ... Thus the *Lustspiel* is often a piece of subdued comedy often set in a bourgeois milieu in which humour is the dominating element. The *Komödie* ... is usually more lively, more cheerful, but also more satirical than the humorous *Lustspiel*.

The "bitterness of impotence", the "ridiculed frailty", lie at the very heart of the modern *Komödie*: it is not mere chance that has made Cervantes' *Don Quixote* a work for our times; the contradiction between the Don's ambitions and his abilities, his futile tilting at windmills, his vain love for Dulcinea, the physical and mental incongruities of his relationship with Sancho Panza — all these are in addition to the basic and comic contradiction between his fantasy, medieval world and the actual *Machtpolitik* of contemporary Spain.

Henri Bergson regarded Cervantes' book as a perfect example of one of his "sources" of comic laughter: "The transposition from the ancient to the modern". But it is important to note also that Bergson saw Quixote as "the general type of comic absurdity" (p.142). He was one of those "runners after the ideal who stumble over realities" (pp.10-11). We laugh at his "mechanical inelasticity" (p.8), at his "automatism" which becomes a "defect that is ridiculous" (p.13).[8]

Bergson's work illuminates many of the trends in the contemporary theatre and the sources of much of the comic laughter in today's *Komödien* can be explained in Bergsonian terms and, in particular, by his basic "Law": "We laugh when we see *something mechanical encrusted on something living*" (p.29). I shall be referring to this work throughout this study, but would note here that Dürrenmatt constantly uses Don Quixote as a symbol of comic futility. In this figure, he seems to see the modern paradox, the comic which is, at the same time, tragic.[9]

For one could argue, with George Steiner, that *pure* tragedy, the tragedy of the Greeks, is "dead". Steiner claimed that, since the tragic vision demanded the unconditional acceptance of one's destiny, the outcome was final: "Tragedies end badly", he wrote.

Neither of the two great ideologies of our day, Christianity or Marxism, admit tragic outcomes. Ian Richards recognized this in 1926:

Tragedy is only possible to a mind which is for the moment agnostic or Manichean. The least touch of any theology which has a compensating heaven to offer the tragic hero is fatal.

The modern writer, living in a demythologized, irrational world, full of doubts, fears and uncertainties, has eschewed tragedy and, on the whole, turned to what is now termed "tragicomedy". The tragicomic, writes Karl Guthke, "always arises where a secure tradition loses its validity and is called into question".[10] It is the result of the contradiction which was noted above, the contradiction between what the character *is* and what he obstinately *thinks* he is, and we laugh, often cruelly, at the disparity. As Bergson wrote: "This inelasticity is the comic, and laughter is its corrective" (ibid. p.16).

★   ★   ★

It can be seen, then, that we are discussing the modern *Komödie* in Platonic or Aristotelian terms: what is comic is akin to the morally or physically faulty; the "ridiculous" is an "offence" against the Beautiful and it is "corrected" by our laughter. Comedy portrayed "inferior beings" and allowed us to deride "ugliness". But who were these "inferior beings" in the Old Attic Comedy? [11]

The Characters of the "Old Comedy" are explained in a work which some scholars hold to be the lost Aristotelian theory of the comic: the *Tractatus Coislinianus*, and it is of interest to this study because I believe that its terminology is valid for the modern *Komödie* in general, and for Dürrenmatt's in particular.

The *Tractatus* says: "The characters (of comedy) are (i) the buffoonish, (ii) the ironical, and (iii) those of the impostors".

The imposter (the *alazon*) is, claims Cornford, the "rigid" man with the "idée fixe", the unwelcome intruder who thrusts himself upon the "hero" and his society and is eventually driven out. Northrop Frye added the categories of the "senex iratus", Plautus's "miles gloriosus", pedants, coxcombs, fops, anyone, indeed, who is "obsessed" and who must inevitably fall.

Allied against the *alazon* are the ironical man (the *eiron*) and the buffoon (the *bomolochos*). The function of the *eiron* in most Attic comedies was the Socratic one of "exposing falsehood and getting at the truth", as Sedgwick put it.[12] He usually makes himself out to be worse than he is. Cicero said of the *alazon* and the *eiron*: "The former simulates, the latter dissimulates" (*De Officio*, i, 30). It is the *eiron* who leads the *alazon* on to his final absurdities, his eventual unmasking and/or rejection.

Northrop Frye saw the *eiron* as the very spirit of comedy, reaching from the Aristophanic "hero", through the "dolosus servus" or "tricky slave" (Figaro, *Leporello*), down to the amateur detective (the one who "unmasks") in modern times. Dürrenmatt's detectives (in *Der Richter und sein Henker* (*The Judge and his Executioner*), *Der Verdacht* (*The Suspicion*) and *Das Versprechen* (*The Promise*) could certainly fit this description.

The function of the buffoons (the *bomolochoi*) is, Frye suggests, "to increase the mood of festivity rather than to contribute to the plot" (p.175).

These characters formed the Chorus (of 24) in Aristophanes' plays, the only complete examples of Old Comedy that have come down to us. It was to them that one looked for the disrespect, the licentiousness, what Schlegel called the "chaotic cornucopia" of comedy to contrast with the "harmonious unity" of tragedy. It was however the Leader of this Chorus (the *coryphaeus*) who was given the task of expressing the views of the author to the public in the *parabasis*, one of the first and best-known examples of *Verfremdung* in the theatre. (The treatment of this comic element, in the form of the *Address to the Audience*, will occupy us later.)

The many performances of Aristophanes' plays in recent years prove that he has something to say to our age. Not only Dürrenmatt would say of Aristophanes (or of his successors, such as Swift): "I have no hesitation in enlisting as one of their spearmen".[13] Today's audiences respond with delight to the savage but witty Aristophanic attacks on "authority" in *The Knights* and *The Wasps*, on canonical literature in *The Frogs*, on war in *The Acharnians* and on the "new" education in *The Clouds*. They rejoice too in the sexual allusiveness of *Lysistrata* and the crazy world of "Cloudcuckooland" in *The Birds*. These plays suited the Athenian spirit, but they speak also to the uncertain, irascible, questioning spirit of our own age. (It was Theodor Zielinski who first put forward the view that Attic Old Comedy presented a "conflict" (the *agon*) in contradistinction to the tragedy which presented a "solution", and we shall find Dürrenmatt insisting on this very point a little later).[14]

Aristophanes wrote about his own times and his own world; Dürrenmatt praises him therefore for his "Einfälle" ("brilliant ideas"):

These are brilliant ideas which burst on the world like shells . . . and the crater they make turns today's world into a comedy . . .[15]

Even the structure of an Aristophanic comedy, the loosely-connected scenes which flash irrationally from idea to idea, can remind a modern audience of a revue-sketch or a ballad-opera — and of their own contemporary theatre or cabaret, since this is a technique which was to be the (unwitting) model for many of the plays of the Expressionist period and of the "distancing" Epic Theatre of Erwin Piscator and Bertolt Brecht. No doubt Dürrenmatt had this development in mind when he wrote in his *Anmerkung zur Komödie* (*A Note on the Komödie*):

"... So once could deduce from this that a contemporary play can only be a *Komödie* in the Aristophanic sense, because of the "distancing" which has to be created in it, for I cannot conceive of any other sensible basis for a contemporary play." (p.136)

So I would suggest that we keep the term *Komödie* in the original German for this very distinctive German brand of comedy, just as we have agreed to retain the term *Lied* for a very distinctive brand of German musical composition.

(ii) DÜRRENMATT AND THE COMIC SPIRIT

In German culture, humour is regarded as something second-rate. Intellectually it expresses itself either as pathos, or as a rather silly sort of wittiness only found in our latitudes and which is obviously meant to be "esprit". The comic is suspect, it is not to be taken seriously or at its full value. Yet I can only be understood from this point of view — from the point of view of humour taken seriously.[16]

This is one of Dürrenmatt's most significant statements and suggests that a critical examination of his important writings on the "comic" would yield profitable results for our study.

Theaterprobleme (*Problems of the Theatre*), a lecture held throughout Switzerland and West Germany in 1954-55 was felt by Frau Brock-Sulzer to be "one of the most important and seminal pronouncements . . . on the theatre of our age and of any age" although Dürrenmatt himself stresses that it is not a work of philosophy, but deals rather with "practical problems in the theatre". It is certainly the best starting point for an examination of some of his major theoretical writings on the *Komödie*.[17]

"Experiment" is a vital clue to an understanding of Dürrenmatt's work. Again and again he stresses the importance which he attaches to the "performance and production" of his plays as against their value as "Literature". For this reason, his plays, like Brecht's, could be called *Versuche* (*Experiments*), existing, as they do, in many versions. They are like music scores on which a cast can and should improvise.

Dürrenmatt is, above all, a man of the theatre and he echoes his countryman, Max Frisch: "It is important that you write *with* the stage ... (p.25), adding: "Writers have always written not only on, but with the stage. I'm thinking for example of Aristophanes' *Komödien* or Nestroy's *Lustspiele*," (p.25).[18] The importance to him of the comic elements in a play are to be found in his emphasis on "stage business", and on stage décor, as well as in the many notes for producers and directors at the end of his works.

The failure to appreciate this point and the consequent criticism of his plays as "belles lettres" may well have led to some of the many misunderstandings about this author. One might recall Gilbert Murray's wise words about literary critics of the Greek classics: "Greek drama has always suffered from a school of critics who approach the play with a greater equipment of aesthetic theory than of dramatic perception".[19]

★   ★   ★

The major part of the lecture deals with the place of tragedy and comedy in our age. Dürrenmatt distinguishes between the tragic and the comic hero; the tragic hero must awaken our sympathy by having his guilt and innocence measured out for us in exact doses according to fixed rules. Likewise, in Greek or Shakespearean tragedy, the "hero" had to come from one fixed social class, the nobility. But, in German literature, the public saw itself in the eighteenth-century "domestic tragedy" as the "suffering hero". Then the hero was firstly demythologized and then "dematerialized" (by Pirandello) as well, just as Thornton Wilder alienated the stage. Dürrenmatt shows that Shakespeare's kings were never portrayed as "fools", but always as a "fate dripping with blood". Only courtiers and handworkers were treated as "comic relief". Now, however, the concept of "hero" has changed: "Thus we see a move towards the *Komödie* in the development of the tragic hero" (p.42), while the "Fool" is becoming, increasingly, a *tragic* figure.

The reason is that such characters represent and portray their world and their times — and *these* have changed. Where Schiller could represent *his* age by a Wallenstein (because a Napoleon was still alive), we now have no more tragic heroes, "but only find tragedies which are produced by universal butchers and acted out by mincing-machines" — and, he concludes, in a most memorable phrase: "We can no longer make Wallensteins out of a Hitler or a Stalin". (p.43)

Schiller's world (Schiller lived from 1759-1805), Dürrenmatt states, was a world where power could be seen and recognized; the powers of today's world are "too diffuse, anonymous, bureaucratic" (p.44). The author sees today's "political happenings" as "supplementary satyr-plays which follow the tragedies acted out in secret", a revealing comment on his own dramatic techniques since the satyr-play followed the tragedy in Greek times — and reversed, by parody, the tragic plot.

But if one wanted to portray the modern world, Dürrenmatt continues, one would have to choose something other than a Wallenstein — one would have to choose "a little spiv-boy" or a "shop assistant", rather than a Federal Councillor or a Federal Chancellor. Works of art cannot reach "those in power" nowadays; if they reach anyone, then only the "little man", the "secretary", thus, "Creon's secretaries deal with Antigone's case" (p.44).

He now argues that tragedy needed a fixed moral order, it presupposes a "world with form", what Una Ellis-Fermor described as an "equilibrium", that is, there is suffering and catastrophe on the one hand, a relation with a fundamental compensating law on the other.[20] Dürrenmatt claims that this does not obtain today, and that only the *Komödie* can therefore reproduce "this formless world, a world developing, ripe for collapse, a world which is about to pack up, like ours" (p.45).

To shape this world, we must "distance" ourselves from it; thus is the task of the "comic". Dürrenmatt chooses first of all the obscene joke (the "Zote") as one example of distancing. It is the same point of view as Freud's in his work on the "joke". *He* saw the "Zote" as the "desire to see sexuality naked". Like Freud's, Dürrenmatt's "obscenity" is "purposive", it creates distance, releases an inhibition and, again like Freud's, its "purpose" is satirical.[21]

Another example of "distancing" would be the "Einfall", the "brilliant idea", the original, inventive germ of a scene or of a whole play. The comic writer must invent his own "Einfälle", whereas the writer of classical tragedies wrote on themes (ie. the myths) known to his audiences. Dürrenmatt repeated here his admiration for the *Komödien* of Aristophanes as the supreme example of "distancing"

("Distanz") set, as they were, in contemporary Athens.[22]

Tragedy, in the Greek sense, is impossible today, he writes:

> Tragedy assumes the presence of guilt, trouble, moderation, the overview, responsibility. In the mess that is our century, this cleaning-out of the white race, there are no longer any guilty men, nor are there any to be held responsible any more. Nobody can do anything about it and nobody wanted it to happen. Things really do happen without anyone. Everything is dragged along and caught up in some rake or other. We are too collectively guilty, too collectively embedded in the sins of our fathers and forefathers. We are only children of children. That is not our guilt, only our bad luck: Guilt nowadays is a personal achievement only, a religious deed. Only the *Komödie* can reach us now. (pp.47-48).

"Pure" tragedy would therefore seem to be excluded because of the absence of the "true hero" and the attendant circumstances; but "we can glean the tragic from the *Komödie*, extract it as one terrible moment, a yawning abyss . . ." (p.48).

Dürrenmatt now admits that one could read into his attitude a belief that the Komödie is an "expression of despair"; but not necessarily so. There is another answer that can be given to the absurd, hopeless situation of today's world — and that would be a "non-despairing", the determination to "endure the world". "It is still possible" he writes, "to portray the valiant man" (p.49).[23]

Here Dürrenmatt's view seems to coincide with that of Albert Camus who interpreted Sisyphus as a happy man because he *knew* that his task was a vain one — but he strove nevertheless. In the case of Dürrenmatt's "valiant men", "the lost world-order is restored in their hearts". They will seek *Freedom.*[24]

★   ★   ★

The lecture finishes with a discussion on parody. By the laughter created by parody, the artist will regain the freedom which he had lost because of the sanctifying influence of the classics on our generation. Through parody, the writer "consciously compares them (the classics) with what they have become" (p.55), and this new material (for every parody presupposes the creation of new material) will affect "those in power" as the classics never did — because it will contain *scorn* and *ridicule*, it will be, in a word, satirical — and satire is the only weapon which those in power fear.

But the difficulty is that the public distrusts the comic: "The comic is seen as inferior, dubious, unseemly . . ." (p.56) and when it becomes dangerous or challenging as well, then it is dropped like a hot potato — which is why such writers are always regarded as "nihilistic". But what the public calls "nihilistic", Dürrenmatt calls "uncomfortable" — and it is the writer's *duty* to make himself uncomfortable." Dürrenmatt ends his lecture with the heretical suggestion that one way to achieve this is to make literature become "so light . . . that it will no longer weigh anything on the scales of modern lit.-crit. Only in this way will it become weighty again" (p.60).

Such a view of literature leads naturally to parody. Like G.B. Shaw, Thomas Mann, Brecht and other writers of this century, Dürrenmatt finds in parody the best means of expressing comic irony, and, through irony, satire. Beda Allemann maintains that parody is "the ironist's speech-form par excellence" and claims that much of Dürrenmatt's comic laughter is gained from irony.[25]

Reinhold Grimm has analysed Dürrenmatt's parodistic method thus: "The formal exterior is retained, but the contents are considerably altered, in such a way that a comical tension, a degree of ridiculousness, arises". The final part of that quotation might also be applied to the concept of the "grotesque".

Grimm calls the grotesque the "basic structure" of Dürrenmatt's work, but disagrees with Wolfgang Kayser's celebrated definition, as does Arnold Heidsieck, in his searching, but opaque study. Both critics found Kayser too concerned with the visual arts and agreed with Heselhaus that the grotesque was rather more than Kayser's "control and exorcism of the demonic elements in the world", which is Phillip Thompson's translation of Kayser in his *The Grotesque* (Methuen 1972, p.18).[26]

Both Grimm and Heselhaus lay emphasis on the *comic* element in the grotesque in Dürrenmatt, ("the farcical as well as the demonic", as Grimm puts it); yet it is the "mere ridiculousness" which Heidsieck attacks. He claims that the grotesque requires a "true, brutal perverseness", and can find this only in *The Visit of the Old Lady* in Dürrenmatt's *oeuvre*. Reality must be "perverted" for a true grotesque to arise, he would claim. Thus, although he agrees that Dürrenmatt's drama is paradoxical, he denies it true grotesque force — an interesting view of a theme which will be more fully considered in later chapters.

★   ★   ★

Two final points remain to be considered: the "loss of the hero", and how "distancing" can achieve the effect of comedy.

William II's Imperial sigh at the outbreak of the First World War: "I didn't want it to happen", might be regarded as the archetypal expression of twentieth-century human impotence. Here, one of the world's most powerful rulers, a "hero" perhaps, in Carlyle's sense, is shown to be helpless in the hands of incalculable Chance. Both Karl Kraus and Dürrenmatt himself echoed these words in their works — Kraus at the end of his monumental "Tragödie", *The Last Days of Mankind*, where the "voice of God" speaks the words against an all-destroying meteoric shower, while Dürrenmatt uses them, as we saw, in *Problems of the Theatre* (above, p.28).[27]

Chance, then, has taken over from "iron" Fate:

> Fate has left the stage where the action is, to skulk behind the curtains, away from the valid dramaturgy, in the foreground everything becomes an accident, the illnesses, the crises. . .

writes Dürrenmatt in the foreword to his *Die Panne* (The Breakdown).[28]

This was how Willy Loman in Arthur Miller's *Death of a Salesman* and Blanche Dubois in Tennessee Williams' *A Streetcar Named Desire* became recognized as "representatives" of our time. Rather than possessing the stature and suffering the fall of tragic heroes, they were often the victims of Life's cruel practical jokes. "I am not a leader of men, Willy," cried Loman's son, Biff, "and neither are you". They lacked the stature to bring about tragic irony and became more like standard comic "types".

Nor could one deny the levelling influence of political developments. The spread of Marxism, and the consequent demythologizing of monarchical power has removed the possibility of depicting power as "heroic" — the modern dramatist parodies the hero to "reduce" him in stature. The machine age, too, has robbed Man of his individuality and freedom. Where Jack is as good as his master, we have little to learn from a tragic hero. Mario Praz has called this "the democratization of the heroic"; Beda Allemann sums it up for our age as the "loss of the hero", while Walter Starkie, as far back as 1926, had coined the term "anti-hero".[29]

When we talk of "distancing", we think willy-nilly of Brecht. His concept of "Verfremdung", translated more satisfactorily as "distancing" than "alienation" fulfils the same function as Dürrenmatt's "Distanz", although perhaps for a different reason.[30] Both writers want to disturb, "épater le bourgeois", to make the audience think critically, to be "uncomfortable" authors. Although Brecht was later to mellow, his original theatrical aim was, of course, the conversion of his audiences to Marxism. Dürrenmatt, in my view, has more aesthetic grounds and a more aesthetic attitude, as my examination of his works will show.

It has been argued, of course, that the very excellence of Brecht's dramatic technique obfuscated his message. Esslin wrote that Brecht "never succeeded in evoking the critical attitude he postulated. The audience stubbornly went on being moved to terror and pity".[31] Brecht's "failure" lies indeed at the heart of Dürrenmatt's belief that a writer cannot change the world; he too felt that "Brecht, the poet, absconds with Brecht, the playwright" (*TP*, p.14).

Brecht's "Verfremdungseffekt" was a comic theatrical device, seen in his use of parody and the grotesque, in his "stage business", sets, lighting and music and in the incongruities and ambiguities of his plots. What T.S. Eliot called "a kind of doubleness in the action, as if it took place on two planes at once" (demonstrated in Eliot's *Sweeney Agonistes*), might well describe the characteristics of Brechtian theatre.[32]

Although Dürrenmatt is admiring Aristophanes in his *Notes to the Komödie* (1952), he makes the Greek poet sound distinctly Brechtian:

> Tragedies present us with a past which is present, they conquer "distance" in order to frighten us. . . Aristophanes goes in the opposite direction. Since his comedies take place in the present, he creates "distance", and I believe that to be an essential for a *Komödie* (or, here, a comedy) (*TSR I* p.136).

This is exactly what Brecht was trying to achieve: "An alienating image" he wrote, "is one which allows the object to be recognized, but yet, at the same time, to appear strange". (Although Brecht rarely discussed the comic *per se*, it has been claimed that his *Verfremdung* is, in fact, a theory of the comic closely allied to Bergson's famous theory of "gestes". It is a point well made and to be borne in mind as we proceed.)[33]

(iii) COMMENTS FROM VARIED SOURCES

While reserving Dürrenmatt's theoretical comments on the plays for the chapters on the plays themselves, I should like to bring together here various comments on the theme from his prose works, essays, interviews and other sources.

Dürrenmatt showed an interest in the paradoxical, ambiguous comic mode (particularly in the theatre) early in his career. In the story *Der Theaterdirektor* (*The Theatre Manager*) (1945), after the new bizarre manager had taken over the theatre, the author describes the macabre change of atmosphere:

> The most devilish thing was, however, that each act imperceptibly took on a different sense and the genres began to intermix, a tragedy was changed to a comedy (a *Komödie*), while a comedy (Dürrenmatt now writes *Lustspiel!*) was falsified into a tragedy.[34]

(Is Dürrenmatt making some distinction between the two words here?)

It will be seen that such a mixing of genres is not just a matter of dramatic techniques, but is, Dürrenmatt believes, a basic quality of life itself. When Arthur Joseph asked him (in 1969) if the "möglichst bittere Ende" ("the most bitter end possible" — an inexact quotation incidentally!) was not a sign of tragedy, the author replied:

> I once claimed that, whether a play was a tragedy or a comedy, depended on the material. I don't believe that now. I think it is a matter of awareness. We are in a different state of awareness nowadays, when we're writing, too. A death on the stage is a death on the stage, not a death in reality. I arrange it, and therefore it is — in the deepest sense — not tragic, that is, everything takes place under the sign of the *Komödie*.

When it was then put to him that this was a "nihilistic" point of view, he defended himself:

> "It's *humour*, and that is, I believe, like irony, one of man's basic philosophical tenets — and it certainly is *not* despair."[35]

Dürrenmatt, like Camus, confronted the greatest of paradoxes, the contradiction of life, the intense physical pleasure of living, against the absolute certainty of dying, and having rejected one possible solution, suicide, had elected Camus' way in *Le mythe de Sisyphe* (1942): "Maintenant il s'agit de vivre". One could certainly say that the comic in Dürrenmatt's work is the expression of a "joie de vivre" which is not however sentimental or thoughtless, but is realistically aware of the temptations of the world and the weakness of Man and is resolutely determined to face them.

Dürrenmatt expresses this, for him, essential truth about the comic in a number of places. The ironical Jew Gulliver saves Kommissär Bärlach's life in *Der Verdacht* (*The Suspicion*) (1953) and, leaving him, says:

"We can only help in isolated instances, not all the time . . . So our aim must be, not to save the world, but to endure it, the one genuine adventure that remains to us in these late times." (p.155)[36]

In the radio-play *Das Unternehmen der Wega* (*The Undertaking of the Wega*) (1954), Sir Horace Wood, the pompous and comical leader of the world mission sent to negotiate with the escaped convicts on Venus, has sadly to realize that they have found a "better" life: "They can have no other idea than to endure this struggle, somehow to hang on to Life, even when this life is so wretched",[37] and in his lecture *Vom Sinn der Dichtung in unserer Zeit* (*On the meaning of Literature in our Age*) (1956), Dürrenmatt developed the theme of the individual vis-à-vis the "collective":

> "Collectiveness" will grow, but its intellectual importance will shrink. Opportunity (=*die Chance*) is with the individual alone. The individual has to endure the world.

And how can an author do this? "By ensuring that he avoids profundities (Tiefsinn)" — by facing the world with *humour*.[38]

Now it is my view that Dürrenmatt's emphasis on the importance of humour, of comedy, in life and on the stage, is largely conditioned by his residence in Switzerland. Again and again, he condemns the earnestness and industry of the Swiss people:

> Now, being Swiss isn't as easy as people think . . . to survive this fate unharmed needs a virtue that most of us don't possess, namely, the ability to laugh at ourselves.[39]

And he humorously reminded another audience that Jeremias Gotthelf (1797-1854) could only carry out his twin professions of pastor and author because he was an early riser, "probably the most Swiss and the most appalling of all virtues"![40]

And is this why Dürrenmatt will not admit the primacy of Reason? The political, social and economic orderliness of a small state would seem to demand a rational ordering of Creation. If one posits then that the world is ruled by *Chance* rather than by Reason, one is mocking: If we are victims of Chance, then pompous endeavour and pedantic planning become ludicrous, futile and, ultimately, comic. Such a comic of the futility of human planning often seems to lead Dürrenmatt to an attitude of cynical resignation; if one studies the "antagonists" of his three novels, however, one sees that it is *their* attitude, their nihilism, which is attacked. His "Fools" have to "grin and bear it", but, in bearing it, they triumph, too, as *human beings*, over the evil in the world.[41]

His three detective-stories and his Novelle-cum-radio-play *Die Panne*, all take this point of view. Inspektor Matthäi in *Das Versprechen* (*The Promise*) (1958) is ludicrously reduced from his former high office in the Zürich Police Force to that of a drunken garageman, through his attempts to solve rationally a crime which irrationally solves itself. As a former Chief of Police explains to the author:

> Our reason only dimly illuminates the world. The paradoxical finds its home in the twilight zone of the intellect.[42]

Similarly in *Der Richter und sein Henker* (*The Judge and his Execution-er*) (1952), comedy is achieved at the expense of Dr. Lucius Lutz (the Dr. is significant for Dürrenmatt!), the rationalist Police Chief and lecturer in criminology at the University of Berne. Lutz returns from the USA to improve the "primeval conditions" of the Berne force by modern scientific and *rational* methods. These fail because of the "confusing intricacy of human relationships". The latter, and not the rational intellect, lead to the discovery of the murderer (*DRH*, p.79). The same point is made in *Der Verdacht* (*The Suspicion*) (1953), where the "criminal", Emmenberger, admits to Kommissär Bärlach that no matter how "careful, thorough and pedantic" he himself might have been, he was bound to be caught: "A crime without clues is an impos-sibility in a world of Chance" (*DVD*, p.131).

Murray Peppard writes of these novels that because "the divine ordering of things seems to prevent comic justice . . . the individual's personal responsibility in seeking the right and just path becomes all the greater". I agree that Dürrenmatt is at all times concerned with Man's personal integrity – which is to say with Man's *freedom*.[43]

★   ★   ★

Dürrenmatt told me during my visit that, after *Problems of the Theatre*, the *Locational Guide to Frank V* and the *Dramaturgical Considerations to The Anabaptists* were his most important contributions to dramatic theory. In the *Introduction* to the latter, the author continues the theme that we have just been discussing.[44] He imagines four ways of treating the heroic story of Robert Falcon Scott: it could be treated (i) as a Shakespearean tragedy, where faults in Scott's character would have brought him down, or (ii) in Brechtian fashion, where, for econo-mic and class reasons, the expeditions's English background would have made them employ ponies instead of dogs (!), or (iii), as Beckett might

have suggested, Scott and his companies would each be entombed
incommunicado in blocks of ice — or, (iv), the Dürrenmattian way —
Scott would have been locked in a refrigerator by mistake before he
even set out:

> Scott, dies tragically, as if stranded on another planet, Scott, locked
> in the refrigerator through a foolish mis-chance, in the middle of a
> big city, a few yards from a busy street. . .

And, thus, "a comic character has grown out of a tragic character", and
this character has been made comical by its "Fate": "The worst possible
turn that a story can take is the turn towards a *Komödie*".

Dürrenmatt then discusses the main character of his play, Jan
Bockelson, as a positively and as a negatively tragic "hero", measuring
him against the "generally accepted laws" of the "Theatre of Identification" of Aristotle, and he comes to the conclusion that there is only
one dilemma for tragedy: "Only what is real moves us tragically". We
need to believe that a man is actually dying in order to be emotionally
affected: i.e. Theatre = Reality, in tragedy.[45]

Dürrenmatt then discusses Brecht's "V-effekt", which, he agrees,
changed theatrical style. "Brecht's theatre . . . is the drama of every
modern theatre", but he claims that here, too, the spectator "identifies",
even though involuntarily, "for the simple reason that he is involved".

The true theatre of non-identification is the *Komödie*, and the best
example is the clown. We laugh at the clown, because we feel superior
to him. "We do not identify with the clown, we objectify him". The
clown is isolated: "What isolates every comic figure is the comic element" — Bergson had defined the comic in almost identical terms:

> Unsociability of the performer, insensitivity of the spectator, these
> are the two essential conditions for comedy.[46]

The tragic figure is not isolated, adds Dürrenmatt, because the audience's sympathy binds him to them.

Since about 1967, Dürrenmatt, like many other major European
authors, has become increasingly aware of the dramaturgical and philosophical implications and possibilities of the figure of the clown, "the
last human beings in end-games" as Dürrenmatt put it in his *Aspects of
Dramaturgical Thinking* (*TSR II*, p.223). Shortly before he took up the
post of *Dramaturg* in Basel, he wrote in the theatre's publication:

> Men laugh at their fellow man when he appears as a clown; the clown
> is the man distanced from other men, the inhuman human being.
> Tragic, comic. The tragic is what is human, comic, what is inhuman.[47]

And in his *Aspects of Dramaturgical Thinking*, he writes of the clown:

> The isolated man appears reduced to mere existence, but also
> stripped of his character, he is relieved of all social functions, he is,
> seen from within, the inner man, purely and simply, and therefore
> an objectified self . . .[48]

Again, in *Gedanken über das Theater* (*Thoughts on the Theatre*) (1970)
he writes:

> If wrestling, when it imitates a contest with a winner and a loser,
> represents the original form of tragedy, then the clown represents
> the original form of comedy.[49]

The comic appears, therefore, when we objectify, that is, when we
create "distance" — "Our laughter is the force which drives the comic
object away from us".

Dürrenmatt now distinguishes three types of comedy: "The comic
can be found in the character and in the plot, in the character alone and
in the plot alone".

The clown's comic lies only in the *character*. In the "social comedy"
from Menander on, both the character, the type (the miser, the nouveau-riche etc) and the plot were comic, but

> if the *Komödie* becomes a *theatrum mundi*, then only the plot need
> be "comical", the characters, in contrast to the plot, are often not
> only "not-comical", but tragic.

Dürrenmatt concludes with a discussion of the *Dramaturgie der Komödie als Welttheater* (*Dramaturgy of the Komödie as a theatrum mundi*):
if the point of a tragic plot is to show a hero's stature, then the plot
itself is irrelevant; therefore the plot becomes *comical* when it becomes
important, when the characters make sense only *through* the plot
(p.106). The point is that the comic plot is a paradoxical plot and "a
plot becomes paradoxical when it is thought through to its conclusion".
Tragedy, Dürrenmatt repeats, in Schiller's terminology, is "naive".
Comedy is "sentimental" — his own term is "bewusst", self-conscious.
It was this very "self-conscious *Komödie* of plot" which Brecht had
demanded from a theatre in a scientific age — but the audience cannot
be "made" to believe in a point of view: "The theatre is a moral institution" (Schiller's phrase), "only in so far as it is made into one by the
audience".[50]

★   ★   ★

The time is possibly not yet ripe to postulate a Dürrenmattian "theory of comedy", yet it is interesting to note from the foregoing summaries how close his critical thinking is to that of Henri Bergson. Both writers view the comic as a "reducing" savage force which punishes ("corrects") those who are rigid or static, in mind, manners or body. Bergson's fame as a philosopher rests on his principle of "creative evolution": the mind must be independent of the body. The consequence is a distrust of "automatism" and a praising of what he called "the ever-changing" or "the truly living Life". Dürrenmatt's works constantly attack those who either fail to realize that the way of the world is an on-going process and that one must move with it, or those who fail to learn from the mistakes made by others and, therefore, who fail to apply the lessons learned to the next catastrophe. But they are not "nihilistic" — Nihilism, Dürrenmatt would claim, is, like Beauty, in the eye of the beholder.[51]

Bergson, through his study of farce and the art of the clown, had tried to trace the sources of comic laughter in society, since it was society who responded to comedy "by a gesture which looks like a defensive reaction, a gesture which makes one slightly afraid".[52] As we now turn to an examination of Dürrenmatt's plays, it will be seen that his methods are not dissimilar.

NOTES TO CHAPTER TWO

(i) THE MEANING OF KOMÖDIE

1. *Reallexikon der deutschen Literatur* (ed. Kohlschmidt und Mohr), Gruyter, Berlin, 2nd. ed., 1958, pp.226-240, here pp.227-228.
2. W.H. Bruford: *Germany in the Eighteenth Century*, CUP 1935, p.134. Dürrenmatt in *Die alte Wiener Volkskomödie* (1953) in *TSR I*, p.142.
3. Tiusanen, rather uncritically it seems to me, assumes that Novalis meant "comedies". He translates: "After a lost war one has to write comedies". (Tiusanen, op.cit., p.74).
4. A.W. Schlegel: *Vorlesungen über dramatische Kunst und Literatur*, 1808, Weidmannsche Buchhandlung, Leipzig 1846, Vols. V and VI (here pp.218-219).
5. P. Kluckhohn: *Die Arten des Dramas*, DVJS, 19 Jg., Band XIX, Heft III, 1941, pp.241-268, here p.260. A Rogge: *Das Problem der dramatischen Gattungen im deutschen Lustspiel*, D.Phil. dissertation, Hamburg 1926.
6. *The English Works of Thomas Hobbes*, Bohm, London MDCCCXL, Vol.IV: *On Human Nature* (1650), p.46.
   Th. Lipps: *Komik und Humor*, Beiträge zur Ästhetik VI, Voss, Hamburg and Leipzig, 1898, pp.39-40.

7. O.Rommel: *Komik- und Lustspieltheorie*, DVJS, Band XXI, Heft II, 1943, pp. 252-286, here p.273.
8. H. Bergson: *Le rire. Essai sur la signification du comique*, Presses universitaires de France (233rd edn.) 1967. Originally published as articles in Revue de Paris, Feb. 1, Feb. 15 and March 1, 1899. The "authorized translation" is *Laughter* by Cloudesley Brereton and Fred Rothwell, Macmillan, London, 1911.
9. In, for example, *The Marriage of Mr Mississippi* (*KI*, p.57); *Evening Hour in Late Autumn* (*Gesammelte Hörspiele* = *GH*, pp. 302 and 315); *Nocturnal Conversation with a despised person* (*GH*, p.105) and in *The Suspicion* (*Der Verdacht*, Benziger 1953, 6th edn. 1965, p.149). In his poem *An mein Vaterland* (*To my Fatherland*), he writes: "O Switzerland, the Don Quixote among nations, why must I love you! (hortulus 48, 10 Jg., Heft 6, December 1960, p.172). (NB *Der Verdacht* has been translated as *The Quarry* by Eva H. Morreale, Cape 1962).
10. G. Steiner: *The Death of Tragedy* (1961), Faber and Faber, 1963, p.129. I.A. Richards: *Principles of Literary Criticism*, Routledge and Kegan Paul, 1960 edn., p.246. K.S. Guthke: *Geschichte und Poetik der deutschen Tragikomödie*, Vandenhoeck und Ruprecht, Göttingen 1961, p.25.
11. *The Dialogues of Plato*, translated B. Jowett, Vol. V: *The Laws* (ii, 935-936); Clarendon Press 1875. *The Works of Aristotle*, (translated by I.Bywater, ed. W.D.Ross), Vol. XI: *The Poetics* 1449a, Chap.5 (Oxford 1946, 1966 edn.)
12 The *Tractatus Coislinianus* was found in a 10th century MS and printed by J.A. Cramer in Oxford in 1839. It is translated and commented upon in Lane Cooper: *An Aristotelian Theory of Comedy*, Blackwell, Oxford, 1924, pp.224-286. F.M.Cornford: *The Origins of Attic Comedy*, Arnold 1914, pp.137-138. N.Frye: *Anatomy of Criticism*, Princeton 1957, p.43. G.G.Sedgwick: *Of Irony, especially in Drama*, Univ. of Toronto Press, 1935, (1948 edn.), p.12.
13. In the programme of the Schauspielhaus Zürich 1953-1954, p.2. See too his remarks on Aristophanes in *A Note on the Komödie*, Weltwoche 22.2.52. (now in *TSR I*, pp.132-137).
14. Th. Zielinski: *Die Gliederung der altattischen Komödie*, Leipzig 1885.
15. *A Note on the Komödie*, op.cit., p.133.

(ii) DÜRRENMATT AND THE COMIC SPIRIT

16. To Horst Bienek: *Werkstattgespräche mit Schriftstellern*, Hanser, München, 1962. (Originally in Neue Zürcher Zeitung (NZZ) 11.3.62.).
17. E. Brock-Sulzer: *Überlegungen zur schweizerischen Dramatik von heute*, Akzente 3, 1956, pp.43-48, here p.47. *Theaterprobleme*, Arche Verlag, Zürich, 1955 (1963 edn.), here p.8. Translated by G.Nellhaus in *Four Plays*, Cape, London, 1962, and by H.M. Waidson in *Friedrich Dürrenmatt: Writings on the Theatre*, op.cit., pp.59-91. It is interesting to note that Dürrenmatt's *Prologue to the Epilogue* to his 1973 play *Der Mitmacher* likewise promises to present the "intellectual background which led to this play through the play itself". (*DMKK*, op.cit., p.82).
18. See Max Frisch: "It is not the theatre's fault if the writer cannot use it. Whoever walks on to a stage and doesn't use it, has the stage against him. Using it means: not writing *on* the stage, but *with* it." (*Tagebuch 1946-1949*, (Suhrkamp 1950) Droemer Knaur 1965, p.265). Dürrenmatt said to Werner

Wollenberger that he only wanted to achieve "theatre" with his plays," as good parts as possible for the actors. As good theatre as possible for the audiences. Give the stage what the stage wants. Play. Stage-play". (*Interview with Dürrenmatt*, in Blätter des deutschen Theaters, Göttingen, Nr.214, 1962-1963, p.184 ff.) (In the Zürcher Woche, 16.2.62)

19. *The Alcestes of Euripides* translated by G.Murray, London 1915, p.vi.
20. U. Ellis-Fermor: *The Frontiers of Drama*, OUP 1964, pp.127-147.
21. S.Freud: *Gesammelte Werke Vol.VI: Der Witz und seine Beziehungen zum Unbewussten (The Joke and its relationship to the unconscious)*, Imago, London, 1940, p.106. 23 years later in *Die Frist (The Waiting Period)*, Dürrenmatt maintains: "Its (the play's) themes stem from the unreality in which reality is lost. I maintain still that one can only get at this through *Komödie*" (p.11). There is much sexual play in *Die Frist*.
22. cf in 1969: "I call a piece comedy in the old sense of Dante's *Divine Comedy*: Comedy is simply play, and the awareness that it is simply play, that it is not divine, that it generates a feeling of alienation: that lies in the nature of theatre itself. I call these things comedy". (See Violet Ketels: *Friedrich Dürrenmatt at Temple University*, Journal of Modern Literature 1 (1971) pp.88-108, here p.95)
23. I choose "valiant man" as the best translation for "mutigen Menschen" because of the effect Bunyan had on the young Dürrenmatt (See *GHLA*, p.14). Note too:
"Forget not Master Valiant-For-Truth/That Man of Courage, though a very Youth/Tell everyone his Spirit was so stout/No Man could ever make him face about/." John Bunyan: *Pilgrim's Progress*: Prefatory verses to the Second Part: The Author's Way of Sending Forth: Marshall, London, n.d., p.156. Later in this study, we shall find Dürrenmatt reviving this concept; the nomenclature will have changed, the talk is of the "ironic hero", but we shall see that he is thinking of the same motif, "the possibility in which I believe, to which I cling, the possibility of becoming nothing but an individual, the possibility of freedom" (*DMMK*, op.cit., p.178) See below p.222.
24. With particular reference to Camus' attitude, see A.Krättli: "*Wie soll man es spielen? Mit Humor*", in *Friedrich Dürrenmatt II*, Nr.56, Text + Kritik, München, October 1977, pp.49-57. (= *FDII*) and to Ketels in 1969: "For me a Christian is a man who sees the world as it is, who is despairing (verzweifelt), but for that reason, is not despairing" (Ketels, op.cit., p.97). Miss Ketels' translations of her conversations are not always felicitous.
25. B. Allemann: *Ironie in der Dichtung*, Neske Pfullingen, 1956, p.24. See too E. Rotermund: *Gegengesänge*, Eides Verlag, München 1964, where, in the foreword, Dürrenmatt and Thomas Mann are briefly compared – as parodists.
26. R. Grimm: *Parodie und Groteske im Werke Friedrich Dürrenmatt*, GRM (Neue Folge XI) 1961, pp.431-450, here p.442 and pp.446-449.
A. Heidsieck: *Das Groteske und das Absurde im modernen Drama*, Kohlhammer, Stuttgart, 1969, pp.87-94. See too W. Kayser: *Das Groteske: Seine Gestaltung in Malerei und Dichtung*, G. Stalling Verlag 1957 (2nd edn. 1961), p.202 and C. Heselhaus: *Deutsche Lyrik der Moderne*, Düsseldorf 1961, p.286 ff. especially p.287, and F. Heuer: *Das Groteske als poetische Kategorie: Überlegungen zu Dürrenmatts Dramaturgie des modernen Theaters*, DVJS 47, 1973, Heft 4, pp.730-768.
Over the year, many scholars have found the grotesque to be the major – and most important – feature of Dürrenmatt's work. I think that this interest is exaggerated and limiting and that there are many more interesting facets of the writer's craft. R.E.Helbling's *Groteskes und Absurdes – Paradoxie und Ideologie – Versuch einer Bilanz* (pp.233-253) and G.P.Knapp's

summary *Wege und Unwege – ein Forschungsbericht* (pp.19-43) in *Friedrich Dürrenmatt: Studien zu seinem Werk* (ed. G.P. Knapp), Lothar Stiehm Verlag, Heidelberg 1976, must surely be among the final words. Disappointingly, this book, only published in 1976, went to press in 1971, although the bibliography has been brought up to 31.12.74.

27 K.Kraus: *Die letzten Tage der Menschheit,* Kösel, München, 1957. Band V, p.771. See too F.Field: *The Last Days of Mankind,* Macmillan, London, 1967. In the foreword to the Zürich version of *Portrait eines Planeten* (*Portrait of a Planet*) (1970), Dürrenmatt wrote that he wanted there to achieve the same effect with the simplest means (*TSR II*, pp.194-202).

28. *Die Panne,* Arche 1956 (1959 edn.), translated as *A Dangerous Game* by R. and C.Winston, Cape, London 1960 and as *Traps* by R. and C. Winston, Knopf, New York, 1960.

29. M.Praz: *The Hero in eclipse in Victorian Fiction* (translated by W.Davidson, London 1956).
     B.Allemann: *Es steht geschrieben* in *Das deutsche Drama*, Vol.II (ed. B. von Wiese), Bagel, Düsseldorf, 1964, pp.420-438, here p.427.
     W. Starkie: *Luigi Pirandello*, Murray 1926, p.170.

30. See alienation as *Entfremdung* and its double meaning (separation and surrender) in R.Schacht: *Alienation,* Allen and Unwin 1971, pp.37-54. See too: "*Entfremdung*" is best translated with "distancing". The usual translation "alienation" is in fact misleading since it carries the Hegelian and Marxian meaning to which the word only alludes but which it does not signify". H.Reiss: *The Writer's task from Nietzsche to Brecht*, Macmillan 1978, p.205 (f.n.43).

31. M.Esslin: *Brecht: a choice of evils*, Eyre and Spottiswoode 1959, p.126. On the Brecht-Dürrenmatt controversy, see my article: *Friedrich Dürrenmatt and the legacy of Bertolt Brecht*, Forum for Modern Language Studies, Vol.XII, No.1. January 1976, pp.65-81.

32. T.S.Eliot: *Essay on John Marston* in *Selected Essays* (1932) revised 1951, London, p.229. He was distinguishing between poetic and prose drama.

33. B.Brecht: *Kleines Organon für das Theater*, No.42 in *GW*, Band 16, p.680. On his "comic theory", see L.J.Bird: *The comic world of Bertolt Brecht*, FMLS, Vol.IV, 1968, pp.248-259, particularly p.253.

(iii) COMMENTS FROM VARIED SOURCES

34. *Der Theaterdirektor* in *Die Stadt*, Arche 1952, p.69.

35. A.Joseph: ... *weshalb man ein Drama schreibt*, Süddeutsche Zeitung 8/9.-2.69. He told me that "no one should write without humour", and claimed it as a "spiritual defence mechanism against absolute theses" in *Gespräch 1971* in *TSR II*, pp.267-282, here p.281.

36. P.Spycher in *Friedrich Dürrenmatt: Das erzählerische Werk*, Huber, Frauenfeld 1972, reminds us constantly of Dürrenmatt's admiration for Swift.

37. In *GH*, p.225. Renate Usmiani's *Masterpieces in disguise: The radio plays of Friedrich Dürrenmatt*, Seminar 7, (1971) pp.42-57 (and then in German by the author in *FD: Studien zu seinem Werk*, op.cit., pp.125-144), is one of the best discussions of these works.

38. *Vortrag an der Tagung der evangelischen Akademie für Rundfunk und Fernsehen*, September 1956, *TSR I*, p.63.

39. *Autorenabend im Schauspielhaus Zürich* (25.6.61) in *TSR I*, p.67. These criticisms appear, interestingly enough, more often in the prose works than in the plays. The reason is probably that the novels appeared as serials in Swiss journals and were therefore thought of more as domestic products!

40. *Schriftstellerei als Beruf,* op.cit., p.51. In *Aspects of dramaturgical thinking* he calls Switzerland "an untragic case in a tragic age" (*TSR II*, p.246).

41. On this point, see P.B. Gontrum: *Ritter, Tod und Teufel,* Seminar Vol.1, No.2 Fall 1965, pp.88-98. On *Zufall,* see U.Profitlich: *Der Zufall in den Komödien und Detektivromanen Dürrenmatts,* ZfdPh, Vol.90, 1971, pp.258-280 and his book *Friedrich Dürrenmatt: Komödienbegriff und Komödienstruktur,* Kohlhammer, Stuttgart 1973, particularly pp.27-33 and Note 125, pp.117-118. He defines Chance as "the improbably disruptive factor" in Dürrenmatt's work. E.P.Wieckenberg reminds us of the Jew Gulliver's comment to Bärlach: "... I am here to restore the old order of things", in *Dürrenmatts Detektivromane,* FD II, pp.8-19, here p.13.

42. *Das Versprechen,* Arche 1957-1958 (5th edn. 1966) here p.187. (= *DVS*) Translated by R. and C. Winston as *The Pledge* (Penguin 1959) (1964). Dürrenmatt often quotes the Russian mathematician Alexander Wittenberg who showed that each logical system automatically ended in a paradox. (cf. to Ketels, p.98).

43. M.Peppard: *Friedrich Dürrenmatt,* Twayne (New York) 1969, p.114.

44. *Die Wiedertäufer (The Anabaptists),* Arche 1967 (= DWT). The *Considerations* are on pp.101-109. This is the "reversion" of *Es steht geschrieben (It is written)* (1947). See pp. 176-185 below.

45. Dürrenmatt continued this theme in a series of articles *Gedanken über das Theater (Thoughts on the Theatre)* printed in his own journal *Sonntags Journal* (formerly *Zürcher Woche*) from Nr.16 of 18/19.4.70 to Nr.35 of 29/30.8.70. They are now gathered as *Sätze über das Theater (Sentences on the Theatre)* in *Friedrich Dürrenmatt I,* Nr. 50-51, Text + Kritik, München, May 1976, pp.1-18. (= *FD I*).

46. *Le rire,* op.cit., p.111. Bergson had mentioned, too, the isolation of the "vice comique" such as "le tartuffe", "l'avare" etc.

47. In *TSR II*, pp.128-131, here p.129. Originally *Zwei Dramaturgien? (Two dramaturgies?)* in the Zeitung der Basler Theater, September 1968, p.2.

48. *TSR II*, pp.206-231, here pp.223-224.

49. *FD I*, No.9, p.2.

50. The reference is probably to Brecht's *Ist das epische Theater etwa eine moralische Anstalt? (Is the Epic Theater really a moral institution?)* in *GW*, Band 15, pp.270-272.

51. Arrigo Subiotto rightly points out that Dürrenmatt, like Büchner, Camus and Kafka, all accused of being "nihilists", is rather a "true realist and moralist". See *The Swiss Contribution* in *The German Theatre,* (ed. R. Hayman), Oswald Wolff, London, Barnes and Noble (NY), 1975, pp.171-188, here, p.182.

52. Bergson's answer to an attack on his thesis in *Le Rire,* published in *La Revue du mois,* tome XIX, 10.11.19, p.154 ff. (Printed as an appendix to our quoted edition).

Chapter Three

BAROQUE BEGINNINGS

(i) ES STEHT GESCHRIEBEN *(It Is Written)* (1947)

(ii) DER BLINDE *(The Blind Man)* (1948)

In an epilogue to his collection of short stories *Die Stadt* (*The City*), Dürrenmatt wrote:

> These prose-works are not to be evaluated as an attempt to tell a few stories, but rather as a necessary attempt to sort something out with myself, or as I put it perhaps better in retrospect, to fight a battle which can only have a meaning if it is lost.[1]

The battle that he fought and "lost" was surely as much the battle between prose and drama, as the battle with his Christian beliefs, as Dr Boyd had suggested.[2] Indeed, Dürrenmatt goes on to admit that these stories are to be regarded as the "front-line" supports to his dramas. Greatly influenced by his Kierkegaard studies, the stories bear hardly any trace of humour. They are the productions of a lonely young man wrestling with his adolescent beliefs. When laughter does break through (in *The Theatre Manager*, for example), it is cruel and despairing. Dürrenmatt agreed in our conversation that the stories are now quite untypical of his work and added by way of explanation: "I was very young, it was during the War and I had come straight from philosophy".

Their importance, therefore, is as the preparation for his first published play *Es steht geschrieben* (*It is written*), the première of which, on 19 April, 1947, is memorable for causing the first scandal in living memory at the Zürich Schauspielhaus.[3] Perhaps the theme and the title (the Biblical guarantee for the truth of the Word) would lead an audience, particularly in Zwinglian Zürich of 1947, to expect a work of high seriousness, especially from a pastor's son. Nor had the young author given the audience any cause for alarm in his programme note:

> I did not want to preach a moral, I just wanted to present something — and what I wanted to present is a world in its decline, in its despair, but also in the radiance which clings to everything that is in decline.[4]

Although Karl Schmid in the same programme put the point: "Tragic and comic elements are inborn in the Anabaptist movement", and added that, to him, this play seemed "one of the most despairing and most daring tragicomedies that we have", the audience seemed nevertheless taken aback by the scurrilous treatment of the theme in general, and by the final "Dance on the Roof" in particular.

While Max Frisch wrote that reading the work had made a deeper impression on him than the stage realisation,[5] it is my belief that the rowdy reception of the play was due as much as anything else to Dürrenmatt's unusual use of the various comic elements. I believe too that the Zürich reaction lead Dürrenmatt to two convictions: firstly, that the comic was, and perhaps always would be, "something second-rate" in German-speaking lands, and, secondly, for that very reason, it would serve him well as an "uncomfortable" instrument with which to achieve his ends – although he had to write *Der Blinde* (*The Blind Man*) to be quite certain, as will be seen. He had discovered his talent *and* his method.

The play has probably vanished from the stage and, since the author has produced a new version *Die Wiedertäufer* (*The Anabaptists*), I shall deal with it more fully later. But Beda Allemann could yet be right when he suggested "that one day this play will attract the attention of the expert as the characteristic early work of a modern author in which all the basics for an effective and fruitful theatrical career are prefigured in a fascinating way".[6]

Gerhard Neumann has tried to show how Dürrenmatt (in his later works) has moved away from the treatment of a "problem" to the treatment of a "conflict": "To consider problems . . . , to weigh them up in scene and counter-scene, has always been the task of tragedy . . ." Tragedies demand consequences and a solution. "Conflicts, on the other hand, here and gone in an instant, without consequences, to be endured but not solved, demand comedy".[7]

Speaking to René Sauter in 1966, Dürrenmatt agreed: "What really interests an author, and what fascinates him, is a conflict" – which takes us back to one of the hastily-composed aphorisms contemporaneous with this play: "As a problem, the world can almost be solved, as a conflict, not at all".[8]

The finding of solutions has been eschewed by the modern dramatist, possibly since Ibsen's "I am here to ask, not to answer". It is surely not coincidental that the comic bulks so large in the dramaturgy of our times and that the outstanding feature of the Attic Old Comedy was the "agon", the conflict.

*   *   *

It *is* of course possible to maintain that *It is written* treated a problem rather than a conflict. Was Professor Waidson therefore correct to call this play (and *Der Blinde*) "experiments in tragedy. . . they seem to point to tragedy or at least to no conscious intention to avoid tragedy"?[9]

It is my view that the play might well have been called a *Komödie* because of the superabundance of comic elements (which Professor Waidson of course acknowledges), and because it can be seen to be not a "problem play" but, as Allemann says, "a fundamental persiflage of all likely problem-plays".

In our discussion of the *Tractatus Coislinianus*, mention was made of the standard characters of the Attic Old Comedy, the "eiron", the "alazon" and the "bomolochoi". Aristotle wrote of the first two: "Pretence, if it takes the form of exaggeration, is boastfulness ("alazoneia") . . . but if it takes the form of depreciation, it is irony ("eironeia") . . ."[10]

The four main characters of *It is written* all display undoubted comic traits — these, allied to the fragmented "open" structure of the work and the parodistical and farcical nature of its language, would seem to indicate that Dürrenmatt meant to make the play evoke laughter, and that he conceived the work in terms of "comedy". Bockelson, for example, is the "alazon"-character. Cornford described these characters as the "unwelcome intruders who thrust themselves upon the 'hero' and his society and are then driven out".

From his arrival in Münster, which he describes in the exaggerated hyperbolical terms of comedy ("The Archangel Gabriel bore me through the air . . . We were just over Münster which we could see spread out beneath our feet when the sun blinded him. He sneezed and let me fall into this barrow where you've found me unconscious") (*ESG*, p.21), to his last grotesque dance on the roof, Bockelson is portrayed as the thrusting intruder-adventurer, the boaster, the Plautinian "miles-gloriosus"-type who attempts to impose his will upon the community until he is eventually driven out; in this case, put to death. His anonymous end demonstrates the empty absurdity of his life; he ends as a number, a non-human being, a "thing" to be laughed at:

> *The Sentinel*: Number 524: Johann Bockelson from Leyden.
> A really nicely preserved corpse (p.112).

Knipperdollinck, Jan Matthisson and the Bishop von Waldeck are likewise all "comic-types"; Knipperdollinck has taken the paradoxes of Matthew xix,30, so literally that he is not only the medieval "holy fool", but also the comic dupe of the classic farce. His obsession with the literal Biblical word "it is written", his "idée fixe", makes him a comic character. He is indeed a *potentially* tragic character — but his comic situation denies him tragic stature.

So, too, Jan Matthisson. Also a man possessed, a clown-like character whom Dürrenmatt instructed should even look like a Don Quixote — "...a very tall, thin actor ..." with a comic phallus-like sword as big as himself (*Stage direction*, p.48). From his opening "Address to the Audience", his rôle underlines the absurdity of the monomoniac who, by the monotony of his insistence on a literal acceptance of an out-dated heroic Christianity, becomes an "automaton", a machine in its unchanging reactions. There is something to admire in this strange figure marching out to its lonely useless death — but the "idée fixe" again robs it too off any tragic dignity. In Bergson's phrase, there is a "certain particular lack of adaptation of the character to society" here.

These characters might be called, in Aristotelian terms, "self-deprecators", but the true "eiron" in the play is the Bishop, 99 years, 9 months and 9 days old! He is the middle way between the fantastic grotesqueness of a Bockelson and the obsessive but useless humility of a Knipperdollinck, for he ends as "the detached but not unsympathetic spectator of the drama ... of human life", J.A.K.Thomson's definition of the *eiron*.[11]

The "bomolochoi", whose function in the Old Comedy was solely "to increase the mood of festivity" are plainly represented here by the participators in what I should like to call the scenes of "pantofarce": the comic Cook, the Street-sweeper. ("the learned menial"), the Chronometric Turk, the drunken Nightwatchman, the pedantic Town-crier, the vulgar and obscene Vegetable-woman. These, with the "automata", von Büren and von Mengerssen, and the Count of Hesse's two wives, represent those boisterous elements of the *mimus* which have come down to us through the *commedia dell'arte* and show the importance that Dürrenmatt attached here to creating laughter.

These brief considerations make me conclude that this play could properly have been termed a "Komödie"; it is an open-ended "agon" between the Anabaptists and the Bishop with no solution offered at the end. The fact that two of its main characters die is, of course, not of itself tragic; at the most, their deaths are sad. Bockelson's might have been tragic since he was brought down by *hubris* — but the absurd anonymity of his death, that "grotesque buffoonery" (which Jan Kott saw in Lear) made his life as if it had never been.

Nor could Knipperdollinck's end properly be called tragic, since his last speech on the wheel can only mean that Heaven's doors would open to him and this "least touch of theology", as Richards called it would be fatal to a tragic hero. His end demonstrates the limitations of Man — a good illustration of Heinz Kindermann's "comic of insufficiency" — and the comic ambience robs the death of any tragic dignity or stature.[12]   Knipperdollinck is a clown — but in contradistinction to the alazon-characters, whom I should like to call "professional clowns", Knipperdollinck is a "spiritual clown", one of those whose rôle is normally a major one and who represents the individual lost in, and alienated from his environment — like Jan Matthisson, also a comic figure, a "clown", who dies a quixotic death bordering on absurdity and, in his case, is saved only by the Bishop's sympathy.

It is in the latter character that we see the true eiron-figure, the man who leads the foolish on to a foolish death and who represents the common-sense which they so obviously lack. Mocked he and his authority may be, but it is in the Bishop's humanity that we hear the voice of the author himself.

I should therefore paraphrase Professor Waidson's remark and say that, here, there was no conscious intention to avoid *comedy*. In the conception of the characters, in the structure of the play and the dialogue, Dürrenmatt's use of the various comic elements makes it clear that, in his very first play, he is obviously following a well-established comic tradition with which he is clearly familiar.

(ii) DER BLINDE (THE BLIND MAN)

That this was to be his forte was clearly shown by the results of his next dramatic work. When Manfred Züfle wrote: "*The Blind Man* is Dürrenmatt's most boring play, although it would like to carry the most profound message", I was tempted to substitute "because" for "although".[13]

In *It is written*, Dürrenmatt skilfully employed the elements of the comic to make what might have been called an "intellectualized farce"; the verbal and physical clowning were part of the serious theme. His change of mood from that baroque extravagance to an almost ascetic severity is a paradoxical gesture reminiscent of his own literary style. As Urs Jenny put it:

> Dürrenmatt's inclination, if not to say his method, always to tumble from one extreme to another, can also be seen in the zig-zag line taken by his works. . .[14]

It was claimed that the first play had some claim to be termed a *Komödie*; I am more ready to treat *The Blind Man* as an "experiment in tragedy" — but an experiment that (fortunately) failed.

We know what Dürrenmatt himself had in mind. He wrote in *Problems of the Theatre*: "It was my aim in *The Blind Man* to set the word against the location of the plot, to direct the word against the image" (*TP*, p.25), a continuation of that struggle to free himself from the tyranny of the visual arts. Thus the play is, in Frau Brock-Sulzer's words, "an attempt at a pure word-drama", an attempt to create the dramatic ambience "through the word alone, through the game that awakes the fantasy of the audience", as Dürrenmatt wrote of Thornton Wilder's dramatic method.[15]

★   ★   ★

In a little-known essay on "Comedy", Christopher Fry wrote: "The Book of Job is the great reservoir of comedy. . ." and it is of some interest that Dürrenmatt, the pastor's son, should choose this book of the Bible for his "experiment in tragedy".[16]

The Blind Man, a story of the tempter and the tempted, is an "agon", a conflict between the two main characters, the Duke, the blind protagonist, and representative of God, and Negro da Ponte, the antagonist and representative of Evil. It has been well said that they resemble the "actors in a mystery play" and have "something of the spirit of the Baroque theatre . . . immanently religious" about them, with a "tragicomic ambivalence".[17]

The Duke is certainly entirely serious as a character. Nothing that he says or does would raise a laugh — yet he is also essentially *un*tragic. The plot shows the absurdity of his "blind" faith in everything; he becomes a "Fool of Faith" as he believes in turn in Negro, in the Players, in Palamedes and in Gnadenbrot Suppe. The play is indeed the "comedy" of his errors, his blind belief, since much of the icy comic that is in the play lies in the rôle-playing of the other characters. Indeed, when Negro tells the Actor, "You can act what you like before him and he will believe everything", the Actor replies: "This will make a jolly comedy (*Komödie*)" (p.130).

The absurdity of the play and the absurdity of the Duke is the absurdity of the demands which Christianity make upon the believer. Dürrenmatt wrote later: "The difficulties that a Protestant has with the art of drama are exactly the same as he has with his faith" (*TP* p.52), and Waldmann has shown how many leading theologians agree with Dürrenmatt's treatment of the Christian paradoxes and absurdities.[18]

The Duke is therefore a "Fool" who acts out the play against a background of absurdity — absurdity in two senses: the absurdity of his "irrational" belief in God and the goodness of Man, and the absurdity of the "play within the play", the illusion of truth. Negro seems to have the Duke in his power, when he himself is robbed of victory by the third absurdity, in the form of Chance, Octavia's unforeseen suicide, and he departs "blind" also, defeated by the Duke's irrational faith: "I leave you, tapping like a blind man", he says (p.191).

One could claim that even in this chilly Existentialist-like work, Dürrenmatt confronts us with the two major characters of the Comedy, the Duke, the self-deprecator, the "spiritual clown" who "accepts worldly absurdity as a sign of divine justice,"[19] and one of those "valiant men" who, as Dürrenmatt himself wrote later, accepts the world as an "enigma of disaster that must be accepted, but before which there must be no capitulation" (*TP*, p.49), while his antagonist, Negro da Ponte, the "black bridge" over which the Duke will reach his faith, is the imposter, the "alazon" who arrives to impose his will upon the community and is driven out. The character of Negro is perhaps the proof that Dürrenmatt could never write "pure" tragedy. There is something Mephistophelian about it, something of that great character's essential untragicality. As Eudo Mason said of Mephisto: "He finds it an immense joke that he should be the devil, it is a fact indeed, but a fact that he himself can never take seriously".[20]

All Negro's planning comes to nought through Octavia's suicide, and he too becomes a "Fool", differing only in kind and not in degree from the Duke. There is no tragedy, no nemesis here, only a sense of waste. It is truly that "allegory of waste" which George Steiner saw in Brechtian drama. Had the circumstances been different, the waste need never have occurred. Chance ruled all.[21]

The "bomolochoi", the "buffoons", as I called them, in the persons of what Dürrenmatt always calls the "Gesindel" (the rabble), are also present in this work. Indeed, they are the sole "laughter-makers": the Actor, the leader and incongruous speechifier, Schwefel, the grotesque gourmand, Lucianus, the comic pessimist, the prostitute-turned-nun, and the negro, who, like Harpo Marx, causes laughter by his inability to communicate. They will play, as the Actor says, "a tragicomedy or a comic tragedy" (p.139). These characters are themselves paradoxes dramatized; none is what he or she seems to be, the comic lies in the contrast between the reality and the illusion. They have, however, that connection with reality which is the mainspring of all comedy. They are realists in seeing the chance to improve their lot and reaching for it. In so doing, however, they have de-humanized themselves, brutalized themselves for, as Dürrenmatt wrote much later in his career, "the clown is the man distanced from other men, the inhuman human being". The clown is always a realistic pessimist.[22]

Only a Swiss writer could "parody ruins", Berghahn has suggested,[23] and *The Blind Man* was quite clearly Dürrenmatt's attempt to come to terms with the philosophy of his age, the *Zeitgeist*. It was an attempt that, just as clearly, failed. Yet out of the experience of writing this play grew the dramatic theory which he later schematized in *Problems of the Theatre* where, as has been seen, he postulated the decline of the tragic hero and the substitution of tragedy by the *Komödie*.

★　　★　　★

In my view, both Professor Waidson who wrote that *The Blind Man* is Dürrenmatt's most consistent tragedy, and Karl Guthke who would have it that this play has "a marked disposition to tragicomedy", fail to substantiate their claims.[24] There is no spirit of tragedy here, essential for a true tragicomedy, but rather a "comedy of despair", of waste. The main characters, like Bockelson and Knipperdollinck, become comic fools; the Duke is the "holy fool" who strives, albeit foolishly, to believe; Negro is the Fool who, like Bockelson, negates Life.

After *The Blind Man* Dürrenmatt realized that he could attain his "philosophical" tragic through his type of comedy — but perhaps more important still, he realized that he had within himself the gift for making audiences laugh and I shall insist that this has always been of paramount importance to him. The sound of laughter in the theatre is music to his ears. "The education of the human race towards humour, to me, that means the same as the education of the human race towards humanity," he said to René Sauter. "There is no humanity without humour".[25]

NOTES TO CHAPTER THREE

(i) ES STEHT GESCHRIEBEN (IT IS WRITTEN)

1. Although *Die Stadt* was published in 1952, the stories were mainly written between 1943 and 1946. Spycher documents the revisions of *Die Falle* and *Pilatus* between 1947-1948 (op.cit., pp.31-32).
2. To be fair, in his later conversations with Heinz Ludwig Arnold, Dürrenmatt said that he had "battles" on both fronts, between prose and drama and between his father and his religion. See U.D.Boyd: *Die Funktion des Grotesken als Symbol der Gnade in Dürrenmatts dramatischem Werk*, University of Maryland, Ph.D. dissertation 1964, p.244. K.A.Pestalozzi in *Friedrich Dürrenmatt* in *Deutsche Literatur im 20. Jahrundert* (ed. Mann und Rothe) Francke, Bern, (5th edn.) 1967, pp.385-402, broadly agrees with me. (See p.387).
3. *Es steht geschrieben. Ein Drama* in *K II*, Arche 1959, pp.12-115 (= *ESG*).
4. Programmheft, Schauspielhaus Zürich, 1946-1947, p.7.
5. Tagesanzeiger, 10.5.47. See too his *Tagebuch* op.cit., p.263. Tiusanen suggests, on the other hand, that "the text does not carry the burden placed on it by the setting" (op.cit., p.51).
6. B.Allemann: *Es steht geschrieben*, op.cit., p.438.
7. G.Neumann: *Friedrich Dürrenmatt: Dramaturgie der Panne* in G.Neumann, J.Schröder, M.Karnick: *Dürrenmatt, Frisch, Weiss*, Fink, München 1969, p.38.
8. Conversation with René Sauter in Sinn und Form, 18Jg, Heft 4 1966, pp. 1218-1232, here p.1219. The aphorism is in: *Hingeschriebenes* (1947-1948) in *TSR I*, pp.87-89.
9. H.M.Waidson: *Friedrich Dürrenmatt* in *Swiss Men of Letters*, O.Wolff, 1970, pp.259-286, here p.264. A shorter version of this is in *German Men of Letters*, Vol.III (ed. A.Natan), O.Wolff 1964, pp.323-343.
10. Aristotle: *Nicomachean Ethics*, translated by J.E.C.Welldon, London 1892, rev. Lane Cooper pp.51-52.
11. J.A.K.Thomson: *Irony*, Allen and Unwin, 1926, p.163.
12. H.Kindermann in *Meister der Komödien*, Wien, München 1952.

(ii) DER BLINDE (THE BLIND MAN)

13. M.Züfle: *Zu den Bühnengestalten Friedrich Dürrenmatts:* Schweizer Rundschau, LXVI, 2, 1967, pp.98-110, here p.100. Tiusanen sees the play as a return to the Kafkaesque world of the middle stories in *Die Stadt* 1945-6, (p.68), but see Note 13 to Chapter One above.
14. U.Jenny: *Dürrenmatt*, Friedrichs Dramatiker des Welttheaters, Band 6, Velber, 1965, (5th edn. 1973), p.24. Now translated as *Dürrenmatt: A study of his plays*, Methuen, 1978.
15. E.Brock-Sulzer; op.cit., p.31. Dürrenmatt in *TP*, p.24. *Der Blinde* is in *K II*, pp.116-191, here p.78. It is called "Ein Drama".
16. C.Fry: *Comedy*, The Tulane Drama Review, IV, No.3 1960, pp.77-79, here p.78.
17. J.Müller: *Max Frisch und Friedrich Dürrenmatt als Dramatiker der Gegenwart*, Universitas Bd.12, No.7 1962, pp.725-738, here p.732. Max Wehrli called the play "stage as *theatrum mundi*" in *Gegenwartsliteratur der deutschen Schweiz: Deutsche Literatur in unserer Zeit*, Göttingen 1961-1962, pp.105-124, here p.120. Sydney Groseclose finds the language of the play "much more archaic than the seventeenth century" and traces it back to the

Old Testament. D.S.Groseclose: *The Murder of Gnadenbrot Suppe*, GLL, Vol.XXVIII, October 1974, No.1, pp.64-71.

18. G.Waldmann: *Dürrenmatts paradoxes Theater*, Wirkendes Wort, 14, Heft 1, 1964, pp.32-35. He cites Brunner and Bultmann in particular: "The contents of Faith are all paradoxes ... essential contradictions in themselves" (Brunner), while Bultmann called the Christian belief "a lost, senseless possibility".

19. R.Holzapfel: *The divine plan behind the plays of Friedrich Dürrenmatt*, Modern Drama VIII, Lawrence, Kansas, December 1965, pp.237-246, here p.240.

20. E.C.Mason: *Goethe's Faust; its genesis and purport*, University of California Press, 1967, p.171.

21. G.Steiner: *The Death of Tragedy*, op.cit., p.297 and p.346.

22. Dürrenmatt shows later that the clown, for him, is the opposite of the hero demanded by our two great ideologies, Marxism and Christianity. Both demand *positive* heroes. (*Aspects of Dramaturgical Thinking, TSR II*, p.226).

23. W.Berghahn: *Friedrich Dürrenmatts Spiel mit den Ideologien*, Frankfurter Hefte, 11 Jg, Heft 2, 1956, pp.100-106, here p.105.

24. Waidson, op.cit., p.264. Guthke, op.cit., p.437. Guthke wrongly dates the play 1944. The première was in Basel on 10.1.48.

25. Sauter, op.cit., p.1224.

Chapter Four

THE "TRAGEDY-TRAP"

(i) ROMULUS DER GROSSE (*Romulus the Great*) (1949)
(ii) DIE EHE DES HERRN MISSISSIPPI (*The Marriage of Mr Mississippi*) (1952)
(iii) EIN ENGEL KOMMT NACH BABYLON (*An Angel comes to Babylon*)
(1953)

The period between 10 January, 1948 (the première of *The Blind Man*)
and 25 April, 1949 (the Basle première of *Romulus der Grosse* (Romulus the Great) marks a caesura in Dürrenmatt's career as a dramatist. As
was suggested at the end of Chapter Three, the failure of *The Blind Man*
on the stage — it ran for only ten performances — and, more important,
Dürrenmatt's awareness of the reasons for its failure, had led him to
reconsider his strengths and weaknesses as a dramatist. Although he was
never to cease swinging violently between various choices and treat-
ments of subjects, the extremes of his first two plays enabled him to
see more clearly where his path should lead. Two simple but inescap-
able facts had emerged: he was unsympathetic to the philosophy of
tragedy — and he was able to write good stage comedy. One cannot
stress often and firmly enough that Dürrenmatt had become at this
stage, and was now to remain, a "man of the theatre".

The next three plays can be taken as evidence of this preoccupa-
tion with the theatre, just as the plays themselves lead us, via his major
critical work, *Problems of the Theatre* (1955) along the road to Güllen
and his masterpiece, *The Visit of the Old Lady* (1956). The financial
backing of Ernst Ginsberg and Kurt Horwitz, who had produced and/or
acted in the first two plays was of enormous significance to the young
writer — but Ginsberg's influence went farther than this, as Dürrenmatt's moving appreciation of him demonstrates.

Dürrenmatt recalls that,when he met Ginsberg in 1946, he was full
of philosophical theories, the theatre was a closed world to him:

> The crisis of my career as a writer occurred after my second play
> *The Blind Man*. That play was still all "message", the illustration of
> a religious problem, a play of language arias whose characters were
> scarcely outlined. I had fled from the characters into fine literature.[1]

Ginsberg's *Hamlet* led Dürrenmatt to a decision about his own playwriting. He asked himself: "whether he should start from a problem or

a conflict" (p.207). His answer: If the dramatist starts with the problem, then he has to solve it, but then, the plot, as an illustration of the problem, can only be presented as a conflict. The solution of the problem is not however the solution of the conflict which lies at the heart of the problem:

> If the dramatist starts with a conflict, then he does not need a solution, only a conclusion, his plot is not the illustration of a problem, but the presentation of a conflict.

where problems are introduced but do not have to be solved.

Dürrenmatt felt that his way was "from now on . . . to start *only* with a conflict", and to leave the *solution* of the problems to the "thinkers". The writer's and the actor's task was "to make the character visible in his conflicts, to document him" (p.209). This would seem to imply therefore that Dürrenmatt's aim now was to present his material in as effective a form as possible for the stage — and thus to agree with his Swiss colleague, Max Frisch, who had written earlier:

> As a playwright, I would think I had completely fulfilled my mission if one of my plays ever succeeded in posing a question in such a way that, from that hour on, the audience could no longer live without an answer . . .[2]

Such considerations led Dürrenmatt to choose as his future theatrical medium that form of "agonistic comedy" on Aristophanic lines which was earlier examined and which, I claimed, could properly be termed *Komödie*.

*   *   *

Romulus der Grosse (*Romulus the Great*) has appeared in four versions: the first, of the première, exists only in manuscript form in the archives of the Zürich Schauspielhaus; the second was published in 1957, the third in 1961, and the fourth in 1964, the version prepared by Dürrenmatt for the Paris production in that year.[3] Its sub-title "An unhistorical, historical *Komödie*" must be read against the background of the historical Romulus — but also against that of the contemporary political situation in Europe, since Dürrenmatt has admitted that he wrote the play with the flow of refugees from Nazi Germany into Switzerland in mind.

This was the period of the later German Federal Republic's economic genius, Ludwig Erhard's, currency reform on 22-24 June 1948, the

ensuing blockade of West Berlin (to May, 1949), and Winston Churchill's neologism, "The Cold War". After the war, Switzerland had
gradually lost her position as the "Hüter der Mitte"; and with it went
many long-cherished concepts about the "defence of the realm", since
she could no longer afford "heroic" gestures. The consequence was a
violent swing to what was called a "defence-neurosis" or a "hedgehog-
perspective", the fear not only of an attack from a foreign power, but
of Communist infiltration from within. To this had to be added the
guilt complex from which many Swiss suffered as a result of the knowledge of dubious transactions with the Nazi economy during the war.[4]

Such historical data are necessary to appreciate Dürrenmatt's comic
intentions in *Romulus*; this is no study-based philosophical treatise,
but a live discussion of contemporary issues. Where in *The Blind Man*,
Dürrenmatt had played with *irony*, here he goes somewhat farther,
to *satire*, or "militant irony", as Northrop Frye has trenchantly called
it. Dürrenmatt's "object" of satire was the Old Guard in Switzerland
who refused to give up the heroic attitudes of the past; his "method"
was to blend the elements of the comic into a "political" *Komödie*.
In his *Note on the Komödie*, he praised the Aristophanic Comedy
which was "too political not to be dependent on politics and too
coarse to be accepted as an aesthetic form" (*TSR I*, p.134).

Romulus must therefore be seen as an Aristophanic "invasion of
reality", a comedy on contemporary politics; Dürrenmatt underlined
this himself in his programme note for the Basle première:

> I beg to look questioningly at the states, and I look at them ques-
> tioningly. It is not a play against the State, but perhaps one against
> the super State.[5]

Although Dürrenmatt has always protested that his characters are
people and not marionettes, only a few critics have agreed with him;
there are those who, like Dr Dyrenforth, would claim that, in *Romulus*,
Dürrenmatt failed to achieve the "distance" that he was seeking, just
as Brecht had failed with Mother Courage, Shen Te and Galileo.[6] The
question to be asked is: Do the elements of the comic create this
distance by making us laugh at the character, or is our sympathy so
strong that his end can appear tragic? Are we dealing with a true
Komödie, a tragicomedy — or perhaps even a tragedy?

★   ★   ★

Romulus has been deceiving his family and court for twenty years, "playing the fool", in order to bring about the fall of the Empire. His wife Julia says: "You've been playing the cynic and the eternally greedy buffoon" (p.51). In Act I, he is presented to us therefore more as a "professional" than a "spiritual" clown in our terminology. We hear that the Finance Minister has decamped — with the Imperial Treasure chest: "Why?" asks Romulus innocently, "... there was nothing in it, after all" (p.13). To pay his faithful retainers, on the Ides of March, he breaks off two gold leaves from his laurel wreath, but asks them to return what is left after deducting their debts. He sells off the busts of his Imperial ancestors to pay for his hen-food. From the outset, then, a character of comic incongruities: in Kantian terminology, one expects an Imperial gesture and receives a clown's. In Freudian terminology, the figure is "unzweckmässig", "ill-adapted" to the rôle it is playing, and one laughs at the incongruity.

It is incongruous that an Emperor should keep hens; the hen is the most banal of creatures and its product, the egg, appears at the least Imperial of meals, breakfast. It is incongruous for an Emperor of Rome to sit down at breakfast in purple toga and laurel wreath to eat the eggs of hens named Tiberius, the Julians, the Flavians, Domitian and Marcus Aurelius (all of which have comically incongruous associations with the historical Romulus).[7]

Throughout Act 1, Romulus is the tinder from which the satire flies. With the speed which, as Freud pointed out, is the essence of the witticism, he mocks the members of his Court. Tullius Rotundus ("Fat Tullius") the Home Secretary, purports to bear a "world-shattering report": "Reports never shatter the world," replies Romulus — "only events can do that — and they have happened long before the announcement arrives" (p.16).

His wife Julia suspects the (Swiss) Grand Master of the Court, Äbius (= Äbi!), of being a spy and Romulus himself of being "a real Germanophile". "Rubbish!" replies Romulus, "I don't like them half as much as my hens" (p.17). Rea, his daughter, has lost her appetite and her fiancé, Ämilian, and has taken to studying Greek drama: "Rehearse the Komödie, that's more in our line", is her father's advice (p.19).

It would seem therefore that Romulus is one of our "professional clowns", even a "Merry Andrew". That this behaviour was carried through to Act IV in the first version, with the result that Romulus' abdication to a caricatured horde of Germani lost its full dramatic significance, was largely responsible for the play's being termed a "farce" by some.

In the second (1957) version, however, after the appearance of *Problems of the Theatre*, Dürrenmatt ensured that the significance of Romulus' abdication was *not* lost. When he reveals to Julia (in Act III) that he has been "playing the fool" and "fooling" the Court for twenty years and that his aim has been to bring down Rome through his very passivity ("I am Rome's judge", p.52), it is clear that the author meant us to sense something more than buffoonery. It is plain now too that he meant this even in the first version. The peripeteia in Act IV (what Dürrenmatt was later to call the "worst possible turn")[8] shows us that Romulus is really a "spiritual" rather than a "professional" clown. Odoaker not only refuses him the "tragic death" that he had planned, but offers him a humiliating pension — mainly because of the "chance" coincidence that Odoaker too is a hen-fancier. He can see Romulus as a fellow human-being: "I never saw a greater man," he says to his Germani, "and you'll never see a greater either" (p.77).

Such an end makes mockery of Romulus' grand design. It is precisely because this end, this "turn", is no working of "iron fate", but rather of incalculable Chance, that Romulus says: "Everything that I've done has become absurd" (p.72). This is indeed a "dramaturgy of hitches", as Neumann has called it.[9] It is this absurdity which makes Romulus an *un*tragic figure, an absurdity deepened by the comic contrast between the many descriptions given of the (expected) barbaric Germani and the (actual) mild-mannered, cultured, poultry-loving Odoaker, dressed not unlike Tischbein's famous picture of Goethe in the Campagna (p.67).

This was the first time that Dürrenmatt had used the term "absurd" in his plays. Because Romulus also uses "Narr" ("Fool") of himself (p.72), since he has allowed his people to perish on the battlefield and his family to perish on the high seas, "and now *my* sacrifice isn't being accepted", it can be seen that we are being invited to pass judgement on him. He *is* a "Narr", a Fool and a clown, but also an "eiron"-type, a spiritual clown, since he is trying to face the world's absurdity as a *human being*, with his attempt "to put sense into non-sense" (p.75). Like Cop in Dürrenmatt's later play *Der Mitmacher* (1973), Romulus wants to say: No!

*   *   *

"It's not my aim to show a witty man", Dürrenmatt wrote for the première in 1949, but in his *Note* to the 1957 version, he wrote:

Look closely at the sort of man I have drawn: witty, relaxed, human, certainly, yet, in the last analysis, a man who acts with extreme ruthlessness and severity and doesn't shrink from demanding the absolute from others ... ,

that is, he now stresses the humour and the down-to-earth humanity of the character. When Romulus accepted reality, he accepted it as a *man*: "Let's act out the *Komödie* for the last time", he says to Odoaker. "Let's act as if our account were being presented down here on earth, as if the spirit were conquering the material man" (p.75). This is the eiron's triumph, a moral one. (It is interesting to note how this attitude was taken to be a Christian one: Max Frisch's 1949 review stressed "the religious element" in the play; Duwe saw "the principle of Christian self-sacrifice" in it, while Frau Brock-Sulzer saw Romulus behave "according to the Christian principle of non-resistance". There is, however, no mention of Christianity in her next book and a reason will have to be sought for this later).[10]

For me, however, Romulus enters his retirement a spiritual clown, one of Bergson's "runners after the ideal who stumble over realities", for, as Romulus says to Odoaker: "Reality has corrected our ideals" (p.75). Thus, although Dürrenmatt writes of "this judge of the universe, disguised as a Fool whose tragedy is actually the comedy of his end, in his being pensioned off ..." (p.79), I see not "tragedy", but what Otto Rommel called the "bitterness of impotence" in his definition of *Komödie*. Romulus' end is serious, yes, but essentially *un*tragic. As he himself says to the servant Achilles at the beginning of Act III: "I am an untragic man" (p.47). Tragedy presents the world as unchangeable, or demonstrates that its changes are beyond Man's control. There is no inexorable logic in Romulus' absurd end; it cannot arouse pity and terror, but, at the most, sympathy, and ridicule, too. The comic elements in his character, and of his situation, destroy the potential tragic of both.

"Ämilian is Romulus' opposite number", writes Dürrenmatt in the *Note*. Here is the "antagonist", an alazon-type character who comes in from outside and tries to disrupt the community: "This Emperor must go!" (p.46). In addition, Ämilian has an *idée fixe*, his obsessive patriotism: "I am a patriot. I've come to visit my Fatherland" (p.37). The "conflict" here is between Romulus' humanity and Amilian's unconditional demand that one's country must come first and should be defended. Romulus had told his daughter, Rea, that one should love a human being before one's country. Dürrenmatt provides no solution to this conflict − simply an end, and Ämilian remains a rather shadowy

character. Yet, in him, the author tries to show the more positive side
of patriotism, that is, he does not condone it but he does appreciate
that Ämilian (and others) are prepared to suffer hardship for their
ideals. Ämilian, that "victim of those in power and soiled a thousand
times over", is an entirely serious character with whom the author can
contrast those laughable elements in an obsessive, narrow patriotism.
Yet, although Dürrenmatt has said that, without Ämilian, Romulus
would have been simply a "nihilist and a cynic", there were those in
Switzerland who did take Romulus to be just that — and Ämilian as a
satirical portrait of a patriot. A.W. Schwengeler wrote:

> Let him ridicule Bubenberg's words: "As long as there is a drop of
> blood left in our veins, none will yield" — the spirit of the man
> who spoke these words outlived generations of nihilists. He will
> outlive Dürrenmatt's *Romulus* as well . . . ,[11]

the reference being to Romulus' earlier remark: "I know the last words
of my generals before they are captured by the Germani: 'As long as
there is a drop of blood left in our veins, none will yield!' They've all
said that" (p.20).

Such people failed to realize that the author was striving to show
the ghastly results of a useless patriotism, results obvious from any
war. Ämilian is indeed "only the ravished victim of the very power
which he is trying to save by his own sacrifice and that of his fiancée".[12]
His death on an unseaworthy raft makes his end "absurd", too. The
comic fanatic has been "driven out".

Odoaker is an even more shadowy figure than Ämilian, appearing,
of course, only in Act IV. His importance for the theme of the play is
that he too is made to look absurd through the comic situation in
which he is placed. Like Romulus, he had made plans which are frustrated by Chance, plans which he feels are guided by Reason: "Even a
German can let himself be counselled by Reason, Emperor of Rome",
he says, a nice touch of Helvetic satire (p.71).

The comic arises from the double contrast which Odoaker offers:
on the one hand, the leader of the "barbaric" Germani who is dressed
"quite unwarlike" (p.67) and is more interested in tracing the progress
of the strain of hen which he had introduced into Italy than sacking
the Empire; on the other, the cultured, rational, peasant-philosopher,
dreading the rule of his brutal nephew, Theoderich, with its German-
cum-Nazi promise of an eventual "world-conquering race of heroes"
(p.71)[13] and laying plans to avoid it, contrasted with the "failed
politician" who must discover, with Romulus, that Man has in fact
no power over his fate: "We have power only over the present which

we didn't take into account and which has brought us both down"
(p.74) that is, *both* men have attained the opposite of what they had
planned — Odoaker had conquered Italy to surrender his people to
Romulus and save them from Theoderich, but, by doing this, he had
prevented Romulus from sacrificing *himself* and his people to Odoaker
to avoid another brutal Roman Empire.[14] Thus, Odoaker too is a
"Narr", a Fool, too shadowy and insubstantial a figure to be a spiritual
clown, but one of those whose "intellect is incapable of directing his
actions sensibly", as Waldmann put it.[15]

★   ★   ★

"The play's real humour lies neither in the plot nor in the theme: it lies
in the language", writes Therese Poser;[16] although my remarks on the
characters, and on the structural elements below, show that I hardly
agree with her judgement, it will nevertheless be useful to consider the
language of the play at this stage of the discussion: for two reasons.

Firstly, Romulus, not unlike Goethe's Egmont, is the sun around
which all the other characters revolve, or, to change the metaphor, they
are mirrors which reflect various aspects of his character; their characters are likewise revealed mainly in their dialogues with Romulus.
Secondly, the minor characters are linguistically satirized caricatures; in
studying their language, we shall also be studying their portrayal as
characters.

Rea, the daughter, is satirized as the pseudo-cultured bourgeoise,
studying "drama", in her case, and significantly, *classical* drama:
"Antigone's Lamentation before she meets her death" (p.18); Romulus
mocks her, and the Classics, with his "Don't study that sad, old text.
Rehearse the Komödie, that's more in our line" (p.19). It is a satirical
parody, both of the Sophoclean text and the bourgeois convention.
Secondly, Rea is satirized as the unthinking bourgeois patriot who,
when Cäsar Rupf offers to marry her and give Rome ten millions in
return, believes this to be clearly her duty — rather than marry her
tortured fiancé, Ämilian.

Romulus' answer to Rea's question is similar to that given by Dürrenmatt to a questioner on his views on Swiss patriotism:

> I don't believe that we have to serve Switzerland. Switzerland has to
> serve us. It's the wrong way round. The country is there for the
> people, not the other way round.[17]

Similarly, Julia, Romulus' wife, is mocked as the selfish ambitious woman whose "terrible marriage" (p.49) is as much a standard comic ingredient as her silly talk. Dürrenmatt satirizes her martial patriotism by making Romulus answer her heroics with banalities such as:

Julia: You must do something! Romulus, you must do something straightaway, or we're lost.
Romulus: I shall draft a proclamation to my soldiers this afternoon.
            p.20.

Romulus' seemingly inconsequential answers show up the language of false patriotism. The contrast is between the (pseudo) serious and the banal; but, as Dürrenmatt wrote once: "There are only platitudes. But unfortunately ours is an age which is only concerned with platitudes. Profundity has become a luxury".[18]

Each of the "bomolochoi", the "buffoons", belongs, we find, to a different language area, whose jargon is satirized — politician, ruler, servant, artist, business man, art dealer and soldier. The language becomes a comic alienating factor.[19]

"Fat Tullius" rushes in with tragic news of the war: "It's terrible! It's awful!" Romulus pricks the pompous balloon with: "I know, my dear Minister of the Interior, I've not paid your salary for years..." (p.15) — expectation is frustrated. In Act II, Tullius is a caricature of bumbling officialdom. Ämilian is astonished at the burning of the Roman documents — Tullius explains in best High German: "Valuable documents of Roman Government may — under no circumstances — fall into Germanic hands, and we lack the financial means to remove them by transport". (p.34).[20]

In the climate of the Cold War of 1948-1949, the character of Mares, the War Minister, was clearly meant as satire. He is a pure buffoon — it is to him that Romulus quotes Bubenberg's "war-cry". Mares, like Tullius, has a stock of martial clichés which are absurdly useless for the circumstances: "Total mobilization" — "Strategy is a matter of intuition . . . inner composure is necessary" (he has just wakened up!) (p.35) — "The strategic position is becoming more favourable by the hour. It is improving from defeat to defeat" (p.36). (Later in his career Dürrenmatt was to suggest that such people equated 1948 Communism with National Socialism).[21]

The laughter is at these clowns who are so absurdly "ill-adapted" to their world, but, by and with our laughter, the author castigates and corrects the institutions that they represent, the world of the professional politician and war-maker who relies on a well-tried but outmoded policy; it is the laughter of derision and superiority.[22]

With Cäsar Rupf, Dürrenmatt is satirizing the world of Big Business
and advertising. Rupf's name is immediately comic; Rupf, from the
German "rüpfen", to fleece, is comically incongruous when united with
the classical Caesar, firstly because of the Germanic-Latin associations,
but also because Rupf has come to deal with the *last* of the Caesars.
(He is, of course, rather more than a simple buffoon; he is an important factor in the play since he offers Rea marriage and this moves
Romulus finally to action.) Rupf is, as Tullius says, "the manufacturer
of those Germanic items of clothing which one pulls over the legs and
which are becoming fashionable here too" (p.27), that is, he is a comic
anachronism within the play itself, the Bergsonian "transposition of
the ancient to the modern".

His language, with its repetitive clichés, is also comically anachronistic: "I am dead certain. . ." − ". . . as a man of crystal-clear conviction. . ." − "A modern state is going to the dogs, sure as death. . ."
− "I've no time for funny business . . ." − "Let's call a spade a spade. . ."
(all on p.28). Dürrenmatt satirizes the morals of twentieth-century Big
Business through Rupf's cynical language and manner. He is inhuman
and insensitive, he seeks a take-over of the Empire; if Romulus will not
sell out, then Odoaker will. When Romulus asks if Odoaker can be
bought, Rupf answers: "Everybody has his price nowadays, Your
Majesty" (p.29).

The audience will laugh uneasily here, for we recognize only too
clearly our own acquisitive society; and it is not surprising that the
character was seen in the east as a welcome attack on capitalist values.[23]

Just as Rupf satirizes the world of twentieth-century business morals,
so Apollyon represents twentieth-century "culture" − or perhaps
"Kultur"!

It should be observed that both these men are "superior" to Romulus; this is shown in their language. When talking to his family or the
Court, Romulus has the last word, usually a witticism. Here, however,
the cynical suavity and savoir-faire of these modern "princes" is stressed
by Romulus' innocence in the face of such duplicity and ingenuity.
He asks Apollyon if the bust of Cicero which he sold him had proved a
success. "A special case, Your Majesty", replies Apollyon. "Was able
to send five hundred plaster casts to the grammar schools which they're
erecting in the primeval Germanic forests" (p.16). (The ellipsis is a
feature of the language of both Rupf and Apollyon; it underlines the
comic anachronism).

Romulus has to haggle with this man over the price of the Imperial
busts:

A: For both Gracchi, Pompeius, Scipio and Cato, two gold pieces
    and eight sesterces.
R: Three gold pieces?
A: OK, but then I'll have Marius and Sulla too! (p.23)

When Julia complains that the busts are all that her father Valentianus
left her, Romulus can answer *her* with: "But you're still here, my dear
wife" (p.21), but when Zeno tries to entice an advance out of Apollyon
on the strength of some "very peculiar Greek relics" which he possesses, the art dealer answers with: "Sorry. I never give Imperial houses a
loan − on principle"! (p.26).

The implication in the character is clear. The classics (i.e. all traditional values and ideals unthinkingly accepted as "good") are worthless
and will end up in the hands of sharp double-dealers like Apollyon. He
sits on top of a ladder throughout Act I, counting and assessing busts
(i.e. old values), and descends from time to time incongruously into the
action, a comic reminder of the tragic fate of this Empire and of others
like it, built on foundations of terror, brutality, greed and hypocrisy.
Our laughter is uneasy. Arnim Arnold says of the Dürrenmatt of
Romulus: "A Kierkegaard has turned into a Spengler − a Spengler with
Parkinson's sense of humour". He might have been thinking of Apollyon.[24]

If these two characters represent the doubtful future of the world,
the more farcical past is portrayed by Zeno, the Emperor of Eastern
Rome, and the Imperial Messenger, Spurius Titus Mamma.

Zeno, a "buffoon", no doubt represents the 1949 division of Europe.
He is a foolish patriot, a defender of "cultural heritages". He tells
Romulus; "We must rescue our culture". "How come?" says Romulus.
"Is culture something that you can rescue?" He impresses on Julia and
Romulus the need to remember their glorious past: ". . . without belief
in our importance for world politics, we are lost". "OK," says Romulus,
"Let's believe". (*Stage direction*: Silence. They sit in attitudes of
believing) (p.24). These "beliefs" prove worthless when news of the
Germani's advance on Rome arrives and Zeno leaves for Alexandria
immediately: "I shall continue my unyielding struggle against German-
ism from Ethiopia" (p.25), words which would almost certainly remind
Swiss audiences of 1949 of the famous "Rütli" speech of Henri Guisan
in 1940.[25] This is a character not prepared to defend beliefs and faiths
(which have already been shown to be worthless anyway by Rupf and
Apollyon).

The language of these characters is often criticized as "gags" or
"bonmots" by those critics who believe, as Dürrenmatt would say, that

"style is what sounds solemn". But these witticisms are often of some importance for the action. For example, Romulus' answer to Apollyon's remark about the worth of the Imperial busts: "Every bust has the style it deserves" (p.17) seems to me to contain the theme of the play: an age has the "style" (of government, culture or morals and so on) that it deserves — and this age deserves "only" *Komödie*.[26]

If Zeno is a caricature of the hypocrisy of "those in power", it is to stress the contempt which Dürrenmatt (like Brecht) felt for that type; only scorn can affect the "tyrants of this planet" — Dürrenmatt's scorn often takes the form of parody (cf. *TP* p.55).

Spurius Titus Mamma, on the other hand, is a miserable "victim". He is a parody of the classical messenger, who sees himself however as a Marathon runner. The comic in the character is mainly in the repetitious remark, the classical "running gag", the comic device explained by Bergson thus: "The living life should not repeat itself" (*Le Rire* p.26). Spurius' gag is "tiredness". It is underpinned by his hyperbolically comic explanation to Romulus: "Seven horses collapsed dead under me on the ride from Pavia, three arrows wounded me and when I arrived, I couldn't get in to see you" (p.31). There then follow, at regular intervals, his comic interpolations on his tiredness: "I'm tired. I'm tired. I'm dead tired" (p.33).[27] Each time, like Apollyon descending the ladder in Act I, (or the idiot son dancing over the stage in *An Angel comes to Babylon*), he disturbs the action, making a comic and alienating contrast; most of all, at the end of the play, when, having finally reached the Emperor and determined to avenge Rome's dishonour by killing the traitor, he is told by Odoaker: "Lower your sword, Prefect. There *is* no Emperor any more" (p.76); the Kantian frustrated expectation demonstrates that his clownish patriotism is as useless, in its way, as Zeno's.

★   ★   ★

In taking a final look at these "situations" which, so often in a Dürrenmatt play, rob the main character of his tragic potential, two points should be made: firstly, Dürrenmatt, in this play, has altered his structural method. Where in *It is written* and *The Blind Man*, he coalesced a large number of scenes into a whole, he presents us here (and in the 1957 version particularly) with a four-acter, almost a "pièce bien faite". Secondly, where in the first two plays, the scenes often consisted of "sketches" containing repartee, or were "parabases" to the audience, he now writes fairly convincing stage dialogue which carries a logical argument. The illogicalities or the illogical absurdities of, say, a Gnadenbrot Suppe, in *The Blind Man*, have given way to the "logical" absurd which Dürrenmatt described to Martin Esslin.[28]

The basic "idea" is Aristophanically comic: an Emperor who keeps hens and plans the downfall of his Empire. (The hen motif is from Procopius.) Dürrenmatt increases the implicit comic by providing an outer dramatic structure which is a parody of the "classical" unities (which are not classical, of course), a device which he uses again in *The Physicists*. Here, Act I takes place "on an early morning in March" in AD 476; Act II on the "afternoon of the disastrous day in March 476"; Act III, "The night of the Ides of March 476", and Act IV on "the morning after the Ides of March". Since, in the first version, the action takes place in *July*, it can be seen how much more conscious of the comic value of parody Dürrenmatt has become.

We are being invited, then, to take this as a "satyr-play", which, however, in contrast to the custom of Greek drama, comes *before* and not after the "tragedy". The satyr-play reversed the action of the tragedy and parodied it into a comedy. Thus we are watching the parody of a parody! By this device, we are invited to read tragic implications into the play. Parody is intended, Highet said, to make us "admire the original a little less". This produces the effect of satire, an "imitation which through distortion and exaggeration evokes amusement, derision and sometimes scorn".[29] The author seeks this particularly in the Julius Caesar parody in Act III.

The scene itself is a brilliant example of the "pantofarce": one by one, the conspirators, all dressed in black, creep from their (unlikely) hiding-places: Ämilian, through the window, Tullius, from under the divan, Zeno and Sulphurides from a wardrobe, Phosphorides from under the bed, Spurius from out of another wardrobe, Mares and a soldier from under the divan again, and finally, the cook, the obligatory farcical figure of old. (Romulus/Dürrenmatt called him "the most important man in my Empire" p.13.)

This scene incorporates many of the devices of the classical comedy: Multiplication (nine characters acting as one); disguise (they are *all* in black); parody (as the cook appears, Romulus groans: "Et tu, Cook?" Since the Cook is still wearing his high white chef's hat, there is a further comic incongruity). But the significance of the comic is deepened by Romulus' great classical rhetorical tirade which follows, since it is given with his purple toga over his nightshirt. This is surely the effect that Wilson Knight had in mind when he wrote in *The Wheel of Fire*: "The comic and the tragic rest both on the idea of incompatabilities and are themselves mutually exclusive; therefore to mingle them is to add to the meaning of each; the result is but a new sublime incongruity".[30] The comic ignominious flight of the conspirators at the cry: "The Germani are coming!" completes the parody, since the Germani are *not* coming and Romulus retires to bed to await them there (p.62).

Like all true farces, this scene takes place in a bedroom (an aptly incongruous setting for an Imperial conference); other stage directions show is Dürrenmatt's comic intentions and his growing awareness of the possibilities of the stage.

The opening of Act I, with Spurius, his arm in a sling, picking his way through "enormous crowds of clucking hens" (p.11) sets the scene. When Zeno comes to pay his visit, the two Chamberlains are kept out of the room in a pantofarcical scuffling scene (p.22); similarly, in Act IV, when the room suddenly fills with "weary, travel-stained Germani", with the pedantic "Storm-trooper" Theoderich at their head (p.75). Likewise the beginning of Act II, as Zeno and the others stagger about on smashed eggshells, Spurius and Mares snore, smoke rises from the burning documents and Zeno finally falls to praying (p.33 ff). Yet these and other scenes are not (*pace* Urs Jenny) a "mere joky ambience", entirely unconnected with the action. They are in fact essential to the establishment of the uselessness of this type of bureaucratic inhuman patriotism.[31] The buffoons and their actions form the rear line of a resistance to Romulus, to humanity, common-sense and freedom, a line that stretches from them through Julia and Rea to Ämilian.

Dürrenmatt has therefore subtly altered the buffoon's traditional rôle in comedy.

> Satire is an exact art, precisely because it exaggerates, for you *can* only exaggerate if you see the nuance and the generalisation at the same time.

These words, on Ronald Searle, the British cartoonist, (*TSR I*, p.290) show why Dürrenmatt constructed *Romulus* as he did; the "objects" of his satire (to speak with Highet) were those aspects of a divided Switzerland and Europe which troubled him in 1949. Deny as he may that he was not parodying them — and he said to me, ". . . I wasn't thinking of Switzerland with *Romulus* . . . Switzerland isn't an Empire, after all. *Romulus* is about a super state, the division of the world, it is the *theatrum mundi* again . . .", the piece did nevertheless arouse much antagonism among those concerned at the time with what was called "drawing-room Bolshevism". There was talk of "Trojan horses", "defeatism" and "traitors to the country". (Indeed, Julia says to Romulus:

"You are a defeatist" (p.48), and, in the first version, Mares talks of "sabotage" and "defeatism". In his *Note* (to the 1949 version), Dürrenmatt wrote: "I am justifying a traitor to his country".)

His most famous aphorism from the play: "Whoever is on his last legs like us, can only understand *Komödien*", while admirably summing up modern literary tendencies, aroused disgust in more conservative Swiss circles.[22] As Professor von Salis noted, the danger was two-fold; those groups in Switzerland who joined fascist and reactionary circles to combat "Social Democracy and Communism", and those who retreated into the "hedgehog rôle of Swiss complacency".[33] Dürrenmatt's *Komödie* could therefore be seen as an attack on both groups.

★   ★   ★

Karl Guthke would not call *Romulus* a "tragicomedy"; because Romulus becomes the "truly human being", the play, he claims, "swerves unambiguously over into comedy . . .". Brock-Sulzer saw it, in 1949, as a "comedy . . . not as a unfulfilled tragedy or drama . . .", but, later, after the 1957 version, she wrote: "Here in *Romulus*, the comedy is near-tragedy", and later still, "In the comic end, tragedy is only just avoided".[34]

I, however, take *Romulus the Great* to be a modern German *Komödie*, as I defined it above. Since there is no "tragic" in the work, it cannot be a "tragicomedy", in Guthke's sense of the term. Romulus does not die the tragic death, but experiences rather "the comic eternal life". Sadness there is, but no tragedy. Romulus, foiled, not by ineluctable Fate but by blind Chance, has what Strelka neatly called the "sceptical resignation" of our spiritual clowns.[35]

Again, the play cannot be called a farce; it is true that it has been shown that most of the characters are "professional clowns" or "buffoons", whose lack of humanity, in the shape of their deceits and conceits, their hypocrisies, their mental and physical rigidities, is only too plain to see. This work is not, however, just "play", as Dr Mahler defines a farce, but is "on the highest level the expression of a philosophy of life", which is how she sees the *Komödie*. (The idea of comedy as "play" was underlined, of course, by Huizinga's celebrated comment: "That tragedy and comedy both derive from play is continually obvious").[36]

This play is, as the author suggested, "a difficult *Komödie*" (*Note*, p.78); the "difficulty" lay in the new juxtaposition of potentially

tragic characters with either actual comic situations or scenes of pantofarce. Dürrenmatt's use of the elements of the comic, ranging through
the entire spectrum from subtle wit to broadest horseplay, place this
work firmly in the great comic tradition while, at the same time,
narrowly skirting Mark Twain's celebrated "tragedy-trap". My conten-
tion is that, having found this pattern, Dürrenmatt has, in essentials,
never departed from it and that he has made the avoidance of the
"tragedy-trap" the groundstone of all his future work.[37]

(ii) DIE EHE DES HERRN MISSISSIPPI
(THE MARRIAGE OF MR MISSISSIPPI)

This, the fourth of Dürrenmatt's plays, had its première under Hans
Schweikart in the Münchner Kammerspiele on 26 March 1952, and was
well received, on the whole, by public and critics.[38]
     Some five months after the première, Frau Tilly Wedekind, the
widow of Frank Wedekind, the "Father of Expressionism" (1864-
1918), announced that she was to take Dürrenmatt to court on a charge
of plagiarism. His defence against her charge that Act I of *Mississippi*
bore a marked resemblance to Wedekind's *Schloss Wetterstein* (Wetterstein Castle), was that his Mississippi was in fact "a continuation of the
Romulus-character who also justified himself by claiming that he was a
judge".[39] Wedekind's *Marquis of Keith* (1900), added Dürrenmatt,
would have been a more likely source of "plagiarism" since that play
had given him the idea of a "dialectic *with* characters . . ." Nevertheless,
he welcomed the opportunity to write about Wedekind. Why? "People
have still not learned to see *Komödien* in Wedekind, that's why he
leaves most people cold. They take him seriously – and that's wrong"
(p.245). (And, indeed, since Dürrenmatt wrote that, Wedekind has
been played much more frequently in all countries). Dürrenmatt used
this to accuse the critics of (once again) looking for "profundity" and
"messages" in everything, a fault which he equates with a lack of
balance and a lack of a sense of humour – and therefore of humanity![40] For, nowhere clearer than in this play can be found Dürrenmatt's
intention to write *with* the stage, in Frisch's phrase; it is fatally easy to
treat this work as a religious or moral tract. But, like *Romulus*, it is a
work for the stage, and to appreciate what Dürrenmatt was trying to
achieve, it is necessary to stress the elements of the comic at the expense

of the religious and philosophical elements, which, interestingly enough, are largely missing from the revised version of 1957.[41]

★   ★   ★

Most commentators on the play have found themselves taxed by the attempt to outline the plot — one of the characters cries out indeed: "If I could understand only a fraction of what's going on here, I'd feel better rightaway" (Bodo, p.123). Saint-Claude sums up as well as anyone when he says in an *Address to the Audience*: ". . . it's about the disquieting fate of three men who, by different means, had got the idea into their head, partly to change the world, partly to save it — nothing more nor less . . . (pp.87-88).

The plot certainly contains some of those Tourneur-like "Jacobean elements" (revenge-motif and power held by the mad) of which Heilmann writes, but I must disagree that there is a "melodramatic intensity which approaches tragedy".[42] For, to understand Dürrenmatt, one has to understand his approach to "comedy" and to accept that on *his* terms. In 1952, there was probably some justification for the charge of "nihilist" being levelled against Dürrenmatt, since the contrast between the traditional picture of Switzerland and Dürrenmatt's satirical levity was a very strong one for contemporary Europe and the USA. Because so many critics have treated his works "with deadly seriousness", they have believed in the evil depicted in the characters and have transferred to the author a nihilism which we now can see is being mocked and condemned. As Dürrenmatt never tires of saying — those who see "nihilism" in him are in fact seeing their own beliefs reflected!

The "comedy" in the play begins with the eponymous main character: the comic incongruity of the name strikes immediately. The parodistic *Florestan* ("the hero of Duty"),[43] redolent of nineteenth-century Schillerian idealism, is matched with the New World dynamism of *Mississippi*: ("My mother was an Italian princess and my father an American armaments king") (p.106).

Mississippi is one of the standard alazon-types of the Old Comedy: the stiff, humourless pedant, "about 50 or 55 years old", suggests Dürrenmatt.[44] The pedantry is seen in his clothes: Saint-Claude describes him as he ". . . hands oyer his coat and top-hat . . . correct as always in his black frock-coat" (p.89); in his formal language and in his regular habits; the executions which Anastasia will have to witness "take place every Friday" (p.102). He has already carried out *200* executions, and when he marries Anastasia, they will live "ten minutes nearer the Court House" (p.102).

The single-mindedness of Mississippi's general thesis, "that only a meticulously observed Code of Law can raise Man to a better, higher Being" (p.104), his plan, "to restore the world from its fundamentals through the Law of Moses" (p.103), to return it to the "original, innocent state of nature" (p.98) (a world which Mississippi now finds only in the old prints which he incongruously collects), present a character of a classical comic stiffness — one of those "blocking characters" of whom Bergson wrote: "This inelasticity is the comic and laughter is the corrective". There is, nevertheless, an undercurrent of horror in this character, which, in conjunction with the undeniable comic in it and its actions, makes it proper to call the source of comic laughter here "grotesque". The laughter is uneasy, the comic is *very* dark.

There is no trace of "humanity" in Mississippi — that is why he is comical; this mad, alienated character, ridiculously misplaced in the twentieth century, striving to introduce a law of 3000 years ago, is an inhuman human being, a clown who evokes grim laughter.

A second classical comic trait must be noted; he is a "cuckold" — and twice over at that. Mississippi is deceived, firstly, by his wife, Madeleine, with Anastasia's husband, François (p.92). His sudden proposal to Anastasia makes an effective comic contrast with the announcement of the cuckoldry (p.98). Mississippi is then fooled for a second time by Anastasia's "seduction" of the Minister, Diego, and the comic intention is underlined at the end when Anastasia "dies" with the lie on her lips:

Mississippi: No other man has ever possessed you, you were never an adulteress?

Anastasia: Never. (p.152)

This means, in turn, that when Mississippi "dies", in the belief that people can be changed by the imposition of inexorable law, he has been made ridiculous once again, since his life's work and philosophy have been shown to be useless. The "marriage" which Mississippi has entered into as a judgement on himself as well as on Anastasia and which he regards as a "triumph of justice", is seen to have been based on false premises. Anastasia was hardly fashioned for the monogamy of the Old Testament, yet it seems that she did not kill her husband out of jealousy at his infidelity, as Mississippi thought, but out of love for Bodo. Her cry, "Bodo! Bodo!" at the end of the proposal scene is, "unfortunately" not heard by Mississippi, since, as he explains in a comic

alienation scene to the audience: "At that time I was out on the stair-
case, perhaps already even in the street" (p.103).

Mississippi "dies" in his idealistic belief, but comes to life again,
with Saint-Claude "in ever new guises, longing for ever more distant
Paradises. . ." (p.156); here, Dürrenmatt is demonstrating the two-fold
absurdity of the character; deceived on the stage and ridiculed by the
audience in the present, he will continue to make the same mistakes in
the future, an example of that "unteachableness" of the human race
that Frisch's *Biedermann* and Dürrenmatt's own *Prozess um des Esels
Schatten* (*The Trial of the Donkey's Shadow* (1951)) set out to deride;
this, too, is an example of that "inelasticity" which is the major comic
trait in the character.[45] Like Knipperdollinck, he is made foolish by his
unconditional demands defined here by Diego: "The world is bad but
not hopeless; it only becomes hopeless when it is judged by an absolute
standard" (p.107).

We castigate his foolishness by our laughter. The alazon is "driven
out of your midst. . ." as Saint-Claude obligingly says (p.156). (Profitlich writes that Mississippi — in the film script version of 1961 —
became a "near-hero" because he finally decides "to restore violated
justice by expiation of his guilt". This is not the case, however, in any
of Dürrenmatt's own stage versions, over which he had more control.
In the 1961 version, Mississippi noticeably remains in the asylum at
the end.)[46]

*   *   *

Jean-Paul Sartre wrote of his "théâtre de la situation":

> What are the issues? Each character will be nothing but the choice of
> an issue and will be worth no more than the issue chosen. It is
> devoutly to be wished that all literature will become as moral and
> problematical as this new theatre.

Such a theatre enabled a dramatist to make his characters the expression of an ideology and nothing more. Dürrenmatt's comment to
Siegfried Melchinger seems to be an answer to that point of view: "The
most dangerous are the ideologies which have a solution for everything.
Ideological Marxism will "solve" anything that remains unsolved. . ."
but ". . . the dramatist has to proceed from insoluble conflicts", and he
continued in the same vein in his *55 Sentences on Art and Reality* of
1977: "Whoever destroys ideologies, destroys the justifications for

force". It is by making his characters just such representatives of ideologies that Dürrenmatt can make them comic by ridicule.[47]

If Mississippi is the ridiculous representative of puritanical and legal pedantry, Saint-Claude (about Mississippi's age, 50 or 55), is the satirized and parodied figure of left-wing idealism. Like Mississippi, Saint-Claude is a risen prole who has become, hyperbolically, "Major in the Red Army, honorary Citizen of Romania, Deputy of the Polish Parliament and member of the Politburo of the Cominform" (p.108). (In the 1970 version (q.v.) "Citizen of the G.D.R." replaces "honorary Citizen of Romania", while the reference to the Cominform is missing. See p.29.)

There is something of the idealistic ardour of 1789 about the character which makes one think of — and made Erich Kästner write about — its relationship to Büchner's, Brecht's and Toller's heroes.[48] He is no Soviet revolutionary (p.109), but, like Mississippi, he is single-mindedly devoted to a cause, in his case, humanism: "We both wanted justice, but you wanted the justice of Heaven and I wanted the justice of earth" (p.112).

Saint-Claude is the bluff picaro, the Wedekindian adventurer, a comic type. His outlook on life is comically cynical, a satire on Brecht's belief that the world can be changed by a new political system. Dürrenmatt attempts to clarify this point by making Saint-Claude an intentionally comic character instead of an unintentional one, as is the case with Mississippi or Bodo. Thus, the comic in the character lies as much in his own non-sequiturs and witticisms as in the dramatic concept.

When Mississippi wants to know why Saint-Claude should want him to lead the new Communist Party, Saint-Claude replies: "The Communist Party of this country has carried out so many purges that it has no leaders left... That's why we've chosen you" (p.109). Mississippi asks him if he will ever break his word: "Of course. Keeping a word of honour is a luxury which our background doesn't allow us" (p.111). It is in this scene with Mississippi that Dürrenmatt establishes the worldly idealism of the character, in the patent impracticability of whose plans the audience sees the author's comic intentions.

And these intentions are clearly shown in Saint-Claude's "parabasis": his plans have come to nought: "Quite simply. I've just been taken in again" (p.143), but, with a certain gay insouciance, he will make the best of it and fly with Anastasia to Portugal — but the only "change" that Saint-Claude has managed to bring about in the world is in himself — he has removed his beard! Although he honestly believes that Anastasia is attracted by his plan to make her the "whore of Babylon" (p.147), the main draw of his Portuguese brothel, he too is "fooled" and "dies", shot by the Communist Party.

"The Communist is the *permanent* hero of our age", quotes Sartre ironically, and Dürrenmatt attempts to create laughter from the absurdity of Saint-Claude's clumsy efforts to become just such a (tragic) hero.[49] The laughter should have Kantian sources — the great expectations come to a miserable nothing, but I am inclined to agree with Züfle's judgement: "Saint-Claude, the revolutionary, remains the weakest character"[50]. For Dürrenmatt, Mississippi was a comic and unreal figure; Saint-Claude was to be a "tragic and real" figure. The characterization is too weak for that, but both he and Mississippi are obvious clown-figures, "Fools", mocked by their human weaknesses, both with "idées fixes", each "non-human" in his obsessiveness.

Against them stands Bodo von Übelohe-Zabernsee (about 35 years old), whose name, like theirs, is already comical.[51] In this *Komödie* on human impotence, Bodo, despite his seeming defeat, is the only character (apart from Diego) to remain truly "alive" at the end, and who will continue to take part in the "eternal *Komödie*" (p.157), a vanquished victor and a spiritual clown.

Bodo is represented throughout as an absurd character, like Kierkegaard's Knight of Faith; he *is* absurd, from his introduction in his "parabasis": "My entry is ridiculous, anachronistic, like me, like my grotesque life" (p.116), to his pathetic realization that Anastasia has "fooled" him too: when Bodo begs her to admit that she killed her husband for love of *him*, she answers: "I killed him because I loved him" (p.139); thus, his years of misery and toil in Borneo have been in vain and he is left with the "love of a fool, the love of a ridiculous man" (p.141).

As Hugo Loetscher wrote in 1957:

> All three fail, if by "failing" we mean that the environment, the world, the situation is more powerful than their own planning. They experience the impotence of human planning and action.[52]

Bodo as the "saviour of the world" is the comic protagonist to Mississippi and Saint-Claude, both of whom want to *change* the world. It is Bodo who recognizes the truth; he tells Mississippi: "We no longer have any say here, History has refuted us" (p.134), one of those quotations from *Romulus* that Dürrenmatt mentioned. He sees (as Romulus had to) that only this understanding can save him and humanity; he finds out, as did the giant Jew Gulliver and, eventually, the Greek Archilochos in Dürrenmatt's "prose *Komödie*" *Grieche sucht Griechin* (*Once a Greek*) (1955) that the Dürrenmattian "individual" can neither save nor change the world, but only *endure* it — with love.

Yet, like the others, Bodo is made ridiculous by his fixed belief in his ability to rescue Anastasia from her sins by sacrificing all for her. The hyperbolical comic is stretched to the limits. When Bodo learns that Anastasia had killed her husband (and not her dog) with the poison which he had procured for her, he mutters: "Has your whole life's work been ruined by a woman . . . Have you had cholera, sunstroke, malaria, spotted typhus, dysentry, yellow fever, sleeping sickness and chronic liver trouble?" (p.125), a passage which might well justify Wellwarth's comment that Dürrenmatt piles on straws until the camel's back breaks![53]

It is true that Bodo has elements of both the professional and the spiritual clown in his characterization. There has always been something buffoonish in the "stage drunk", for example. Drunkenness implies lack of human reason or reason out of control; it is a Bergsonian "comic vice". Our very first sight of Bodo is during Mississippi's speech: *Stage-direction*: Count Übelohe staggers past the window (p.143). Again, Saint-Claude has shown us a picture of Bodo who "blind drunk, is trying to cut out the appendix of a drunken Malayan" (p.88), and he describes himself as "drunk, clapped-out, as you can see" (p.115), and as "a ruined Count, sodden in bad alcohol" (p.142).

The qualities of the spiritual clown, on the other hand, are shown in two main scenes: firstly, in the pantofarcical scene during the bombardment when Mississippi and Bodo crawl to the (very important) coffee table in the middle of the room. Mississippi asks Bodo why he fled to Borneo:

Ü: I was sorry for Mankind.
       (Salvo. They duck.).
M: You loved them all?
Ü: All of them.
M: In their dirt and their greed?
Ü: In all their sinfulness.
       (Salvo. They duck.)   (p.136)[54]

There is an immediate comic contrast between Bodo's unshakeable and naive belief in the goodness of Man and his farcical position brought about by Man's all too obvious evil.

The second scene occurs at the very end of the play, when Bodo, "a battered metal helmet on his head, a bent lance in his right hand, moving in and out of the circling shadows of a windmill" (p.156) appears, quixotically, to challenge the evil of the world. There is, of course, no tragic hero here; his too laughable fate and his ridiculous apparel "distance" us from the tragic — as does his unheroic message to the windmill: "... See me ... often beaten-up, often laughed at/ Yet defying you still" (p.156).

We know that characters like these will always be vanquished "Fools", spiritual clowns, since they demonstrate Man's frailty and fallibility in the sight of powers beyond his comprehension.

Thus Bodo is: "... An eternal *Komödie*/ so that His glory may shine/Fed on our impotence" (p.157). And since Bodo also describes himself as "the only one that he (i.e. the author) loved with real passion. . ." (p.116), it would seem that we are invited to mingle sympathy with our ridicule, since Dürrenmatt surely means us to accept Bodo's views as his own.

★   ★   ★

All three characters are linked together by Anastasia. There is little that is comic here. She is a "woman whose consumption of men is enormous" (Saint Claude, p.146) which led Urs Jenny to call her a "Super-Lulu ... Frau Welt and the whore of Babylon at the same time".[55] There is something in this remark, although I miss the "youth and freshness" which Frank Wedekind expected to see in his Lulu.[56] Instead, there is an earnest stolidity, lightened only by some grotesque Expressionist outbursts which are not really grotesque either, since there is, as I have said, hardly any comic in the character — only a certain horror, underlined indeed by the name of her maid: Lucretia.

Only in the proposal scene is there any trace of comedy — and there it is the "involuntary comic". She and the Prosecutor, both dressed in black, are made to act like automata; there is, in Bergson's words, "something mechanical encrusted on something living". (*Stage direction*: They sit down, Anastasia on the left, Mississippi on the right. The following scene at the coffee table is to be produced very precisely, with the same movements as they drink; thus, both put the cup to their mouth at the same time or stir with their spoon at the same time etc. (p.90).)

The comic is increased by the contrast between the grave topic of conversation (the death of her husband), the sober black attire of both parties, and the comic machine-like unanimity of their actions. It is Reason versus Automation, man in control versus man controlled from without.

But Anastasia is also the block over which all the characters in the *Komödie* finally, and ridiculously, stumble; they are made to look ridiculous by their inability to conquer her, a "mere" woman, Mississippi poisons her — but she "dies" with a lie on her lips; Saint-Claude thinks that he can blackmail her to leave with him — but she betrays him, while Bodo is reduced to a farcical begging-scene on his knees to try to make her admit her love for him.

Like Anastasia, Diego, the Minister of Justice, is the essence of practicality and adaptation, but, unlike her, he has a sense of humour.[57] Dürrenmatt satirizes here the chameleon-like politician of our days, ready to change his policies and politics to save his seat (or his head). Having approved of his friend's (Mississippi's) rather drastic justice to begin with, he then advises him to be merciful, to play it both ways. Only he sees through Anastasia, for he is like her: "Nobody can understand you, whoever relies on you will go under and only the person who loves you, as I love you, (i.e. in an unhuman way) will possess you for ever" (p.120).

Similarly, he satirizes Mississippi's "grand design" to change the human race: "Everything in the world can be changed, my dear Florestan, except Man . . ." (p.107) whereby Brecht is also satirized!

There is something truly Aristophanic about Dürrenmatt's portrayal of politicians. They are "reduced", in word and deed, as later, when Diego, rushing hither and thither, is terrified that the Foreign Minister will be given the vacant post of Prime Minister. A few minutes later, he rushes back on to, and then again across the stage, pitiful in his terror (p.125).

The laughter should arise out of our Lippsian feelings of "superiority", yet it is to this type that Dürrenmatt would seem to be granting the victory, the artful politician who counts on the weakness of the masses and who wins Anastasia in the end. He, "greedy for power and nothing else", she, "a whore who goes unchanged through Death" (p.155), represent the victory of an evil and immoral world.[58] The answer to them both was Bodo, who, like Sisyphus, knew that his task was a vain one, but also, that he must not capitulate. In his actual comic fate is mirrored the potential tragedy of this modern chaotic world.

*   *   *

This chaotic world is depicted in many of the stage-directions which clearly indicate Dürrenmatt's comic intentions. The play is not divided "classically" into scenes and acts, as was *Romulus*, and the time-scale is

also far removed from any classical model, but Dürrenmatt does con-
centrate his action on one place: in his *Note*, indeed, he calls the work
"the story of a room" (p.158).

It is a comic parody of European culture through the ages; we see a
mixture of Gothic, Louis XIV, fin-de-siècle, Louis XVI, Spanish, Japan-
ese, and Meissen art styles, plus a Biedermeier nineteenth-century little
coffee table ("the true main character of the play round which the
action revolves") — this becomes literally true in the 1970 version
where this bric-à-brac is placed on a revolving stage! (cf.p.8).

The room is thus a visual satire — culture is satirized through parody,
and then the room is gradually and symbolically reduced to a shambles
by the violence of the Modern Age. Gottfried Benn was not the only
one to find the set confusing in 1952. The author had demanded a view
of a cypress and a temple from one window, an apple tree and a Gothic
Cathedral from another.[59]

The coffee table is an important element. Mississippi and Anastasia
sit and stand round it — the mechanical play with the table has already
been described; there is a scene of pantofarce as the two dance around
it "in the excitement of the battle" (p.97), while the farcical encounter
between Bodo and the Prosecutor takes place *underneath* the table.

Thus "coffee" and "table" are closely connected visual elements of
the comic. Indeed one could say that they are the "agentia" of the plot,
since the coffee is a visual pun, an "ambiguity". No character is certain
whether or not the coffee is poisoned; Mississippi drinks four cups in
his first scene with Anastasia (p.98); when Bodo (now "completely
short-sighted") finally recognizes Anastasia, he calls for black coffee,
but, by the time it arrives, he has already heard too much about what
coffee means in this house and says: "You surely cannot expect me to
drink any more coffee *here*!" (p.124) and eventually consumes five
bottles of cognac (p.132). When the shooting is over at the end,
Saint-Claude asks for a coffee; Anastasia immediately poisons it. Saint-
Claude puts it down without drinking it — "There was sugar in it!" —
but drinks Anastasia's when she leaves the room. The audience is thus
prepared for the final "comedy" when Mississippi enters, sees Anastasia's empty cup, fills it, drops in the poison — and drinks the other cup.
This was the dramatic situation which the author described in *Problems
of the Theatre* as the "trick of the coffee-drinking", a masterpiece of
"ambiguity" (*TP*, p.33). The sugar, the table, the uncertain décor and
the pantofarcical scenes are satirical symbols of what Hans Bänziger
called "bourgeois *Kitsch*".[60]

In this play, Dürrenmatt returned to direct comic alienation scenes
such as he had created in his very first play. One of Brecht's earliest

"V-effects" was this stage-direction in his *Threepenny Opera* of 1928:

> Song illumination, golden light. The organ is illuminated. Three
> lamps descend on a pole and on a board are the words. . .

usually of a song. One could say, indeed, that Dürrenmatt's first involvement with the "Brecht legacy" occurs in *Mississippi* where he
savagely parodies the V-effect.

In *Mississippi*, the stage direction reads:

> Three pathetic busts . . . representing from left to right Saint-Claude,
> Übelohe, and Mississippi, the two at the extremes draped in black.

and this slowly descends; or two pictures, one showing Saint-Claude
starting the Romanian Revolution, the other, Bodo cutting out a
Malayan's appendix (p.88). Later, pictures of Mississippi and Anastasia
at the executions are lowered (p.104); when Bodo is supposed to fly off
to Chile, the sound of an aeroplane is heard: "A board with a painted
aeroplane flying through the clouds covers the scenery" (p.142).

All these intended comic effects occur, noticeably, during the alienating "parabases" of which there are eight in the play, some indication
that Dürrenmatt found this well-tried comic technique very useful.

★   ★   ★

The pantofarce scenes in the play are of particular interest. The buffoons are seen, firstly, in the comic persons of the three "men with
arm-bands" who appear only at the beginning and end of the play
(although they are given more important rôles in the film where they
bear the alienating names of McGoy, van Bosch and Santamaria. In the
1970 version, they are, more sinisterly, "three men in raincoats"! (p.9)).

More important, however, are the clergymen and the doctors; the
former, "a Protestant, and Catholic and an Israeli", (the classical
"comic trio") enter to thank Anastasia for her attendance at the execution. The choric form in which they speak gives the impression of
puppetry – which is heightened by the knowledge that such a class is
usually independently voluble.

The third group of buffoons, the doctors, under their leader, Professor Überhuber (comic enough), come to take Mississippi to the asylum.
They arrive – as in *Romulus* – in typically farcical fashion (from
windows and grandfather clocks), the comic of "multiplication" and a
satire on the white-coated efficiency of Swiss clinics. When Mississippi

tries to convince them that he is a murderer and should be taken to prison, they can only murmur in a Bergsonian chorus: "Fixe Idee" (Idée fixe!) Truth itself has become a casualty in the twentieth-century, since Mississippi is carried away protesting: "I've told the truth, the whole truth and nothing but the truth", a satirical reference to his own legal profession. The contrast between the farcical comic structure of these scenes and their potentially tragic content deepens the significance for the action.

Finally, an ancient comic device. Since the Greeks, comedy has known the device of the "ritual death." Frye writes: "The ritual pattern behind the catharsis of comedy is the resurrection that follows the death, the epiphany or manifestation of the risen hero". He goes on to show how this classical pattern (which gave rise to the comic satyr-play following the tragic trilogy) is repeated in Christian "tragedy" where tragedy is only an episode in the "divine comedy", "the larger scheme of redemption and resurrection".[61]

In this play, the ancient myth is parodied: the characters rise from the dead at the end (and *Anastasia* means "the risen one", of course), not to redemption, however, but to the same life of futility and stupidity.[62] Saint-Claude and Mississippi display the stupidity of all obsessive monomaniacs, alazon-characters, who believe that there is an absolute justice on earth or in heaven; but a justice without love and mercy is an inhuman justice, and it is inhumanity which is mocked in this play.

Yet, one might ask, who *did* gain the day? Was it not Anastasia and Diego, those who lived only "for the moment" and for the chance? And if it is so, must we not charge Dürrenmatt with nihilism, as we have seen that some critics have done? At this stage of the study, the answer is no. Dürrenmatt attacks false beliefs, but also false illusions, with his weapons of comedy. While he attacks the (to him) erroneous belief that the world can be changed by an ideology, he is also attacking the equally false idea that the present and the future can be lived like the past. His Bodo — what he was later to call his "valiant man" — is in comic conflict with the inhuman forces of the world who seek to make him unfree. There is no positive solution to this conflict, but, with our laughter, we have castigated and corrected certain human "vices", religious and legal pedantry, impractical (and inhuman) political idealism, public opportunism and private sinning; the comic in the work removes the inherent tragic implications, but, at the same time, deepens their significance, as we have seen.[63]

For me, this play is a *Komödie*. It is true, as Werner says, that "the aggressiveness of this *Komödie* often becomes so malicious that the audience gets afraid at its own laughter", but I believe it to be a

Komödie on the Aristophanic model, satirical, purposive (in the Freudian sense) and agonistic. Many critics, overlooking these comic elements, decided that the play was a problem-laden "discussion-piece" and brought the wrath of the misunderstood author down upon themselves.[64]

His next play compounded the confusion.

(iii) EIN ENGEL KOMMT NACH BABYLON
(AN ANGEL COMES TO BABYLON)

After the coldness of *The Blind Man*, Dürrenmatt produced the warmth of *Romulus*; if one bears in mind Urs Jenny's remark about the "zig-zag line" taken by his works, it is perhaps not surprising that the "dark" comedy of *Mississippi* should be followed by the dancing lightness of the *Angel*. In *Zwei Äusserungen zu seiner neuen Komödie* (*Two remarks about his new Komödie*), Dürrenmatt wrote that he saw *Angel* as an "attempt to get out of the dramaturgical cul-de-sac which *The Marriage of Mr Mississippi* had tempted me into. The new play was to be self-contained, strictly proportioned and colourful".[65]

Dürrenmatt had attempted to tackle the theme of the new play as early as 1948, under the title of *Der Turm zu Babel*, and had written almost four acts before abandoning it. The second attempt became a "fragmentary *Komödie*" and received its première (again in the Münchner Kammerspiele under Hans Schweikart) on 22 December, 1953, and was repeated in Düsseldorf, Zürich and Vienna. But, as the author pointed out in the *Note* to the (second) 1957 version:

> It didn't satisfy me. One needed a break. I had to work on something else in order to gain distance, to shape the *Komödie* dramaturgically from the direction, to let it become plot and nothing else.

This version was performed in the Deutsches Theater in Göttingen on 6 April, 1957.[66]

Dürrenmatt had now produced a work in which the structural elements and the plot were of paramount importance. The view he expressed to Rainer Litten in 1967 was obviously no new one: "Writing a play really means directing it as well — in a rough sort of way".[67] As we have seen, his interest is now firmly in the theatrical technique: "... to write *with* the stage ... I'm thinking of the *Komödien* of Aristophanes or the *Lustspiele* of Nestroy" (*TP*, p.25).

*   *   *

The last words above, which appeared in *Problems of the Theatre*
shortly before the staging of the second version of *Angel*, give the clue
to the work which has so much in common with Attic and Viennese
Comedy. It is perhaps no coincidence that the first Akki was Erich
Ponto, the famous Viennese comic actor. The Aristophanic "invention" of "Cloudcuckooland" in *The Birds* and Socrates "Thinkery" in
The Clouds can be compared with Dürrenmatt's "invention" of the
descent of the Angel and Kurrubi to earth from Heaven, the "myster-
ious starting-place of the action" (*TP*, p.26)[68], but there is also something of the contradictory and bizarre comic of Raimund and Nestroy,
as Dorothy Prohaska's remarks on their comedy remind us:

> The heroic action was made trivial, and serious characters made
> ridiculous, largely by virtue of their incongruous settings . . . The
> serious thought of Raimund was earnest rather than tragic and he
> could express it successfully through his comic characters.[69]

In *Problems of the Theatre*, Dürrenmatt showed that he had intended
the structural elements to be among the main comic devices in this
play. Heaven was to be regarded "not so much as an infinite place as
an incomprehensible one", and therefore the rear of the stage was to be
taken up with a gigantic picture of the Andromeda nebulae, a recurring
figure in Dürrenmatt's works and obviously intended to represent the
vastness of space made visible to insignificant Man.

The visual comic element is in the incongruous contrast between this
vast "incomprehensible" backcloth and the "little square" on which the
heavenly pair arrive. In contrast to the cleanliness and innocence of
Heaven, Babylon is to appear as an incongruous "array of palaces, sky-
scrapers and cottages, lost in the yellow sand of the desert, magnificent
and filthy at the same time, inhabited by millions.(*Stage direction*, p.163).

This first scene is a satire on today's world; the author contrasts the
original state of the world with the depressing consequences of modern
"civilization".[70] His parodistic "old Babylonian gas lamp" is a poor
thing compared to the light of Heaven. Heaven is still invisible, but we
now find ourselves "sous les ponts de Babylone", as the *Neue Zürcher
Zeitung* neatly put it (1.2.54), with all the refuse of modern culture.
It is the same visual comic as was used in the first scene of *Mississippi*;
here, Akki's dwelling is "a wild mélange of the most diverse objects of
all ages, sarcophagi, negro gods, old royal thrones, Babylonian bicycles
and car tyres . . ." (p.191). The sand outside is littered with the culinary
("planned obsolescent") symbol of our age — the food tin — but also

with the poets' manuscripts. The joke in the contrast between the classically sublime and its ridiculous, but, alas, all too common fate in our times, is summed up: "Parchments of poems and clay tablets hang all around . . ." (p.191). The author demands an aural anachronism: "From high above the sound of the traffic of a vast city. The rattle of Old Babylonian tramcars . . ." and a visual one: "On house walls and poster columns some torn posters such as: 'Beggars damage the Fatherland' — 'Begging is unsocial' — 'Beggars, join the Civil Service' " (ibid.). to complete the comic incongruity. This is the "fantastic comedy" of Nestroy's "Volksspiel", a "fantasy Babylon".

The directions for Act III mirror the "darker" act which follows the two "lighter" ones: The comic moves now to the other end of the spectrum and lies in the savage satire of the set, in the "bestial horror" of the Kings' throne-room: "In the midst of the most sublime culture, there is something hideously negroid" (p.219). Everything is exaggerated; the background stretches out "to infinity" — all is "deformed", as the historian of "mannerism", G.R.Hocke, might have put it. There is a comic here, but it is the comic of the abyss, uneasy, uncertain, Hoffmann's fantastic grotesque, the ludicrous combined with the demonic. He is mocking the corruption which absolute power brings and comparing satirically its bestial enormity with the pure enormity of the heavenly background of Acts I and II.[71]

One other comic element on the stage must be mentioned: the coffins or sarcophagi. Akki's favourite resting-place is the coffin "of the lovely Lillith who was once my mistress . . ." All around his dwelling are coffins which, at one point, open up to reveal the poets (p.196). In this play (in which there are no deaths, an unusual feature for a Dürrenmatt play), the coffin represents the death of culture; the poet, the lowliest in the state but for the hangman, is consigned to the tomb, although, as we shall see, there is a "way out" for him, too.[72]

Comedies have always known the "comic disguise". We noted Dürrenmatt's use of it in *The Blind Man*; in that play, the characters were "disguised", in the sense that the blind Duke could not see them for what they really were, and the comic arose from the discrepancy. Here, Dürrenmatt employs the more traditional device of disguise through clothing, an element rarely lacking in the Viennese Comedy and an essential feature, of course, of the masked Attic Old Comedy. One thinks of Christopher disguising himself as Maria in Nestroy's *Einen Jux will er sich machen*, the manifold disguises of Titus Feuerfuchs in *The Talisman*, and, in the Viennese Mozartian operas, too, where Cherubino changes into Susanna's clothes in *The Marriage of Figaro* or where the old hag is revealed as Papagena in *The Magic Flute*.

It is a form of comic irony in that the audience knows what the third party does not — and laughs over its (possible) discomfiture.

Great emphasis is laid on clothes and costumes in *Angel*: The Angel himself, "disguised as a ragged beggar with a long red beard", arrives on earth (p.163); Nebuchadnezzar wants to find out why Akki has not entered the nationalized begging association and so disguises himself in "the old beggar's cloak" (from the Court Theatre) and a red beard (p.168); he pretends to be a beggar from Nineve and is therefore taken for Akki by the heavenly pair. Finally, when "a ragged and wild figure with a red beard" (Akki) appears, we have not only one real and two disguised beggars on stage — but a comic trio, an example of comic "multiplication", in addition to the basic comic element of disguise. Freud noted that one could employ this device "in the service of malevolent and aggressive tendencies" (*Der Witz*, op.cit. p.215); here the King and the Angel are both satirized, the former's power and the latter's innocence and idealism.

We see it again when Akki outwits the hangman by exchanging his "antique shop" for the latter's clothes (p.209 ff.) There is also an element of satire here, since the hangman is portrayed, cynically and paradoxically, as, on the one hand, the guardian of culture, and, on the other, as a tasteless glutton. (This disguise is of prime importance for the action, since it allows Akki finally to outwit the King and to escape with Kurrubi, p.245.)

The *topos* is noted for the third time when Kurrubi is brought face to face with what she calls the "Double Being", the two Kings, in Act III. It is clear that the device is used ironically; in order to appear as Kings, the two characters wear "golden masks" (p.229); but, when the masks are dropped, the characters are still disguised, since Kurrubi can only see her beggar ("Anaschamaschtaklaku") whom she met by the Euphrates:

> *Nebuchadnezzar:* I was never a beggar. I was always a King. That
>   was just a disguise.
> *Kurrubi:*   Now you're disguised.   (p.231)

One can see the comic intention here when one recalls the King's proud remark to Akki in Act I: "It is one of the most important matters for mankind that everybody keeps his name, that everybody is what he is" (p.170). At one stage or another, all the characters "play rôles" and, as will be seen, it is their failure to play these rôles convincingly, their failure to match up to their conception of themselves, which, set in the comic ambience, provides the comic contrast between their "intentions" and their "performance".

We might finally consider another "structural element", pantofarce. Although Dürrenmatt returns in this play to the more conventional dramatic structure of three acts with curtain drops, there remain nevertheless many revue, or cabaret-like scenes with pantofarcical elements within them. The scene in Act I, where the King orders his courtiers to remain hidden while he talks to Akki, is perhaps the best example. The half-hidden courtiers react comically to whatever the King says or does on the stage. This is a scene in the oldest comic tradition of popular pantomime theatre (pp.168-190).

In Act II, the poets provide the comic pantofarce. When Akki is threatened by the policeman, Nebo, the poets ask for his "maquama" on the theme: *Stage direction*: The sarcophagi open up. Poets get up quickly or crawl out from under all sorts of things" (p.196). When the King later orders the "hangman" (Akki in disguise) to hang all the poets, Akki pardons them – and is then embarrassed when first one, then two . . . "stagger in . . . with beer-mugs and legs of mutton" (p.233) and have to be ushered out.

This pardon, and Dürrenmatt's indication that "a few poets" at least might accompany Akki and Kurrubi as they flee the doomed Babylon, give cause for believing that the author would not include *all* writers so satirized in these pantofarcical scenes; for the satire takes the form of "unmasking" – each of these characters has to be shown as hollow and insincere.[73] In the same way, the scenes of pantofarce involving Nebuchadnezzar and Nimrod mock the assumption of power. The two fight like children for possession of the throne – and are mocked by their own people in the statue of Gilgamesh with the changeable head which emphasizes the ephemeral nature of power (p.234). These scenes indicate clearly the author's efforts to create a comic ambience for his characters.

★   ★   ★

In many ways, Akki is a traditional comic character. He can be regarded as the "dolosus servus", met with in Plautus and Terence, the "tricky slave" who, like Palaestrio in Plautus' *Miles gloriosus*, arranges the comic action from the outset. Frye saw this character as the "spirit of comedy", Puck and Ariel together, carrying out the will of the author to reach a happy ending. (Frye, op.cit., p.174). He is one of those positive figures, whom on the whole we support in their comic conflict with the rigid characters. There is also about Akki something of that

quality of "poneria" which Whitman noted as a characteristic of an
Aristophanic "hero": ". . . the ability to get the advantage of somebody or some situation, by virtue of an unscrupulous but thoroughly
enjoyable exercise of craft". Whitman names specifically as examples
of the "poneros", Falstaff and Brecht's Azdak in *The Caucasian Chalk
Circle.*[74]

There is perhaps little point in embarking here on a lengthy comparison between Azdak and Akki; they are both representatives of a long
comic tradition, manipulated by their creators for different purposes:
Brecht makes a socio-political point, Dürrenmatt, a socio-religious
or cultural one. *Both* writers strive to make their character a genuine
human being.[75]

Like many of Dürrenmatt's comic protagonists, Akki is a realist;
his comedy is likewise down-to-earth and has a good deal of Bernese
"Bauernschläue" ("peasant shrewdness") in it, (a trait which Herbert
Lüthy noted about the Bavarian Brecht, calling him "the oddest, slyest
and craftiest poet who ever walked on God's earth"!)

The *locus classicus* for this trait in Akki is the fine begging-scene
with the King in Act I (p.170 ff.) It is a microcosm of the whole comic
"agon" — the eiron against the alazon, the beggar against the king, the
lowly against the mighty. As Akki wins each round, the audience laugh
at the collapse of the pompous Freudian "demi-god". The scene shows
us, too, how Dürrenmatt establishes the character of Akki through his
comedy and also shows us what he was trying to achieve through the
character. It is Akki's ability to deal realistically with a situation with
humour and guile which saves him and Kurrubi. As Kurrubi becomes
more and more depressed with the situation on earth, Akki shows her
how one must accept such unhappiness and, if need be, turn it to one's
advantage.

Even Akki's begging has a paradoxical goal, however, since everything superfluous to his needs is thrown into the Euphrates: "Extravagance is all," (cf. Goethe's: "Feeling is all") ". . . this is the only way
that the world can get rid of its riches", and he adds, "Since I can't
live on this earth, I've decided to live off it and have become a beggar"
(pp.192-193).

Akki, like Romulus, has *chosen* this comic life. Both have dedicated
their lives to bringing down their crumbling culture and hypocritical
civilization, "so that people see that everything ends up with beggars
in our declining age" (p.183).

Can Akki be called a "Fool", then? Does he become one of our
spiritual clowns? I think not. The difference between Romulus and
Akki is plain. Akki is a *victor*, indeed, as was mentioned above, he is

the "vice" of the classic comic tradition. As Frye observed, this character was often combined with the "hero" to produce a "cheeky improvi-
dent young man who hatches his own schemes and cheats his rich
father or uncle into giving him his patrimony along with the girl".
Mutatis mutandis, there is something of Akki in this description.[76]

Akki is a mixture of our professional and spiritual clown: his rôle
of beggar, his clothes and way of life qualify him for the latter rôle;
his belief that heroic struggles against authority are useless — "heroic
deeds are useless, they only betray the impotence of the weak, and
their despair makes those in power laugh" — (p.217); his struggle
against the "perfect" state and its unenlightened bureaucracy, and his
insistence that the only sensible way to order one's life is to recognize
the stupidity of all Heaven-storming enterprises, certainly all add up to
that mood of "sceptical resignation" that we noted in Romulus. Yet
Romulus was a true spiritual clown, because his plans were foiled by
the workings of Chance — the acceptance of his pension was simply
the acceptance of the inevitable and, as was noticed, there was a dark-
ening of the comedy because there was some sense of the tragic, "the
tragic of his greatness" (*Romulus*, Note, p.79). Akki, on the other
hand, simply chooses to flee the crumbling Babylon which "blind and
empty, crumbles with its tower of stone and steel", a fall symbolized
by the figure of the idiot prince. Akki flees as a victor, because he is
the only character to sacrifice himself for love, but, in fleeing, he
avoids tragedy and its burden of responsibility. It is therefore possible
to argue with Madler when he claims that Akki is the only one of the
four characters named by Dürrenmatt in *Problems of the Theatre*
(p.49) as "valiant men", who actually fulfils the criteria.[77] He certainly
"orders his world," as Berghahn suggests, but, for us, he is important
as Dürrenmatt's first purely *comic* character.[78] The elements of the
comic in his character and situation are presented in such a way as to
ensure that he is not laughed *at*, but laughed *with*. There is no ridicule
to take away the sympathy which the author wants us to feel for him,
the only character who has the courage to remain a human being. He is
the nearest Dürrenmatt has come to creating a solely comic personality
who mocks the mighty but escapes with his life, "for the man without
grace is always confronted by the man with grace" (*Two Remarks*,
op.cit, p.7), in a visual sense as well.

The "man without grace", the antagonist in this comic conflict, is
Nebuchadnezzar, the King. Although described as "still a young man,
not at all unsympathetic and somewhat naive", all his actions and
words make him appear unsympathetic and comically unscrupulous.
He is the alazon-type of heavy comic "raideur". His very first appearance

is laughable:

> Since my armies in the north have reached Lebanon, in the south,
> the sea, in the west, a desert, and in the east, a mountain range that
> is so high that it never stops, I have conquered the world . . . (p.166).

The "running gag", that "beyond Lebanon" the world stops, makes
him the all-powerful, short-sighted provincial ruler and tyrant, supported by his sycophantic lackeys, the Archminister, the Theologian, the
General and the Hangman who chorus, one comic soul in four puppet-
like bodies: "We congratulate His Majesty on the New Order of the
world" (p.166).

The laughter here is at the mortal who believes that he can create
perfection. The King is one of Dürrenmatt's monomaniacs who, like
Knipperdollinck in *It is written*, demands "unconditionally", in this
case, that God's grace should be given to him as he demands it — as a
King and not as the poorest of men. By this demand, he renounces his
right to be thought of as a "human" being; we must regard him as the
inhuman incorporation of an office — as such, he can become a comic
figure, laughed *at* but not *with*. (His treatment of Kurrubi proves the
point, cf. p.189).

Having established the King as a comic type, the author underlines
Nebuchadnezzar's true impotence by giving him a second soul in his
body; Nimrod, the ex-King, who has ruled for the last 900 years with
Nebuchadnezzar at his foot-stool, but who has now been captured by
the Queen of Sheba. Nebuchadnezzar is something of a match for Akki
in Act I, but when Nimrod appears in Act III, Nebuchadnezzar becomes
merely comic.[79] Stage setting and dialogue combine to give comedy:
on the throne "sits Nebuchadnezzar, Nimrod's head between his feet
which rest on the latter's shoulders". The pair are made to speak simultaneously; thus robbed of their individuality and humanity, they act like
marionettes, impotent wielders of useless authority. "We are chained to
one another, me and you", says Nebuchadnezzar (p.221); the farcical
throne-changing scenes make mock of their assumption of authority.[80]

These farcical scenes and their more sinister implications lead us
from the comic light to the darkness of the abyss, when the idiot son
of the two Kings dances grotesquely across the stage. Whose son is he?
"We both slipped in to see his mother when we were drunk," the Kings
say. The boy hops stupidly over the stage again just when the Kings
have assured Kurrubi that she is standing before the true King of
Babylon (p.229). The grotesqueness shows up the impotence of a
power whose successor is an idiot. It is the furthest limit of Dürrenmatt's comic spectrum in this play.

Nebuchadnezzar's enraged impotence expresses itself, of course, in his fixed determination to build the Tower of Babel (p.246), but, "the grandiose conception of Man which proves to be his "most senseless" when the world is completed", shows itself when the King learns that all the prisoners on whom he would vent his rage have escaped — and he is left alone, or rather, not quite alone, but with his successor, the idiot son:

> *Stage direction:* Grinning, the idiot son walks like a tight-rope dancer over the stage. Nebuchadnezzar covers his countenance in *impotent* rage, in *impotent* sadness (p.246).[81]   (my emphases)

Jacob Steiner writes: "One hesitates more than with *Romulus* to use the genre-term *Komödie* here", but changes his mind slightly later and says, "Thus this dramaturgical *hic et nunc* is the basis of the *Komödie*, of a *Komödie* certainly which has all the essentials for tragedy".[82]

But surely there is no "tragic" in the end of this play? Nebuchadnezzar is shown to be an example of that absolute power that corrupts absolutely, but which Dürrenmatt continually shows to be impotent in the face of a true humanity. It is such impotence which is ridiculed, and it is the ridicule which removes tragedy from the conclusion. We are left — again — with Otto Rommel's "bitterness of impotence".

Guthke writes that the *Komödie* is, "as far as genre is concerned, clearly defined. Considered logically, it ... conceals tragicomic possibilities, but they are not actualized", and one of the more perceptive "instant" critic-journalists wrote: "It is a *Komödie* with a strong inclination towards tragedy. Dürrenmatt wants to show what happens when certain ideas clash in men who take them seriously".[83]

★   ★   ★

The Angel and Kurrubi might be considered as two halves of an "alazon"-type. They come in from the outside, disrupt the community and are then driven out. They are, too, the optimist-pessimist duet not unknown to comedy. The Angel can only see Good wherever he looks: "Whatever is created is good, and what is good is happy" (p.165). His wit and optimism make him a sympathetic character at the outset, but, on closer examination, one can see that he, too, is deluded — his innocent, impractical idealism has become an obsession. Firstly, he is tricked into giving Kurrubi to Nebuchadnezzar instead of to Akki.

The chance presence of the King then leads to the contest with Akki, and the King's defeat means that *he* is chosen as the "least of men" (p.184).

So it is the Angel's mistake that "disrupts the community" — but *is* it a mistake? The "least of men" (one assumes a beggar) does eventually receive Kurrubi; indeed, Akki receives her *twice*, once when he exchanges her for Nimrod, a second time, when, disguised as "the hangman", he is handed Kurrubi by the King. But, firstly, Akki is not the least of men — he could be a millionaire if he wished (cf. p.192), and, secondly, Kurrubi does not love him, but rather the beggar on whom she first set eyes, her beggar from Ninive, as Nebuchadnezzar had introduced himself. Thus it does look as if the Angel had made a mistake — and he makes a second, when he returns at the end to say farewell to Kurrubi. He is shown to be an extremely naive Angel, maybe even a stupid one, since he fails to perceive the unhappiness of mortal men amidst earth's beauties. Kurrubi's frantic pleas to be taken with him are unanswered: he flies away, as the gods do in Brecht's *Good Woman of Szechwan*, ironically "leaving you, o happy one, on Earth" (p.245).

It does seem as if Dürrenmatt wanted to stress that the ways of Heaven were incomprehensible even to angels — we recall that Heaven was to appear "incomprehensible" rather than "immeasurable". Indeed, the Angel says to Kurrubi: "We shall never comprehend what comes from the hand of Him who created you, my child" (p.165). In this respect, the Angel is a comic figure; he has failed in the task allotted to him — instead of bringing "grace" to the world, he has set in motion the most ludicrous enterprise imaginable, the building of the Tower of Babel.

Kurrubi is yet another of Dürrenmatt's humourless female characters.[84] She is all fear and trembling, the "innocent abroad". She, the other half of this alazon-figure, is the second "agens" of the action. She is responsible for the whole "comedy of errors" and she becomes a "comic character" since, like many of the others, she is obsessed by a fixed idea. She *will* secure her "beggar from Nineve". This insistence becomes comic because the audience knows that she is being deluded:

Nebuchadnezzar:	You seek one who does not exist.
Kurrubi:	He does exist because I love him.
Nebuchadnezzar:	You love one whom you will not find.
Kurrubi:	I shall find him I love, sometime, somewhere.

This is a demand for the "unconditional", for the audience knows that it must remain unsatisfied. She has grace and dignity, but it is sadly and paradoxically comical that she, descended from Heaven with an Angel, should have to flee at the end through a desert sandstorm accompanied by a beggar whom she does not love, and still seeking one she does.

The "bomolochoi", the buffoons, divide themselves neatly into four groups; the *Volk* (the populace), minor buffoons, who, caricatured and characterized as automata, have walk-on rôles only. The second group: Tabtum, the high-class prostitute and purveyor of the "Zote", the comic obscenity; Enggibi, the banker, a gentle satire on the Helvetic love of money and lack of culture (as in the old proverb: "Point d'argent, point de Suisse"!) and continuous and continual cantonal rivalry; Gimmil, the goat-milk dealer with his comic slogans (eg "With cow milk for Progress").[85] Then a third group, led by one of the "learned menials", the comic policeman, Nebo, who composes poems on traffic duty and whom the Swiss audience would identify from their newspaper "Nebelspalter" (lit. "Fog-Divider"); then Dürrenmatt's favourite hangman whose paratactic sentences lend him a grotesque air — as does his garb: "Dressed in a solemn shabby black, a little case in his hand" (p.209). To these two, one must add the comic chorus, the fifty poets.[86] It would seem that these poor souls, living off Akki (the "coryphaeus") under a bridge, will nevertheless be among those who will escape to a land "full of new promises, full of new songs", when the rotting social fabric of this civilization crumbles away. But, be it noted, this land will also be "full of new persecutions", Dürrenmatt, the eternal realist, adds.

The fourth, and final group is the duet Utnapischtim-Chamurapi, a much-scorned pair of time-servers, clowns representing, as Werner rightly says, the "all-dominating power of Bureaucracy", distanced from us and objectified by their blind inhumanity and their stupidity.[87] We see here, in this savage attack on institutionalized religion, how Dürrenmatt was already beginning to work with a "theology without God", as Hans Meyer put it.[88] Yet one has the feeling that Dürrenmatt, in creating Utnapischtim, was creating him as one who "is not so sure that he would act differently", to quote from the *Note* to *The Visit of the Old Lady*. But there is certainly no such saving grace for the Archminister, the archetypal, ruthless, scheming politician who sums up his own behaviour in a typically Dürrenmattian aphorism: "The more often a politician contradicts himself, the greater he becomes" (p.236). These two in high office are "maladjusted and inappropriate" to their situation, as William McDougall would have said.[89] Their maladjustment can be comic *and* dangerous to the rest of humanity — and Dürrenmatt is constantly attacking their like.

★　　★　　★

Space must be made for mention of an unusual feature of this play and one which is certainly part of the comic fabric — Akki's "maquamas".[90] In *Problems of the Theatre,* Dürrenmatt explained why he used them: "With these I am trying to express what is Arabian in this character, the joy in composition, in the battles with words, in the play on words . . ." (*TP*, p.36). He is clearly hoping that the audiences will find them funny.

Dürrenmatt uses a wide range of linguistic devices in the three maquamas (p.197, p.215 and pp.217-218), but relies mainly on incongruous rhymes and alliteration. In the final maquama however, the "last, most bitter maquama", Akki-Dürrenmatt philosophizes: "To endure the world, the weak must know it well, so that they will not blindly follow a path which vanishes, or run into a danger which will lead to Death". To attack "those in power", "humble yourself and you'll smash every wall" (p.217). This is a classic statement of the "spirit of comedy" — Frye says: "The tricky slave often has his own freedom in mind as the reward of his exertions" (Frye, p.174). Like Ariel in *The Tempest*, Akki "longs for release" and finds it in the end. (Brecht, too, abhorred the "useless sacrifice": cf. "Courage is nothing, but/ arriving is all / Whoever sails out to sea / and drowns, is a damned fool . . ." (*Ozeanflug*)).

★　　★　　★

For me, then, this is Dürrenmatt's "purest *Komödie*". The "tragic", the stupidity of Man who refuses to sacrifice his political or religious power or his material possessions in return for divine grace, is achieved through the "comic" in the structural elements and the characters, a practical example of the theories to be enunciated shortly in *Problems of the Theatre*, and practised — in Güllen. These potentially tragic figures are placed in comic situations and accidents which underline the frailty and fallibility of us all (angels included!). No answer is given here, there is no "Happy End" to his *Komödie*; it is a conflict, not a problem, a conflict between naked power (inhumanity) and goodness. It is interesting that a Zürich reviewer only saw a "silver lining" in the play; this came certainly from what Scherer called the "joyful, positive worldly wisdom" of Akki,[91] or perhaps from the heroism, "although a modest heroism within human limits", which Oberle saw, a humanity beside which the comic attempts at "heroism" in the play, in the guise of power-politics, of the inhuman and puppet-like buffoons, appeared ridiculous.[92]

It is a comedy of errors and in the "fairy-tale atmosphere" which Frau Brock-Sulzer always finds in this play, there lies too the "sharpness of satirical rage or the bitterness of impotence" that Otto Rommel mentioned.

"Stay calm, my child", says the Angel: "A simple accident which doesn't affect the harmony of things" (p.180). There is indeed a similarity between this work and Voltaire's *Candide*; in this story of the best of all possible worlds in which nothing but misfortunes occur, there is the same comic pattern — order and chaotic nonsense.[93]

For the third time, Dürrenmatt had avoided the "tragedy-trap". He now had the confidence to go as near to the edge of the "yawning abyss" as he had ever done.

NOTES TO CHAPTER FOUR

(i) ROMULUS DER GROSSE (ROMULUS THE GREAT)

1. Ginsberg produced the première of *Romulus*, with Horwitz in the title rôle. A translation by Gerhard Nellhaus is in *Four Plays*, Cape, London, 1957-1962, 1964. Dürrenmatt's *Gedenkrede (Memorial speech)* on Ginsberg was held in the Schauspielhaus Zürich on 7.2.65. The text is in *TSR I*, pp.195-209, here p.205.
2. Max Frisch: *Tagebuch 1946-1949* (Café Odeon, p.108).
3. My quotations are taken from the 1964 version in *KI*. pp.7-79. Only Act IV of the 1957 version (Arche 1958) differs from the 1949 version and these have been compared with the other two versions. See H.U.Voser in the Schauspielhaus programme of 1957/58, pp.3-10 and C.M. Jauslin: *Friedrich Dürrenmatt — Zur Struktur seiner Dramen*, Juris-Verlag, Zürich 1964, p.46 for details.
4. Switzerland's Janus-like attitude in the war has been dealt with in E.Bonjour: *Geschichte der schweizerischen Neutralität*, Helbling und Lichterhahn, Basel, 1965-1970. There are six volumes, Vols. IV-VI deal with the war. See too P.Lyon: *Neutralism*, Leicester University Press 1963, pp.151-164, and also Dürrenmatt: "Switzerland's policy had only one aim . . . to avoid war . . ." in *Zur Dramaturgie der Schweiz (On a dramaturgy for Switzerland)* *TSR II*, pp.232-256, here p.235. (Dürrenmatt's son became a conscientious objector and was jailed during the anti-Vietnam period).
5. *Theaterzeitung der Stadt-Theater Basel*, No.33, 33 Jg., 115 Spielzeit, 22.5.49 p.15. The second version was produced in Zürich on 24.10.57.

6. See the *Note* to *The Visit of the Old Lady* 1956 (in *KI*, p.341): "I describe human beings, not marionettes", while N.Pawlowa finds "modesty and kindness" and a "lively, remarkable naturalness" in his characters: *Theater und Wirklichkeit*, Kunst und Literatur XIV, 1966, pp.76-86, here p.80. See too H.Dyrenforth: *The Paradox and the Grotesque in the work of Friedrich Dürrenmatt*, Ph.D. dissertation, University of California 1963, p.324. For another favourable view, see H.Haller: *Friedrich Dürrenmatts ungeschichtliche historische Komödie "Romulus der Grosse"*, Germanistische Studien I, Braunschweig 1966, pp.77-106.

7. The historical Romulus Augustulus (= little Augustus) was only 16 when created Emperor on 31st October AD 475 by his father Orestes. He was defeated and deposed on September 4th AD 476 and sent to relatives in the villa which Lucullus had built near Naples, with an annual pension of 6000 solidi. Dürrenmatt's Romulus is "about 50", married, with a grown-up daughter, Rea.

8. See *The Physicists*, Point 3: "A story is thought through to a conclusion when it has taken its worst possible turn". (*K II*, p.353).

9. Neumann, op.cit., p.27. *Point 4* to *The Physicists* says: "The worst possible turn cannot be foreseen. It occurs by Chance". This is comic in Kant's definition — it is "an emotion caused by the sudden conversion of a tense expectation into nothing". (In *Kritik der Urteilskraft*, 1790). Interestingly enough, Dürrenmatt takes up Neumann's point in his *Sentences on the theatre* (1976) where he calls it the "dramaturgy of an accident" (p.15). He writes: "Reality is an unlikely event which has occurred"!

10. M.Frisch in Weltwoche, 6.5.49. W. Duwe in *Deutsche Dichtung des 20. Jahrhunderts*, Orell Füssli, Zürich 1962, Vol.II, p.457. E.Brock-Sulzer: *FD* p.51 and *Dürrenmatt in unserer Zeit*, Reinhardt, Basel 1968, pp.24-27. We cannot agree with T. Tiusanen that Romulus is a "megalomaniac" like Knipperdollinck and the blind Duke. Does he mean a "*mono*maniac"? If so, then we still cannot agree. The monomaniac is our *alazon* and Romulus has too much "humanity" to be so classed. (Tiusanen, p.83).

11. In *Der Bund* 18 January 1951. Schwengeler supported the concept of "geistige Landesverteigung" (Spiritual defence of the country), first used to discourage acceptance of the Nazi ideology in Switzerland, but later adopted by those who wished to uphold the older Swiss traditions against "modern" ideas. See A.W. Schwengeler: *Vom Geist und Wesen der Schweizer Dichtung*, St Gallen 1964 and also T.Lengborn: *Schriftsteller und Gesellschaft in der Schweiz*, Athenäum, Frankfurt, 1972, p.11. This attitude is called "Kantönligeist" in Switzerland.

12. J.Scherer: *Der Mutige Mensch*, Stimmen der Zeit, Band 169, 1961/1962, pp.307-312, here p.308.

13. Odoaker says: "I am a peasant and hate war" (p.72), a comic "Helvetic incongruity". The historical Odoaker, a Scythian, reigned over the Germani as King of Italy until 493 AD when Theoderic, King of the Ostrogoths, killed him in battle. It would seem that Dürrenmatt mirrored Theoderich in his "mythical" Alaric the Goth in *Titus Andronicus* (1970): "World domination is our great goal" (*TA*, p.46).

14. See *Point 9* to *The Physicists*: "Chance strikes them (i.e. men who plan) hardest when it makes them reach the opposite of their goal" (*K II*, p.354).

15. G.Waldmann: *Dürrenmatts paradoxes Theater*, p.28. He is one of those who overstress the "*Komödie* of the Christian faith" here and fails to see the play as a *stage-work*. Above all, it is a fine play for the stage.

16. T.Poser: *Friedrich Dürrenmatt*: in *Zur Interpretation des modernen Dramas*, (ed. Rolf Geissler), Diesterweg, Frankfurt (n.d.), 4th edn., pp.69-96, here p.87.

17. In *Das Schönste*, München, November 1961. Brecht named this "bourgeois trait", "rotten mysticism". See *GW*, Band 18, p.231. Martin Esslin reports that Brecht enjoyed *Romulus* but the authorities would not allow him to stage it. See *Brief Chronicles*, Temple Smith 1970, p.123.
18. Theaterzeitung, Basel, op.cit. The phrase recurs in *Nocturnal conversation with a despised person* (1951-1952) in *GH*, p.109 and is used again as a "defence" in the Foreword to his *Portrait of a Planet* (1971): "For the world which we live in is neither sane nor profound; it is a mass of unhealthy banalities" (p.10).
19. See on this point H-J Syberberg: *Interpretationen zum Drama Friedrich Dürrenmatts*, Verlag Uni-Druck, München 1965, pp.68-87. This was Syberberg's D.Phil. dissertation. He is now, of course, a distinguished and much-discussed film-maker! This work is, as Bänziger suggests, "rather tiresome to read".
20. See Shaw's *Caesar and Cleopatra* where the library is burned down. Other parallels are: the drinking of Falernian wine and the Imperial bath. Dürrenmatt wrote himself: "The play will settle down somewhere between Theo Lingen (a German comic actor) and Bernard Shaw" (KI, p.78). Hugo Garten mentions the similarity, but believes that the Swiss lacks the "moral zeal and rationalism" of the Irishman. H.F. Garten: *Romulus der Grosse*, Methuen 1962 (1968), p.xxix. A.D. Klarmann calls it Dürrenmatt's most Shavian play ". . .full of fine repartee and irony" in *Friedrich Dürrenmatt and the tragic sense of comedy*, TDR 4, 4 May 1966, pp.87-88.
21. In his fragment, *On a dramaturgy for Switzerland*, op.cit., p.238.
22. Freud called this the "reduction of the sublime" and expanded the remark in a famous phrase: "This and that man worshipped like a demi-god is after all just a man like you and me" (*Der Witz*, op.cit., p.231).
23. See F. Philipp: *Dürrenmatt im Spiegel der sowjetischen Kritik in Die Tat, No. 285, 3.12.65*. Tiusanen mentions Dürrenmatt's "early and lasting popularity in Poland" and Jan Kott's 1959 essay on Romulus in his *Theatre Notebook 1947-1967*, Methuen 1968. (Tiusanen, p.92).
24. A. Arnold: *Friedrich Dürrenmatt*, Colloquium Verlag, Berlin 1969. (Köpfe des XX Jahrhunderts, Band 57), p.33. Dürrenmatt accepted that his *Titus Andronicus* could well be considered as a repetition of the Romulus theme. "The classical world is brought to an end here too" (*Notes to TA in TSR II*, pp.187-193, here p.193) and see too Titus' speech on ". . .the world/to which justice brings but murders and no order" (*TA*, p.22).
25. Marcel Pilet-Golaz and Henri Guisan (as Foreign Minister and "General" respectively) were the two Vaudois who led the Swiss at the beginning of the war. Pilet-Golaz's policy was to conciliate Nazi Germany – Guisan's to resist. The latter made a famous and symbolical speech to that effect on the Rütli mountain in July 1940, promising to defend the "Alpen-Reduit" to the death.
26. The aphorism is a parody of the Comte de Maistre's (1753-1821): "Toute nation a le gouvernement qu'elle mérite" (in a letter of 27.8.1811).
27. The phrase is then repeated, with variations, eleven times. Amédée Scholl has made a most interesting study of Dürrenmatt's language in *Zeichen und Bezeichnetes im Werk Friedrich Dürrenmatts*, in *Dürrenmatt, Studien* (1976) op.cit., pp.203-217.
28. "I am concerned with logical thought in its strictest application, so strict that it sets up its own internal contradictions" (M. Esslin: *Durrenmatt. Merciless observer* in Plays and Players, March 1963, pp.15-16).
29. G.Highet: *Anatomy of Satire*, op.cit., pp.68-69.
30. G. Wilson Knight: *King Lear and the comedy of the grotesque* in *The Wheel of Fire*, Methuen 1949, 4th edn, rev.1960), pp.160-176, here p.160.

31. Max Frisch wrote delightedly about the cackling hens in the programme of the première in 1949. He found them a perfect theatrical metaphor.
32. *Romulus* has proved to be Dürrenmatt's most popular play with amateurs and school-groups according to N.Baensch: *Dürrenmatt und die Bühne* in *FD I*, pp. 65-72, here p.70.
33. J.R.von Salis: *Die Schweiz im kalten Krieg*, op.cit., p.187.
34. K.S.Guthke, op.cit., p.381. Brock-Sulzer in a) Die Tat, 3.5.49. b) *FD*, op. cit., p.54 and *Dürrenmatt in unserer Zeit*, op.cit., p.27.
35. Romulus' situation is therefore not unlike Dürrenmatt's view of Switzerland herself: "It (Switzerland) is not a tragic object, but an untragic case in a tragic age" (*On a dramaturgy for Switzerland*), p.246. (J. Strelka in *Friedrich Dürrenmatt: Die Paradox-Groteske als Wirklichkeitsbewältigung* in *Brecht, Horváth und Dürrenmatt*, Forum-Wien 1962, pp.114-158, here p.144).
36. See J.Huizinga: *Homo ludens*, Pantheon: Akademische Verlagsanstalt, Amsterdam 1939, p.232 and H.Mahler: *Das Tragische in der Komödie*, D.Phil. dissertation, University of Munich 1949, pp.1-2. Reference might be made here to P.Kurz's interesting article *Der Narr und der Zweifel: Zu einem Aspekt im Werk Friedrich Dürrenmatts*, in *Über moderne Literatur 3*, Knecht 1971, pp,49-72.
37. Despite its success with amateurs, *Romulus* has not been a great success with professional critics. Gore Vidal's adaptation (New York, January 1962) was criticized for its lack of drama. John Simon suggested that Vidal was more to blame than Dürrenmatt. See The Hudson Review 15, 2, Summer 1962 (pp.264-265). For Twain on the "tragedy-trap", see the letter to Howells quoted in Arnold, op.cit., p.45.

(ii) DIE EHE DES HERRN MISSISSIPPI
(THE MARRIAGE OF MR MISSISSIPPI)

38. Dürrenmatt still regards this as one of the few "really good performances" of any of his plays (to Dieter Fringeli in 1977). He produced the play himself in Berne in 1954. The second version was directed by Leopold Lindtberg on 11.4.57; the third version, from which my quotations are taken, is a slightly altered version of the second: *Die Ehe des Herrn Mississippi: Dritte Fassung : Eine Komödie* in *KI*, pp.80-158 (= EHM). The first *book* version appeared in 1952 (Zürich-Oprecht). The second version came from the same firm in 1957. The play was translated by Michael Bullock in *Four Plays*, Cape 1964. See too on the film version, Note 46 under. For criticisms of the première, see *Komödie mit vielen Leichen*, Stuttgarter Nachrichten, 31.3.52; Bruno Werner in Neue Zeitung, München, 28.3.52 and *Ideen fressen Menschen* in Der Spiegel, 2.4.52. Dürrenmatt himself sees this play as the breakthrough for him in Germany (inter alia, *GHLA*, p.19).
39. *Bekenntnis eines Plagiators*: Die Tat, 9.8.52 (now in TSR I, pp.239-246) here p.245. Dürrenmatt has continued to insist upon this: "In *The Marriage of Mr Mississippi*, for example, I quite consciously quote a few sentences from *Romulus* to show where in *Romulus* this *Marriage of Mr Mississippi* came from": J.Preuss: *Wie ein Drama entsteht* (Jan.1969) in Literarische Werkstatt, Oldenburg 1972, pp.9-18, here p.14.
40. R.Carew: *The plays of Friedrich Dürrenmatt*, Dublin Magazine IV, 1965, pp.57-68, gives an account of the "surrealist" production at the London Arts Theatre in 1959 (p.65). Titled *Fools are passing through*, and directed by Maximilian Slater, it was Dürrenmatt's first American première in the Off-Broadway Theatre on 2.4.58. Brooks Atkinson compared Dürrenmatt's "despair" with the traditionally happy image of Switzerland (New York Times, 3.4.58). See Bänziger, pp.281-282 for further particulars.

41. His novels of this period, *Der Richter und sein Henker* (serialized in the *Schweizerischer Beobachter* December 1950-March 1951 and published by the Benziger Verlag in 1952); *The Judge and his Hangman*, trans. Cyrus Brooks, Penguin 1954 (1969); and *Der Verdacht*, serialized similarly September 1951-February 1952 and published by Benziger in 1953, certainly prove the point. Bärlach, the Kommissär in the latter work, is a spiritual clown trapped by the evil in the world (the ex-SS doctor Emmenberger) and rescued by the giant Jew, Gulliver, who acts, like Mississippi, "according to the Law of Moses". Gulliver calls Bärlach, whom he significantly titles "the Sad Knight", "You fool of a detective", since "the age has taken you ad absurdum". (*DVD*, pp.149-151). Peter Spycher's book on the stories is the first full-length study but he rarely gets to the heart of them since. as he admits, "there is a good deal of paraphrasing" (Preface, p.10). Although Dürrenmatt called his works "pot-boilers" (cf. "I am a Sunday novelist" to L.W. Forster in *DRH*, Harrap 1962, p.9), they have been best-sellers since their publication. A film of *DRH* (directed by Maximilian Schell and with Dürrenmatt in the rôle of Fortschig) appeared in 1978.

42. R.B.Heilmann: *Tragic elements in a Dürrenmatt comedy*, Modern Drama XX, May 1967, pp.11-16, here p.11. Gottfried Benn called it an "existential tragedy" in *Die Ehe des Herrn Mississippi* in *Autobiographische und vermischte Schriften: Gesammelte Werke*, Band IV, Wiesbaden 1961, p.299.

43. In Beethoven's only opera *Fidelio* (1805/1806/1814) Florestan, the endungeoned hero, sings: "Sweet comfort in my heart / I have done my duty".

44. Cf. "The tendency to treat pedants, often by their own consent, as laughing stocks for the delectation of the court, was carried to much greater lengths in Germany than in either France or England", E.Welsford: *The Fool, His Social and Literary History*, Faber and Faber 1968, p.188.

45. See the final chorus in *Biedermann und die Brandstifter* (1958) and the despairing question of Anthrax's donkey at the end of *The Trial of the Donkey's Shadow* (1951): "Was I the ass in this story?" In *GH*, p.87.

46. The present *Dritte Fassung* is largely the same text as the stage production: Kurt Hoffmann's film version appeared in 1961 (*EHM: Bühnenfassung und Drehbuch*, Arche 1966), (Drehbuch, pp.83-150), and finally the *Fassung 1970*, (Arche, via Europa Verlag, 1970) which was to have been produced in Basle in 1969, but, as Dürrenmatt wrote in the *Notice*: ". . . it fell victim to my disagreements with the Basle Theatre management" (p.81) (q.v.) *Mississippi 1970* is not significantly different from the *Dritte Fassung*: "It only seeks to clarify them (i.e. earlier versions) in theatrical terms" (p.81). Ulrich Gregor called the film a commercial vulgarization of the intellectual acrobatics that make up the charm of the stage play, (in *Verfilmtes Theater*, Theater Heute, 8.8.61, p.4 (Profitlich op.cit., p.62).

47. J-P.Sartre: *Qu'est-ce que la littérature?*in *Situations II*, Gallimard 1948, p.313. and see too, I.Murdoch: *Sartre*, Collins 1953, pp.118-119. Dürrenmatt in *Theater ist Theater* in Theater Heute, September 1968 and also in S.Melchinger: *Theater im Umbruch*, dtv 1970, pp.76-79, here p.78. For Dürrenmatt's dislike of Sartre, see his review of *Le diable et le bon dieu* in Weltwoche 9.11.51, now in *TSR I*, pp.311-313. Dürrenmatt's *55 Sentences on Art and Reality* in *FD II*, pp.20-22.

48. Kästner's review runs: "Each time it was a case of: *Tua res agitur*. And Dürrenmatt certainly deals with everybody's problems", Weltwoche 28.3.52. The character's full name is interesting: Frédéric (from Chopin?) – René (from Chateaubriand?) – Saint-Claude (Saint-Simon?) – whose first names were Claude Henri!)

49. Sartre, op.cit., p.281. He is quoting from the *Action francaise*. Mona and
    Gerhard Knapp see Saint-Claude as the beginning of a development in
    Dürrenmatt's dramaturgical thought (his "concentration on the individual")
    which, they claim, reaches its climax in *Der Mitmacher* (*Recht-Gerechtig-
    keit-Politik* in *FD II*, pp.23-40).
50. M.Züfle: *Zu den Bühnengestalten FDs*, op.cit., p.101.
51. Marahrens suggests that the name might be derived from the Alsatian town
    of Zabern (Latin "tres tabernae") and might refer to Bodo's "lake of alco-
    hol". (G.Marahrens: *Friedrich Dürrenmatts Die Ehe des Herrn Mississippi*,
    in *Dürrenmatt. Studien*, op.cit., pp.80-124, here p.96.
    Dürrenmatt told Violet Ketels that the character was based on Kierkegaard
    who was a hunchback and had to suffer "the greatest test for a Christian –
    Paul wrote this – namely, ridiculousness" (p.105). I think she means "ridi-
    cule".
52. H.Loetscher: *Die Groteske der menschlichen Ohnmacht*, Programmheft,
    Schauspielhaus Zürich 1956-57, pp.7-10, here p.10.
    Pace Dürrenmatt, we cannot see anything "grotesque", in the modern sense,
    in the characterization of Bodo – comic and fantastic, yes, but there is little
    of Kayser's "attempt to control and exorcize the demonic elements in the
    world" (op.cit., p.202) or, in his earlier work, the "alienation" which "takes
    the ground away from under your feet" (*Das Sprachliche Kunstwerk*,
    Francke, Bern, 1948 (12th edn. 1967), p.384). Anastasia, on the other hand,
    has the horror but not the comic in her character; only Mississippi combines
    the two. We agree with Jennings' view: "The grotesque is the demonic made
    ludicrous . . . if the disarming is carried to completion, the result is some-
    thing ludicrous not demonic". He describes Hoffmann's figures ("human
    heads moving about on grasshopper legs, human-faced ravens, a man whose
    chest is a fiddle on which he accompanies his daughter's dance . . .") as
    properly grotesque. There is none of this in Bodo. See L.B.Jennings: *Klein
    Zaches and his kin: The grotesque revisited*, DVJS, 44 Jg, Heft 4, Dezember
    1970, pp.687-703, here p.690 and p.695. Peter Johnson attributes Bodo's
    "lover of cruel fables and useless comedies" (*EHM*, p.116) to Dürrenmatt's
    own character. P.Johnson: *Grotesqueness and injustice in Dürrenmatt*, GLL,
    XV, No.4, July 1962, pp.264-273, here pp.265-266. Heidsieck however
    agrees that much of what has been called "grotesque" in Dürrenmatt is only
    "ridiculous" or "farcical comedy" (op.cit. p.89). Margret Dietrich, too, lays
    a good deal of emphasis on the comic element of the grotesque in *Theater
    im Gespräch*, München 1963, p.277, as does Grimm with his "element of
    play", in his *Parodie und Groteske* . . . op.cit. p.448 ff.
53. G.E.Wellwarth: *The Theatre of Protest and Paradox*, London 1965, p.140.
    In the 1970 version, Dürrenmatt added "worms" to the list of diseases!
54. The scene is much altered from the 1952 version where Mississippi launches
    out on a religious tirade which is not so much farcical as impossible. The
    1957 and 1970 versions are much more "comical" and more dramatic (See
    EHM 1952, pp.68-71 and the 1970 *Fassung* pp.58-59). See too L.R.Phelps:
    Dürrenmatt's Die Ehe des Herrn Mississippi: The revision of a play: Modern
    Drama, Vol.8, 1965, pp.156-160, although the material is rather thin.
55. U.Jenny, op.cit. p.41. Saint-Claude calls her "whore" (p.145) and the
    "whore of Babylon" (p.147), while she calls herself "a whore who goes
    through Death, unchanged" (p.155).
56. cf Wedekind: "With my description of Lulu, I was trying to describe the
    body of a woman through the words she speaks. At each of her utterances I
    asked myself if it made her young and fresh". On *Erdgeist*, 1893-4 in *Prosa,
    Dramen, Versen*, Langen, Müller, München 1960, p.945.

In the 1970 version, however, Dürrenmatt insisted that Anastasia should be played by "as young a woman as possible" to offer as great a comparison as possible with Mississippi. "Anastasia should be almost a 'Lolita' while Mississippi should be about 50 or 55" (To Ketels, op.cit., p.107). See too the *Notice*, p.82.

57. I really cannot believe that Dürrenmatt chose the name "Diego" because of the "-ego" section! (cf Marahrens, p.99).

58. In Hoffmann's 1961 film version, Diego (now renamed Sir Thomas Jones) gains a more decisive victory, marries Anastasia and gets rid of his adversaries. Mississippi is last seen in an asylum, muttering (three!) times: "The world must be changed . . ." (Film script, op.cit., pp.83-150) See too *Dürrenmatt auf der Leinwand*, NZZ, 25.8.61. for a good review of the film, and *Der Spiegel (Justizkrise)* of 1.3.61.
     A propos the film, Dürrenmatt said to Horst Bienek that "they made a political farce out of a perhaps more religious-slanted *Komödie*". (*Werkstattgespräch*).

59. See M.Hodgart: *Satire*, Weidenfeld and Nicholson 1969, p.133: "*Satura lanx* = a full dish, hence a kind of cornucopia . . . a medley, farrago or hotchpotch". For Benn, op.cit., p.299. In the 1970 version, Beethoven's 9th Symphony is extensively used as a symbol and parody of a dying culture (cf. ". . . not to be heard as background music – the individual themes are to be used as motifs" *EHM*, 1970, p.66). They occur frequently from this point in the play on. It is clear, however, that the set was meant to arouse laughter. See the pictures of the 1952 set in U.Jenny, op.cit., pp.98-99 and Dürrenmatt: *Teo Otto: Begleittext zur Aufführung in Frankfurt* 1964 in *TSR I*, pp.165-170, here p.168.

60. In *Problems of the Theatre*, Dürrenmatt said that he stressed the "uncertainty of the location . . . in order to suspend the play in a joke, in a *Komödie*" (p.25).

61. cf. N.Frye: *Anatomy of Comedy*, op.cit., p.215.

62. Murray Peppard mentions the appropriateness of the title of the American translation: these "fools" are only "passing through", "but they will return since they are eternal, recurrent types" (Peppard, op.cit., p.48. See above, Note 40).

63. C.Cases in *Friedrich Dürrenmatt: Die Ehe des Herrn Mississippi: Stichworte zur deutschen Literatur* (trans. F.Kollmann) Europa Verlag, Wien 1969, sees the author as "one who radically and defiantly perpetuates those tendencies characteristic of nihilistic decadence" – but writes as a communist approving Dürrenmatt's attacks on capitalism. Ruth Blum grants that he is one of those "who wants to express the positive by showing the negative side: *Ist Friedrich Dürrenmatt ein christlicher Schriftsteller?* Reformatio 8, 1959, pp.535-539, here p.536, while Otto Mann believed that this type of pessimism played directly into the hands of the Communists. (*Geschichte des deutschen Dramas*, Stuttgart, 1963, p.625). See Dürrenmatt's answer to those "who see the world only as despair" in *Two Remarks on his Komödie*, op.cit., pp.7-8. In 1977, Dürrenmatt said to Dieter Fringeli that Schweikart's *Ehe* gave the picture of Dürrenmatt as a "nihilist" which has dogged him ever since.

64. H.G.Werner: *Friedrich Dürrenmatt: Der Moralist und die Komödie*, Wiss. Z.U., Halle, Band XVIII, Heft 4, 1969, pp.143-156, here p.153. See too Dürrenmatt's *Der Autor zu seinen Kritikern*: "I'm not writing *about* our age, but rather a *Komödie of* our age" (First book version, 1952) and G.F.Hering: *Der Ruf zur Leidenschaft*, Kiepenhauer & Witsch 1959, pp.33-40 for a hilarious account of Dürrenmatt's comically disguised appearance before the public at the Munich première. Grimm is very critical of the later versions (*Nach zwanzig Jahren*, Basis, Vol.3, 1972, pp.214-237).

(iii) EIN ENGEL KOMMT NACH BABYLON
(AN ANGEL COMES TO BABYLON)

65. In the Programmheft of the Schauspielhaus Zürich 1953-1954, p.7 but see
M.C.Feller: "His development from *Romulus* to the *Marriage of Mr Missis-
sippi* shows that he has understood that plays *about* which there is discussion
are, in general, better than plays in which there is discussion", in Münchner
Merkur, 28.3.52). And Dürrenmatt: "My next attempt (i.e. *The Tower of
Babel*) grew out of hand, I had to break it off . . ." (in *Zum Tode Ernst
Ginsberg*, 1965, in *TSR I*, pp.195-209, here p.205).
66. *Ein Engel kommt nach Babylon: Eine fragmentarische Komödie in drei
Akten: Zweite Fassung* 1957 in KI, pp.159-248 (= *EKB*). The "fragmentary" refers to Dürrenmatt's plan to write a trilogy. "According to my
plan, my next play *Die Mitmacher* (ie The *men* who never said: NO!) should
present the building of the tower itself. All are against the Tower – yet it is
still built". *Der Mitmacher* (i.e. in the singular) of 1973 could certainly be
seen as a continuation of the theme (See below pp.220-225). The first version appeared in book form as *Ein Engel kommt nach Babylon: Eine Komödie in drei Akten*, Arche 1954. The first Act was left untouched later.
(William McElwee's translation is in *Four Plays*, Cape 1964). On June 5th,
1977, Rudolf Kelterborn's opera on the theme to a new libretto by Dürrenmatt had a successful première in the Opernhaus Zürich. The libretto was
published by Bärenreiter in 1976.
67. R.Litten: *Dürrenmatts Team-Theater*, Christ und Welt, XX Jg., No.49,
8.12.67, p.11.
68. See William Arrowsmith's wonderful translations in the Mentor Press 1962.
On Dürrenmatt's "Einfall" in general, see C.Kaelb: *The 'Einfall' in Dürrenmatt's theory and practice, Deutsche Beiträge zur geistigen Überlieferung*,
(1972) pp.240-259.
69. D.J.Prohaska: *Raimund's contribution to Viennese popular Comedy*, German Quarterly, Vol.XLII, May 1969, No.3, pp.352-367, here p.353. Dürrenmatt's radio-play *Stranitzky und der Nationalheld* was given in 1952. It is
interesting that Joseph Anton Stranitzky (1676-1726) was the greatest
"Hanswurst" ("Merry Andrew") of the Wiener Komödie at the Kärtnertor
from 1711 on. There is surely more than a fortuitous connection between
the two Stranitzkys – and the "national hero", Baldur von Moeve, and the
Babylonian "national hero", Gilgamesh, in *EKB*.
70. Although Dürrenmatt tried to convince Dieter Fringeli in 1977 that it had
been wrong to play *Engel* as a satire, he admitted to Violet Ketels that, when
it was produced in Warsaw, "Stalin's skyscraper" was projected on to the
stage as the "Tower of Babylon" (sic). (To Ketels, p.104). In *Der Mitmacher*,
of course, "civilization" is about to vanish.
71. G.R.Hocke: *Manierismus in der Literatur*, Rowohlt, 2 Vols., 1959, See
Vol.1, p.303, and also E.R.Curtius: *Europäische Literatur und lateinisches
Mittelalter*, Francke, Bern, 1948, pp.275-284, where mannerism is described
as ". . . a general term for all those literary tendencies . . . opposed to classicism . . ." (See too Note 52 on the grotesque above). This scene was given
the most dramatic music in Kelterborn's opera!
72. Hans Mayer, among others, has commented on Dürrenmatt's "penchant,
always to fill the stage with mountains of corpses" (in *Dürrenmatt und
Brecht oder die Zurücknahme*, in *Der unbequeme Dürrenmatt*, op.cit.,
p.105) and refers to Beda Allemann's article on *Es steht geschrieben*. But
just as George Steiner and Theodor Adorno had asserted that Death had lost
its significance for writers after the monstrosities of Auschwitz, so too
Dürrenmatt treats "death" in the manner of the detective story, "so nobody

thinks of having any sympathy with one of the obligatory victims, since all that matters is to find the murderer and bring him to justice" (Mayer p.106). Thus, Dürrenmatt's "deaths" are the "stage deaths" of traditional comedy, not to be taken seriously. There, the "doctor" restores the "dead" to life, as in the Medieval Mummers' plays. In Dürrenmatt's works, too, the dead are often restored in one way or another (as in *Mississippi* or *The Meteor*), or their death is treated as a comic interlude (as in the burial scene in *DRH* or Fortschig's death in *DVD*, Böckmann's in *Frank V* – and Edgar's many "deaths" in *Play Strindberg*). Where the death seems genuine, the work takes on the hue of tragedy (as Ill's death in *The Visit of the Old Lady*). Note too: "A tragicomedy is not so called in respect of mirth and killing, but in respect it wants deaths, which is enough to make it no tragedy, yet brings some near to it, which is enough to make it no comedy" (1608): The Preface to *The Faithful Shepherdess* (Fletcher). When I told Dürrenmatt about a dissertation on him entitled *The Problem of Death in the Works of Friedrich Dürrenmatt*, he smiled and said: "Death? That's no problem"!

73. "In farce, unmasking occurs all along. The favourite action of the farceur is to shatter his appearances, his favourite effect being the shock to the audience of his doing so": E.Bentley: *The Life of the Drama*, Methuen 1965, p.242.

74. C.H.Whitman: *Aristophanes and the comic hero*, Harvard U.P. 1964, p.30. Dicaeopolis in *Acharnians* wants peace for one reason only – to go to bed with a girl.

75. Cf. Brecht: "It must be an actor who can play a completely decent man. Azdak is a completely decent man, a disappointed revolutionary who plays a man in rags, just as, in Shakespeare, the wise men play the Fools. Otherwise, the judgement with the Chalk Circle would lose its validity". (*Advice for the casting of Azdak*: *GW*, Band 17, p.1206). For some of the more interesting comparisons between Akki and Azdak, see Jauslin, op.cit., p.84; Bänziger, op.cit., p.166 and Note on p.285; Waidson, op.cit. pp.269-270; Mayer, op.cit., p.488. Durzak finds in this play "the strongest divergency between Dürrenmatt and Brecht", because Brecht tries to expound the need to change historical processes – Dürrenmatt simply unmasks *a priori* the stupidity of all history. (M.Durzak: *Dürrenmatt, Frisch, Weiss*, Reclam, Stuttgart, 1972, p.84). See too H.Lüthy: *Of poor Bert Brecht* in Encounter, Vol. 7, No.1, July 1956, pp.33-53, here p.53.

76. Profitlich places Akki in the group of ". . . characters perhaps the least tinged with comical and ridiculous traits of any sort" (op.cit., p.93). True, we laugh *with* and not at Akki, but I cannot agree that Akki is in any way as "serious" a character as, say, Ill in *The Visit of the Old Lady*. Akki is a truly *comic* character. See too Profitlich's article on *Zufall* (above p.279) footnote 41, where he discusses Neumann's categorisation of Akki as a "pseudo-hero". See Neumann, op.cit., p.45.

77. H.P.Madler: *Dürrenmatts mutiger Mensch*, Hochland, Band 62, 1970, pp.36-49, here p.45.

78. "Akki outwits a mad and absurd power and tempers the Angel's confident bliss, intoxicated by the beauty of Creation. The world really belongs to the man who knows how to handle it without getting in too deep" (Berghahn, op.cit., p.105).

79. Brock-Sulzer notes how much funnier this "Double Being" has become in the 1957 version. Walter Kerr established the "technical reason": "Twinners invite comedy because identity – which is a spiritual thing – is denied by the body", (in *Tragedy and Comedy*, Bodley Head 1967, (UK 1968), p.166). This is surely Bergson's concept of "the body stealing a march on the soul"? (*Le rire*, p.40).

80. Cf. "Me on top, you beneath, me beneath, you on top – and so it goes on" (p.221). They speak "simultaneously" on pp.226-7, again on p.229, pp.235-37 and on p.239, during which time Nimrod claims the throne only to be replaced some minutes later (p.240). In this way, "those in power" are mocked. (The theme of the "struggle for the throne" reappears in *The Waiting Period* (1977)).

81. D.Daviau attempts to ascribe Nebuchadnezzar's failure to the "chance" intervention of Kurrubi and the Angel. This element seems to me much less strong here than in Dürrenmatt's other works. See D.Daviau: *The rôle of 'Zufall' in the writings of Friedrich Dürrenmatt*, The Germanic Review, Vol. XLVII, No.4, November 1972, pp.281-293, here p.285.

82. J.Steiner: *Die Komödien Dürrenmatts*, Der Deutschunterricht, 15, Heft 6, 1963, pp.81-98, here p.89 and p.91.

83. Guthke, op.cit., p.382. The review was in the Neue Zürcher Nachrichten on 13.4.57.

84. In *Quellen: Zur Genesis meiner Stoffe* (*Sources: On the genesis of my themes*), printed in the programme to the production of Kelterborn's 1977 opera, Dürrenmatt relates how the character of Kurrubi grew out of the fragment of a 1946 radio-play similar in theme to Kafka's *An Imperial Message*. That, plus a passage from Kierkegaard's *Sickness unto Death*, in which an Emperor wants to make the poorest worker his son-in-law, gave Dürrenmatt the impetus: "Themes are public property", as he writes!

85. For Dürrenmatt's love of slogans and his expertise in drawing them, see his charming *Die Heimat im Plakat* (*The Homeland in Posters*), Diogenes 1963, vicious cartoons drawn for his children. See too the slogans in the radio-play *Hercules and the Augean Stables* (1954).

86. Cf. Akki to the hangman: "What remains, I leave to the poets" ("Was bleibt, stifte ich den Dichtern"), a parody on Hölderlin's "But what lasts, is created by the poets" ("Was bleibet aber, stiften die Dichter") in *Andenken, Hymnen*, (1799-1803).

87. H.G.Werner, op.cit., p.145. Utnapischtim is a deep bass in Kelterborn's opera. The opera was conducted by Ferdinand Leitner and produced by Götz Friedrich. It was composed between November 1974 and August 1976.

88. H.Mayer, *Friedrich Dürrenmatt*, op.cit., p.483. This essay is essentially on *The Anabaptists* (1968).

89. W.McDougall: *The theory of laughter*, Nature, Vol.67, 1903, p.318.

90. The *Makame* (maquama) is an "oriental poetic form in rhymed prose with isolated verses", introduced into Germany by Friedrich Rückert with his *Die Verwandlung des Abu Seid*, 2 Vols., 1826, 1837. See *Der Grosse Brockhaus*, Band 7, (1955 edn.), p.464. Dürrenmatt introduces the maquama into his later work *Der Mitmacher* (1973). There too he emphasizes the importance of the *rhymes*. (*DMMK*, pp.185-190). It also incidentally, Dürrenmatt claims, makes *Der Mitmacher* into a *Komödie* (p.186). In his fascinating *Laudatio*, August Everding showed that Dürrenmatt so constructed the maquamas because he was convinced that conventional speech would destroy the characters who only lived "from the language". (Speech at the ceremony of the award of the Buber-Rosenzweig Medal to Dürrenmatt in the Paulskirche, Frankfurt, on 6.3.77).

91. "That Dürrenmatt, despite all the tragic and tragicomic in the world, does not hide the silver lining . . . but points the way confidently forward, is a reason for us to thank him", NZZ, 1.2.54. See too *Dürrenmatt in der Stiftsruine*, Theater Heute 4, 1963, p.43. (Performance at Bad Herzfeld). J.Scherer in *Der mutige Mensch*, op.cit., p.310.

92. W.Oberle: *Grundsätzliches zum Werk Friedrich Dürrenmatts*, in *Der unbequeme Dürrenmatt*, op.cit., p.26.

93. Neumann, op.cit., p.58. For a good discussion of the opera. see the Stuttgarter Zeitung, 19.9.75: *Rudolf Kelterborn vertont Dürrenmatt's Ein Engel kommt nach Babylon*. Kelterborn was born in Basle in 1931.

Chapter Five

THE MASTERPIECE

DER BESUCH DER ALTEN DAME *(The Visit of the Old Lady)* (1956)

In 1956 Dürrenmatt published his radio-play *Abendstunde im Spätherbst (Evening hour in late autumn)*, in which Maximilian Korbes, a famous writer and recipient of the Nobel Prize for Literature, tells his peculiar visitor, Fürchtegott Hofer:

> I've been interpreted from the point of view of depth psychologists, of Catholics, of Protestants, of Existentialists, of Buddhists and of Marxists (*GH*, p.300).

Such, too, has been the fate of Dürrenmatt's most striking international success *Der Besuch der alten Dame (The Visit of the Old Lady)*. (The British translator, Patrick Bowles, agrees with me on the illogicality of the American title *The Visit*) (See *Note* 2).

Interpretations of the play[1] range from the conventional: Bänziger's "Probably *the* tragicomedy of our age" or Weber's "A sort of second national drama for the Swiss", through the political; a play about the "secrets of Fascism" (Tolschenova) or Kühne's "judgement on the philistine bourgeoisie", to the Biblical: "A modern presentation of the Passion Play" (Hortenbach) or an illustration of the "victory of grace" (Buri) or of the "principle of moral steadfastness" (Profitlich) to the psychological, economic and political interpretations of Askew, the cheerfully admitted bafflement of a younger critic, Hugo Dittberner, and Murray Peppard's summing-up: "There is no single, simple message or moral in *The Visit*, but rather a powerful action with a wide range of suggestibility". Max Frisch saw it, *tout court*, as "the greatest play in the German language since Brecht", while one of the latest pronouncements is Gerhard Knapp's: "So we can see that the way to over-interpretation leads over rough places, because of an exaggerated love of pre-pigeon-holing".

It was significant that a performance of the play in Basle, almost ten years after the première, reprinted the report of a Basle discussion group in 1957, when the group decided that the play had been over-treated "from the theological, philosophical and psychological point of view" and that people had forgotten "that the author is writing for

the stage". And this must be my point of view, too, since I have been
striving to show that Dürrenmatt's concern *at all times* is with the
living, critical theatre.

The *point de départ* is the sub-title: "A tragic *Komödie*". For the
first time, the adjective "tragic" appeared in the title of a Dürrenmatt
play, and it is surely no coincidence that his *Problems of the Theatre*
was published in 1955, shortly before the première of this play in 1956.

These theoretical writings were dealt with above (pp.25-29), but it
will be of value to recall here the cardinal points in close proximity
to the play to which, above all, they refer.

Dürrenmatt had compared the tragic and comic modes of writing
and had concluded that "pure tragedy" was not compatible with our
age:

> Tragedy assumes the presence of guilt, trouble, moderation, the
> overview, responsibility. In the mess that is our century, this
> cleaning-out of the white race, there are no longer any guilty men,
> nor are there any to be held responsible any more. (*TP*. p.47)

In this chaotic, disintegrating world, a fate is decided by "bad luck"
rather than by "guilt". "Guilt nowadays is a personal achievement
only, a religious deed". Tragedy is no longer possible, and "only the
Komödie can reach us now".

Dürrenmatt elaborated on this a little during my conversation with
him in Neuchâtel: "Tragedy is a naive art and we no longer possess this
naivety. Yet comedy is not simply external form (in the theatre) —
comedy is not just the act of getting married. . ." (A reference to the
end of most classical comedies).

Dürrenmatt was trying to define what William McCullom had called
a "tragedy for the time being". All of the plays considered to date
have had, to a greater or lesser degree, something of these contradictory,
contrastive and paradoxical elements of comedy which were discussed
in Chapter Two. Why, then, did Dürrenmatt call this play specifically
"A tragic *Komödie*"?

If we look at the *Problems of the Theatre* again, we note that the
author went on to discuss the possibility of depicting a tragic hero
today; one cannot portray a "hero", say in the Schillerian sense,
because the times are out of joint for that — the pathos and moral
earnestness would be unbearable. So the author has to bring the "tragic"
and, with it, *his* type of "hero", through the back door, as it were:
"We can glean the tragic from the *Komödie*, extract it as one terrible
moment, a yawning abyss. . .", and the man who can withstand this
"terrible moment" and who will not flinch in front of this "yawning

abyss", who "sees the senselessness, the hopelessness of this world" and yet who will not capitulate to it — he will be called "the valiant man". Dürrenmatt claimed that he had already depicted this "model" in the blind Duke, in Übelohe, Romulus and Akki, but I have shown that there was no true "tragic" in any of these characters, that the various elements of the "comic" had made them, in one way or another, "comic characters" in *Komödien* of the 20th century.

★   ★   ★

The Visit of the Old Lady was produced by Oskar Wälterlin at the Schauspielhaus Zürich on 29 January 1956, with Therese Giehse (who was Brecht's Mother Courage at the same theatre on 19 April, 1941) as Claire Zachanassian and Gustav Knuth as Alfred Ill.

In his *Note* to the *Angel*, Dürrenmatt had written that "according to plan, my next play *Die Mitmacher* should present the building of the tower itself. All are against the tower — yet it is *still* built" (*KI*, p.248). In *Problems of the Theatre*, he wrote: "No one can do anything about it and no one wanted it to happen" (p.47). My examination of the play will reveal how these twin concepts intertwine and what part the comic plays in the process.

In their discussion of the play, Soergel and Hohoff say that, apart from the conclusion, it is a classical comedy, a statement which begs, of course, a rather large question. Although this view of the work accords more with mine than, say, the Italian one (after Strehler's première in Milan on 31 January, 1970) or the many performances that I have seen of Maurice Valency's "adaptation", I feel that it goes too far.[2] Where producers of the latter sort have failed to note the author's admonition in the *Note:* "Nothing will damage this *Komödie* (which ends tragically) more than deadly seriousness" and have played the work as a pure tragedy, producers of the former brand have treated the play as a too-typical Dürrenmatt *Komödie*.[3]

I have tried to show that the other plays to date (with the possible exception of *The Blind Man*) were meant to be played as *Komödien*, where the sense of the tragic is nullified by the overriding significance of the elements of the comic in structure, language and characterization. But *The Visit of the Old Lady* is clearly different; where, in the other plays, one was dealing with a *potentially* tragic character in an *actual* comic situation, here we are dealing with an *actual* tragic character in an *actual* comic situation. The examinations of these plays revealed that the main characters were "spiritual clowns" whose laughable fates might evoke sympathy, but certainly not Aristotelian "pity" or "terror". The elements of the comic in the concept of the character and in the situation had removed any sense of the tragic. For this reason, I called the plays *Komödien* rather than "tragicomedies", where there must be a true sense of the tragic present.

H.M. Waidson rightly asserts that "humour in this play. . .is for the most part demonstrated in the minor characters". There are four such groups: the Teacher and the Parson; the Mayor and the Policeman; Ill's family, and fourthly, the popular (*das Volk*) of Güllen. Although it would appear, at first sight, that these groups could all be classed as "buffoons", whose rôle was simply the creation of a "mood of festivity" and little else, it will be shown that this is not the case. They are, in fact, an important and essential ingredient of the plot.

These characters are, however, all "impostors"; they possess many of the characteristics of the classical alazon-type; pedantry, pretentiousness, hypocrisy, mendacity, static obtuseness and obsessiveness. The comic here is "reductive", in the Hobbesian sense; it aims at "bringing down", at stripping them of their illusions. But, when we laugh at them, we have here the uneasy feeling that we are laughing at ourselves.

The Teacher is portrayed as a weak rather than a wicked man. In Act I, the comic lies in his ossified pedantry and pretentiousness:

> Madam (*to Klara*), as Headmaster of the High School of Güllen and worshipper of the noble Saint Cecilia, may I be permitted to present you with a simple folk-song, performed by the mixed choir and the youth group? (p.263).

The song is symbolically and comically lost in the rattling of a passing train; then the Teacher feels "classical grandeur" coming into Güllen with Claire's arrival and likens her parodistically to a Clotho, a Lais, a Juliet and, finally, to a Medea. Yet it is the Teacher who makes the final plea to Claire not to drive the villagers to murder Ill and, when that fails, he takes refuge in drink which alone can give him the courage to tell the press-men the truth. But even this "valiant" attempt to restore honour is rendered ridiculous when the Painter breaks his picture over the Teacher's head.

This scene is his last attempt to become "human" — he then joins the others in accepting Claire's offer and participating in Ill's execution. The clichés mouthed at the meeting of the villagers bring him back to the rôle of a comic character: "In the name of God, we must take our ideals seriously, deadly seriously" (a sinister pun) (p.331). The comic is pointed up by the misunderstandings of the Press who report the remark as a "moral greatness which, alas, we do not find all too often nowadays".

Through the character of the Teacher, the author attacks what he believes to be the hypocritical support for cultural, humanistic values which are no longer valid. Like Romulus' servants, the Teacher is a "monument passé", a comic thing, but the sympathy which we feel for his attempt to retain his humanity saves him from complete "buffoonery" and makes him, as was said, a weak rather than a wicked or stupid man.

The Parson, probably Protestant,[4] the second figure of "authority", is also depicted with something approaching sympathy. He is satirized as a "fellow traveller". The Mayor suggests that Claire is the town's only hope. "Apart from God", adds the Parson dutifully. "Apart from God", repeats the Mayor. "But he doesn't pay", adds the Teacher and shows up the Parsons's hypocrisy (p.256). When Ill, on his symbolical flight, turns to the Parson for help, the latter is too busy hunting Claire's missing panther and preparing for a baptism. His advice to Ill ends on a comically deflating and incongruous note: "One should not fear Man, but God, not the death of the body but of the soul. . .Button my cassock up at the back, Verger"! (p.297). He too has sold his soul to Mammon by buying a bell for his church.[5] When he hears this news, Alfred cries out: "Et tu, Parson! Et tu!" and the difference between this tragedy-laden cry and Romulus' comic: "Et tu, Cook?" to his servant (above, p.64) well sums up the difference between the two plays.

Only the Parson's cry: "Flee! We are weak, Christians and heathens. . .Flee, lead us not into temptation by staying here. . ." (p.299), shows that he is moved by some innate humanity. The sympathy gained here is hardly enough to counteract the earlier satire; nevertheless, the fact that he does not appear again means that the elements of the satirical comic are softened and that he is to be regarded, with the Teacher, as slightly less reprehensible than the others.

The second group is led by the Mayor who is portrayed without redeeming features. The comic in the character of this petty bourgeois official lies in the ossification of its attitudes, its inability to adapt itself to new situations, a perfect example of Bergson's "mechanical inelasticity"; one laughs at the likeness to a non-human talking machine.

He is presented as pompous, hypocritical, mendacious and stupid, the last familial quality being underlined by his wife's maiden name, Dummermuth (= "stupid mind"), who was comically "the top of her class" in Güllen! (And Güllen itself means "liquid dung" in Swiss

German). His hypocrisy is shown by the names of the (comic) twin
grandchildren, Hermine and Adolfine, who must have been born in
1948 – some latent Nazi sympathies are suggested.

After the Mayor has given his hypocritical instructions for Claire's
reception, he tries to impress the V.I.P. with a pompous speech:

> Madame, honoured guest, I, as Mayor of Güllen, have the honour
> to welcome you, honoured guest, Madame, a child of our town,
> an honour which. . . (p.261),

which is followed by the stage direction: "Because of the noise of the
departing train, the remainder of the Mayor's speech – and he speaks
on unconcernedly – can no longer be understood", which reminds us
of the similar ridiculing effect of the Teacher's earlier attempt
to impress.

At the banquet for Claire, the Mayor's inability to digest Ill's (and
others') previous instructions, lead him to make wonderfully comic
and hypocritical errors of identification: "Yet we have never forgotten
you, Madame, our Kläri (applause)". He remembers her wonderfully
healthy mother – (*Stage direction*: Ill whispers something to him . . .)
"unfortunately snatched away from us all too early by tuberculosis";
he remembers her father who built a "much visited" (Ill whispers to
him) "eh, much *admired* building" (the station toilet!); he remembers
Kläri as a "blonde. . ." (Ill whispers to him) "eh, red-haired tomboy";
he praises hypocritically her school marks in "the most important
subject" (biology) in which, we heard the Teacher say earlier, she had
just managed a "genügend" ("satisfactory"), and the Mayor makes out
of this an "expression of your sympathies for all God's creatures"
(p.275).[6]

When Claire's offer is made known, the Mayor refuses it grandilo-
quently: "We are still in Europe, we are not heathens yet. In the name
of the town of Güllen, I reject your offer. In the name of Humanity.
We would rather stay poor than be stained with blood" (p.279). The
subtle overtones of the antiquated diction (in the German) mark the
pomposity which becomes hypocrisy when his "humanity" disappears
at Ill's execution, since it is he who intones the oath at the conclusion
when the money is finally accepted by the people of Güllen: ". . .for
we can no longer live if we tolerate a crime in our midst. . ." (p.333).

The Mayor has therefore something of the "comic type" about him;
like "l'avare" and "le tartuffe", he represents a wide section of
humanity and very traditional sources of comic laughter. The audience
will see the character in this way in Act I; the darkness descends later.

The Policeman is likewise portrayed as a hypocritical time-server
only too ready to turn his coat. The laughter here comes from a similar
"reduction" of Authority, but, since he represents perverted "bourgeois" justice, the character becomes a "perversion of reality". There is
a demonic, frightening quality about this man which makes me ready to
call the characterization "grotesque". As Dürrenmatt put it in the
Marginal Notes under the rubric "Fear": "The Void enters as a gold
tooth (see Policeman)". This is certainly no simple laughable caricature.[7]

He has to admit at the very outset that he is corrupt: "Do you turn
a blind eye now and then?" asks Claire. "Of course, Madame. How do
you think I could get by otherwise in Güllen?" (p.264). This is the
classical contrast between what is and what should be, but, within the
context of the play, the contrast carries a potential tragic within it, for
it is clear that this character lacks a humanity — which is shown in
many more subtle ways than simply by calling him "The Policeman".[8]
Although he is undeniably a source of our laughter, he is too important
for the action to be typed as a simple buffoon.

Like these two characters, Ill's family have no redeeming features.
They are just as stupid and selfish, but, like the others, they are too
important for the plot to be regarded as mere "laughter-makers".
Although Dürrenmatt attempts to defend the family in the *Note* —
"they are not wicked either, only weak like us all" — Ill's conversation
with Claire in the Konradsweilerwald shows the hellish life that he has
led with them; "I am always fighting with my family who throw our
poverty in my face every day" (p.270). Mathilde, his wife, is portrayed
as "scrawny and embittered"; the first sign that the village will desert
Alfred Ill is given when the son and daughter refuse the family meal
which Alfred proposes. As he says pathetically to Claire, they are
"without any feeling for ideals" (p.270).

They, their nouveau-riche manners and their language, Karl's new
Opel, Otillie's daring dress, her French, English and tennis lessons,
Mathilde's fur coat ("on appro.") and her plans for rebuilding, are the
main sources of our laughter during the last symbolical journey in the
car. As Hobbes wrote: ". . . Men laugh at the infirmities of others by
comparison wherewith their own abilities are set off and illustrated".

These are all portrayed as "comic characters", but with an underlying sense of the tragic in their actions, which makes us take them
more seriously than the normal "buffoons". Nevertheless, when Dürrenmatt said that he wrote as one "who does not distance himself
from these people and is not so certain that he would act differently"
and then goes on: "They are not to be depicted as wicked, not at all;

they are quite determined at the outset to reject the offer. They do, of course, incur debts, but not with the intention of killing Ill, but simply from lack of thought, with the feeling that it will all sort itself out in the end" (p.343), then we can be fairly certain that he had only the Teacher, the Parson (and probably the Doctor) in mind.[9]

It is true that the audience will take them all as "buffoons" in Act I; in Acts II and III, as the comedy darkens, as the Teacher and the Parson struggle to retain their humanity, sympathy will creep in for these men and our scorn will be blunted. As J.L.Styan wrote in his summing-up of "dark comedy": "The detachment of comedy is not allowed us, nor the sympathy of tragedy".[10] When we see from the final chorus that all is as it was, that these people have shown themselves to be unteachable, then we may laugh out of a feeling of superiority — but, in their case, our laughter will almost certainly be cathartic. "But for the grace of God . . ."

The true "buffoons" would seem to be the people of Güllen. These are "mechanicals", in every sense of the word. From their paratactic, elliptical sentence structures and automatic head movements at the beginning of the play as they watch the trains go by and bemoan their misery, through the simultaneous remarks of the two women as they buy from Ill, to the end-farce of the final parodistic Sophoclean chorus, we have an almost perfect example of the Bergsonian "Law":

> The attitudes, gestures and movements of the body are laughable in exact proportion as that body reminds us of a mere machine.
> (*Le rire*, pp.22-23).

Although these buffoons are undeniably part of the Güllen "collective", an audience can laugh more heartily at them than at the last groups, since they lack both persona and humanity and are effectively "distanced" from us by such mindless and mechanical behaviour.

In the opening scene, Dürrenmatt cleverly establishes the background to the plot through these buffoons. The four men speak in a choric structure which is not stychomythic in the strict sense, but rather a "distancing" process:

The Painter:	The train!
First Man:	stops!
Second Man:	in Güllen!
Third Man:	In the poorest
Fourth Man:	lousiest
First Man:	most pitiful dump on the line from Venice to Stockholm! (p.259).[11]

The Stationmaster observes that "the laws of Nature have been suspended"; following this syntactically perfect, but comically deformed sentence, this suggests that the author wanted to stress the comic in these automata — that *all* natural laws have now been suspended and that what follows is unnatural, non-human and, (I should say), comic.

Such unnaturalness and non-humanity is revealed particularly in the two forest scenes. (The forest and the barn link the past with the present, guilt with punishment, innocence with despoilment). In the first scene, the comic intention is plain. The alienated Shakespearean settings: "*Stage direction*: The First Man climbs on to the bench, he has a huge cardboard heart with the initials AK hung round his neck, the others arrange themselves in a semi-circle round him, they spread out branches and simulate trees" (p.268). These "hempen home-spuns" are the comic background to the tragic situation. Their rhythmical chant parodies the traditions of German Romanticism, just as the later choruses parody those of Greek Classicism:

First Man:	We are spruces, firs, beeches.
Second Man:	We are dark-green pine trees.
Third Man:	Moss and lichen, ivy thickets.
Fourth Man:	Undergrowth and fox-holes.
First Man:	Scudding clouds, bird-calls.
Second Man:	Genuine German wilderness of roots.
Third Man:	Toadstools, shy deer.
Fourth Man:	Murmuring branches, old dreams.

Dürrenmatt suggests that they act as trees to make the "somewhat painful love-story" more bearable, but I am certain that he is suggesting that we should see these people of Güllen as the buffoons of the play. One has to hop over the stage like a deer, another pretend to be a woodpecker — he comically knocks a rusty key against an old pipe — and another pretends to be a cuckoo. In the second forest-scene, when Alfred and Claire both know that the end is near, the four men reappear as trees, but this time, absurdly, in full evening-dress, to deepen symbolically the significance of the leave-taking; the "tree" is dying and the "leaves" are yellow. E.S.Dick has said of these scenes that they are "an essential contribution to the explanation of the meaning of the dramatic action", which is, of course, true, but he fails to note, as so many other commentators do, that there is a *comic* principle involved here.[12] Having deprived these clowns of their humanity in Act I, Dürrenmatt paradoxically makes them the carriers of the action, the darker comedy of Act II. It is grimly comical that the action should be precipitated by such unlikely characters. It also means that they too have become something other than *simply* conventional stage buffoons. Indeed, they become the true *Mitmacher* ("those who string along") whom Dürrenmatt will castigate in his plays from now on.[13]

As they come in to buy dearer cigarettes (Hofbauer), full-cream milk instead of the ordinary brand, dearer chocolate and white bread (the two women), cognac instead of Schnaps, (Helmesberger), all on credit, Ill's suspicions grow and are confirmed by the sight of the new yellow shoes worn by all.[14] (Duden notes that in "colour symbolism, yellow has almost always a negative connotation, eg. as the colour of deceit or jealousy"). The comic situation, here, the "comic of multiplication", provokes the tragic response. "What are you going to pay with?" cries Ill. "What are you going to pay with? With what? What with?" (p.287). The change from the "we" in the earlier to the familiar German plural "ihr" (= "you") demonstrates that he has already become an "outsider" in this inhuman society.

By the end of the play, these automata have become the unthinking emotion-swayed mass who chant at the Mayor's behest and repeat the empty, hypocritical responses which Urs Jenny saw as a travesty of the famous oath on the Rütli Mountain, but which could also be taken to be a parody of liturgical responses (Jenny, p.69).

Thus, the main sources of laughter in the play *are* to be found in these four groups, but they cannot be regarded *simply* as mindless buffoons, as could some of the characters in the earlier plays. Here, I would suggest, they form in fact *one* main antagonist to Ill, a permanent record of Man's inhumanity to Man. This is no *Komödie*. Nevertheless, as these figures lose their humanity and become unthinking stereotypes, they do become clowns whose automatic gestures and responses evoke comic laughter. Jacob Scherer has rightly noted how Dürrenmatt's "attack on our age for its loss of humanity becomes more urgent with each play",[15] and it has seemed to me that this strongly political element in his work can best be illustrated by studying the use he makes of the traditional comic techniques which mercilessly reveal the in- and non-humanity of his chosen characters.

★   ★   ★

It might be of some use here to interpolate a few of the more provocative interpretations of the play. East German critics have taken the comic in the characters just treated as a satire on western capitalism. Erich Kühne praises Dürrenmatt for his attack, but suggests that he has missed his target, or, rather, that he has chosen the wrong one: "The weapon of his comedy-based satire does not strike at the major class of imperialistic society but at an intermediate class, the petit bourgeois fellow-travellers and the hangers-on of the monopolistic bourgeoisie...". Jürgen Kuczynski, defending Dürrenmatt against another East German, Rainer Kerndl, who had called the play 'social criticism, but anti-human", since it was not truly "realistic" in the "socialist" sense, finds the play "a parable of a people who succumbed to fascism until it 'honestly believed in it', of a people who are succumbing today to the psychological warmongering of the imperialists".

Hans-Georg Werner, seeing Dürrenmatt as a "moralist" praises the "accuracy of his attacks on the capitalist social system" and sees the theme of the play as "the corrupting force of money". Maurice Valency, the author of the American "version" agrees. He writes: "The propulsive force of the action is neither external fate ... nor guilt; it is the power of money — not even money itself only the smell of it, its influence".

Now, all of these are fairly predictable, but they do show, firstly, the reason for Dürrenmatt's popularity in the Eastern bloc countries, and, secondly, the reasons for the suspicions of some of his critics in the west. Here, the play, a masterpiece of the twentieth century by common consent, has been interpreted from an all too narrow "religious" standpoint. The approach is, of course, a valid one, but the vast theses built up on a purely religious argument seem, to me anyway, often wide of the mark. Jenny Hortenbach's attempt, for example, to find Biblical parallels everywhere is too full of remarks like "... this advent (Claire's arrival) has *something* of the horrifying descent of Yahveh upon Mount Sinai ..." and again "... the words (of 2, Peter iii, 8) *seem to be* applicable to Claire also" (my emphases in both cases). Certain parallels are, of course, obvious, (Ill's "One of you will hold me back" with Matthew 26, xxi), but Miss Hortenbach is much too inventive. The same could be said of M.Askew's psychologically-orientated study which energetically seeks to prove that Ill was a sufferer from the classical castration-complex, that he was a modern Oedipus. A recent study by Ulrich Profitlich perhaps concentrates too much on the "minor" works and he sees Ill as one of that group which is "exempted ... from comic and ludicrous characteristics" which, as will shortly be seen, is not quite accurate.[16]

Some of these writers seem to me to have overstrained theses (which are useful in themselves), and omitted to relate the work closely enough to the stage — its only and proper medium. Not that the work need lack a "message" — but its meaning lies in the performance on the stage and not in the professional study. It is a dramatic work — not a theological, political or psychological tract — not "theatre as dissertation", as Dürrenmatt once remarked. This is what Dürrenmatt always has in mind when he speaks on the critics' love of "profundity". "Stick to my flashes of inspiration" he wrote in the *Notes* to *The Visit of the Old Lady*, "and forget about profundity". He has always wanted to be treated as a "sort of conscious Nestroy" (the nineteenth-century Viennese comic author). It seems to me that a performance which emphasized more the elements of the comic in those "minor character-istics" and which would ensure the "atmosphere of mad hilarity" which H.P.Guth claimed should appear in a performance (see *Note* 2), would not only please the author, but would also deepen the play's significance by creating that "new sublime incongruity" of which Wilson Knight wrote (above pp.64-65), and which is the peculiar merit of this "tragic comedy".

★   ★   ★

It would seem at first sight that Alfred Ill was to be one of our "spiritu-al clowns"; when Claire arrives, he seems ready to deceive himself into thinking that she will be as susceptible to his charms as she was 45 years before: "Look, teacher, I've got this one where I want her", he says (p.262). As has been seen, one of the attributes of the comic character is his proneness to be perpetually deceived. It is clear, however, that Ill has a feeling of guilt from the outset, for the opening scene shows a petty bourgeois with a conscience; the bribe of the next Mayorship hangs heavy over Ill's head, making him a party to the hypocrisy of his fellow-citizens. When he talks to the others of his relationship with Claire, the words ring almost sentimentally true: he remembers her coming towards him "with flowing red hair, supple and yielding, slim as a twig, gentle, a devilishly beautiful witch" (p.257).

Our suspicions that Ill might become a spiritual clown are strength-ened during the first forest scene with Claire: "I lead a laughable life", he says, "I've never really been out of the village. A journey to Berlin, one to the Ticino, that's all" (p.270). Jacob Steiner has written that "the tragic hero need become laughable only once — and he is finished as a tragic hero".[17] There would seem to be no "heroic" in this self-pitying little man. Part of the comic here lies in the grim incongruity of Claire's teleological comments on Alfred's statements of despair. He claims that he married Mathilde for Claire's sake: "She had money",

Claire answers. The future belonged to Claire, so Alfred renounced his future for her: "And now the future is here", says Claire. Alfred has lived in a hell since Claire left him: "And I've become Hell itself", is Claire's frightening answer (p.270).

When Claire says that she will not abandon him, Alfred is "fooled" and the deception is comically symbolized by the "false" bird-calls of the "unnatural" people of Güllen and by his discovery of her artificial limbs!

But — do we laugh here? Perhaps. But Hebbel once wrote of *his* tragicomedies: "We would freeze with horror, but our laughter muscles twitch at the same time; we should like to free ourselves with a laugh from the whole sinister situation, yet an icy hand closes over us again before we can".[18] Such is the laughter here, Claire's external appearance, her grotesque false limbs, are all grotesquely comic; her incongruous, often illogical ("absurd") answers are comic — but the two characters, the one ridiculous in his hypocritical self-pity, the other mysteriously paradoxical, are diffused with an emotion which is patently *un*-comic and which "freezes" our laughter.

Alfred is a comic character up to the banquet scene: ". . . Klara has a golden sense of laughter! These jokes'll kill me!", he says innocently (p.273). The "indescribable joy" and the comic gymnast's routines rival Alfred's ecstasy when Claire announces the gift of a milliard — and contrast dramatically with the deathly silence when she continues: "I'll give you a milliard and I'll buy justice for myself with it", and even more so later: "A milliard for Güllen if someone will kill Alfred Ill" (p.276 and p.279).[19] From that point on, Alfred Ill ceases to be a comic character. Some, the Mayor, the Policeman, Ill's family, the people of Güllen, become more ridiculous, others, the Teacher, the Parson, the Doctor, less so, but they all still serve as sources of comic laughter. Alfred detaches himself from them; by going his own way, he ceases to be the generalized "typed" character of the comedy and becomes an individual, a "human being".

I have tried to show in the earlier chapters how all of Dürrenmatt's characters met with fates which were perhaps sad, but not tragic. Knipperdollinck's end was sad, but untragic, since it was brought about by his own ridiculous obsessions and his obtuseness; the Duke's fate was sad, but he did eventually triumph over Negro da Ponte; Romulus' end was untragic, since it was brought about by Chance, and Übelohe ends as a brave but ridiculous Don Quixote. Akki, of course, runs away to fight another day!

Ill is like none of these. Calvinistically conscious of his own guilt, he must now wrestle with his conscience like the tragic hero of old. The whole point of Act II is to make Ill aware of his guilt and the comic situation throws Ill's agony into high relief. From "The village will stand by me" (p.281) to his anguished cry: "What are you going to pay with?" (p.287), is his step on the way to self-knowledge, to be followed by *his* visits to the Policeman, the Mayor and the Parson where his demands for justice are rebuffed by inhuman hypocrisy.

As will shortly be seen, the sources of laughter in Act II lie mainly in the juxtaposition of Claire's remarks with those of the buffoonish populace. Yet the accumulation of the small symbolic details – the Policeman's new gold tooth, the hunt for the panther, the rifles, the new typewriter, the new Church bell, all have some comic significance too – but the laughter is uneasy since the audience is laughing at the tragic ironies. *It* knows the meaning of what Wolfgang Kayser would call the "emblematics", the "symbols", but neither Alfred nor the Güllener can do so. The people, acting as a collective, follow like sheep, "not wicked but weak". "It is a community which slowly yields to temptation", writes Dürrenmatt in the *Note* (p.343).

The "agon" between Alfred and the people has commenced and reaches its climax at the end of Act II when he is accompanied to the station, but, surrounded by the collective (who now speak as one, that is, as "Alle" (All)), he cannot get on the train and, overcome by guilt and terror, he sinks to the ground: "I'm lost", he cries. The greatness of this scene on the stage lies in its simplicity – there is no need to add to it.[20]

In Act III, the people become more inhuman and likewise more comical; on the other hand, Ill attains a true humanity by accepting the burden of his guilt: "I've made Klara what she is and me what I am, a dirty, big-headed shopkeeper" (p.317). Later, to the Mayor, who has tried to make him commit suicide, Ill says: "But now I have made my decision, conquered my fear . . . I shall submit to your verdict, whatever it may be. For me it is justice – what it is for you, I do not know" (p.322), for, to commit suicide, would be to avoid the consequences of his guilt and (incidentally) would remove the guilt for his death from Güllen.

This is what makes the village meeting comically ironical for the audience. It knows that all that is being said and done is ambiguous – the people of Güllen swear to stamp out injustice because they cannot tolerate a crime in their midst and so on – but we know that this very vow implies a crime. Only Ill's dramatic and parodistic cry: "My God!" – his horror at the hypocritical inhumanity of the proceedings – is genuine; it alone cannot be repeated *ad libitum* when requested by the camera crew after the TV lights have dramatically and comically failed:

"What a pity that the cry of joy: My God! wasn't repeated – that was really effective", says the cameraman (p.334).

Does Ill die a tragic death? Hans Mayer thinks not: "The vast nexus of relationships between the Old Lady and the town of Güllen did not allow the normal play between guilt and repentance. . ." Jan Knopf, on the other hand, has no doubt that the *end* is tragic: "And in the analysis of what has gone before, Ill's guilt is gradually revealed. He atones by his death, by the tragic conclusion".[21]

The importance of this death for my study is whether it nullifies the effect of the various comic elements which have been examined. Where is the weight to be laid? On Ill's "tragic" death – or on the comic situation? Is the play a *Komödie*, is it a tragedy in the guise of a tragicomedy, or is it an actual tragicomedy as, say, Karl Guthke has defined the genre? Is a "tragic *Komödie*" in Dürrenmatt's terminology something quite different? Are the comic elements to be treated simply as "comic relief", or do they in fact help to create Wilson Knight's "new sublime incongruity"?

★   ★   ★

Dürrenmatt's portrayal of the character of Claire Zachanassian will help us to answer these questions.

It has been demonstrated in preceding chapters that I am unhappy with those attempts to table all of Dürrenmatt's comic elements under the heading of "grotesque", however defined. I do not deny the presence of the grotesque in his work, of course, but I believe that much of what has been termed grotesque is, in fact, only a dramatization, a sensationalization, an exaggeration of the comic. The grotesque is indeed in danger of becoming what Dürrenmatt said the absurd was: a superficial catch-phrase.

My own view is that the grotesque should show three major traits:
<blockquote>
a) an ugly "deformation",
b) a dark and ludicrous comic,
c) the demonic or fearsome.
</blockquote>

I believe, too, that it has much more relevance in and to the pictorial arts from which it derives, after all, than in or to literature where it has often been used, on the one hand, for what is really "comic" and, on the other hand, for what was merely weird or macabre.[22]

In the figures of Claire and her retinue, and in the nature of her impediments, one must acknowledge the presence of the true grotesque.

Our laughter is not only uneasy, it is often "frozen" when we have had time to consider the retinue in its entirety: The butler Boby "about 80, with dark glasses" — are these not perhaps *the* grotesque symbol of twentieth-century stage, screen and TV?; Boby, after whom, we learn, all Claire's (seven and eventually nine) husbands have been named. Claire possesses him for life since he was the judge at Alfred's successful paternity-suit trial. The duos, the two "Herculean, gum-chewing monsters" who carry her sedan-chair and who are acquitted murderers, and "two little fat old men with gentle voices", the castrated witnesses bribed by Ill to swear that they were "the father" of Claire's child. The underlying demonic makes the normally merely "comic" multiplication (of husbands) and "automatism" (of the eunuchs) grotesque.

For similar reasons, Claire herself is grotesque. "62, red-haired, pearl necklace, huge gold armlets, dressed up to the nines, impossible, but then again, and because of this, a lady of the world with a strange graceful charm despite all the grotesqueries" (p.259). (It is as well to bear in mind, of course, Dürrenmatt's explanation of Claire's grotesqueness. Since he wanted the first scene set in a railway station, Claire had to arrive by train. The only reason why a rich woman like her should use a train was for her to have been involved in a serious accident — hence the artificial legs, etc. "Out of theatrical necessity, there arise elements of the action which only seem to be flashes of inspiration!" he said to Horst Bienek.[23]

From her first action, the unheard-of stopping of a train in Güllen, it is made clear to us that Claire is not of this world. She is the stranger "from outside", certainly, but she is no alazon, although she is, like most of these characters that we have studied, "inhuman" and, like them too, she sets the action in motion. Their "inhumanity", however, is figurative and usually makes them ridiculous. Claire's is literal and it makes her fearsome and awe-inspiring.

Claire even seems to speak a different language, full of ambiguities. Since she is above the world, she has the gift of prophecy, all her remarks bear on the yet-to-come, most notably in her conversations in Act I with the Policeman, the Parson and the Doctor. There was laughter at the seeming illogicality of her remarks — they were, in fact, grimly prophetic.

Yet this is not all grotesque; Claire's revue-like dialogue with the train-guard, for example, is simply witty, the laughter arising from the contrast between her colloquial, even vulgar language and the stiff, formal German of the official. Again, she shocks the bourgeoisie with her indelicate remarks (her "Zoten"), as in her reference to the pissoir which her father had built: "I used to sit on the roof and spit down. But only on the men"! (p.263). There is no horror or demonic in these opening remarks — the true grotesque begins at the banquet.

Claire's other-worldiness is presented literally in Act II by her balcony where she sits throughout like a Greek goddess spinning the threads of Fate. "The events of the play turn like a merry-go-round, almost like a Dance of Death, round the balcony", wrote the first producer, Oskar Wälterlin.

The sources of laughter lie here partly in the juxtaposition of her remarks with those down in the village and partly in their own incongruity. Claire drinks whisky, while Helmesberger exchanges Schnaps for cognac; Husband VIII admires Güllen's peace and quiet, but soon (and sinisterly) finds "no sense of greatness, no sense of tragedy. I miss the moral stamp of a great epoch" (p.297) — but the "tragedy" is being prepared below where Ill is visiting the Parson to seek moral support and is finding only moral cowardice.

Although we are expressly warned in the Note that Claire represents neither "justice. . .the Marshall Plan, and especially not the Apocalypse", her name and her world-wide connections show that she represents the world beyond Güllen.[24]

So, what lies behind this comic situation? Sinister implications for Alfred Ill, since this woman can do with him what she will, she has his fate in her hands. Critics have called Claire "fearful Justitia", Alfred's "Jocasta-Mother-Lover-Sphinx" (!), she is "Frau Welt" in Baroque terminology — and many other symbols of spiritual or temporal authority. Such absolute authority is underlined in the dusty barn in Act III where Claire, resplendently incongruous in her wedding-gown, the even more incongruous St Matthew Passion still in her ears, informs the plaintive Teacher and Doctor that the destitution of Güllen is entirely her doing. Their hopes that her money would revitalize their (comically named) industries are set at nought when they hear that she already owns everything in Güllen: "Your hope was an illusion, your waiting senseless, your self-sacrifice stupid, your whole lives a useless waste", she tells them (p.308). The Teacher's plea: ". . . try to see your way to be truly human" — to prevent them murdering Ill — is senseless, since, as has been seen, Claire is *literally* inhuman. They must now themselves become "inhuman" and participate in the execution.

*   *   *

To return then to our question: Was Ill's death tragic? Is the play a tragedy rather than a "tragic comedy"? Claire's words to the Teacher may answer the first question: If he had really wanted to better Güllen with Claire's money, then his true humanity would not have permitted him to take part in the execution. Since he did take part in it, the money was a bribe and his humanity (the humanity of traditional culture, of "Goethe and Brahms", be it remembered), a sham. Claire shows him that her money meant nothing to her — she wants *revenge* only. By "stringing along with her", Güllen executes Alfred Ill for the money alone. His death is therefore no Grecian tragedy; it becomes death by executioner (he is clearly strangled by the gymnast) in surroundings of hypocritical rôle-playing. The Doctor diagnoses "heart failure", the Mayor says "Death from joy" and the whole event takes place — on a stage. But it is no "comic death" either, unlike the death of the characters in, say, *Mississippi*. Alfred does not come back to life.

Further, the parodistic Sophoclean ode to a dehumanized economic boom which closes the work shows clearly that Alfred's life has been what George Steiner might have called "an allegory of pure waste", rather than a tragedy. The two choruses, in evening-dress in the middle of their rebuilt town, a universal "Happy Ending", sing finally the joys of prosperity. There is no remorse, no sense of guilt. They (like Frisch's *Biedermann* chorus) have learned nothing. Ill's sacrifice, like Romulus', was in vain.[25]

Yet Alfred Ill *has* risen once to the greatness of the tragic hero, this was his "personal achievement"; his fate was brought about, not by Chance, but by *hamartia*, that "great error on his part", as Aristotle put it in *The Poetics*, an error which he sought to correct. The "lost world order", lost, as was noted, when Claire's arrival suspended the natural laws, is restored to him when he refuses the Mayor's suggestion to commit suicide and decides to face the judgement of Güllen. It is however restored to *him*, the "individual", the only citizen willing to accept the responsibility for his actions as a human being — to stand up and say: NO! Nothing has been changed with his death and nothing will change or can change until, as the drunken "half-human" Teacher tells the people of Güllen, an "Old Lady" comes to *them*. As has been noted, *The Visit* is one of Dürrenmatt's answers to Brecht's maxim about the changeability of the world.

Such fates are warnings; they do not necessarily depict what has happened, but what might happen if mankind continues to deny Freedom to Man. The "valiant man" shows the way, but, as Dürrenmatt wrote in 1969 in his *Gigantic Lecture on Justice and the Law*: "It is not the individual who changes reality, reality is changed by us all. Reality is all of us, and we are always individuals". He had already reminded us of this in *Point 17* to the *Physicists*: "What concerns all of us can only be solved by all of us".

We have therefore a practical demonstration of the "theory" expounded in the *Problems of the Theatre*. Ill is placed before a decision, before the "yawning abyss" of his guilt. He faces the "sense-lessness, the hopelessness of this world", this "enigma of disaster", accepts his guilt and goes to his death, at first a "thoughtless man, a simple man. . .who suddenly becomes aware of something, through Fear, through Terror. . .who personally experiences justice done" *because* he acknowledges his guilt and will defend his human dignity. His death is both "meaningless" and "meaningful", adds the author (in the *Notes*) but it could only be truly meaningful (that is, truly tragic) "in the mythical realms of a classical *polis*" (a City State), that is, against a firm, ethical background, for, as Walter Jens has written, "the existence of the tragic hero is bound to the existence of the *polis*, the existence of the *polis* to the existence of the gods".[26]

But this death has taken place in the *hic et nunc*, in Güllen, the "liquid dung" found at the foot of the ubiquitous Swiss dung-heaps, a name which the inhabitants now want to change to "Golden" (Gülden)[27] — but it is also the town which represents Hebbel's "morass of foul relationships", an image of the modern faceless world, of shifting uncertain relationships where there are no longer any clear-cut issues, only paradoxes, no answers, only questions.[28]

Ill becomes a "hero"; he recognizes his "great error" and "suffers a terrible experience". Yet, as this study has shown, Dürrenmatt has continually moved the mood away from the heroic by evoking comic laughter. Ill's tragic is played out, not against a moral background which "raises" him, but against this farcical "morass of foul relationships" which "reduces" his death from "pure tragedy" to "comic tragedy" by turning the "religious deed" into a farcical butchery. The inscrutable Greek Fates are replaced by a grotesque Old Lady, the ancient *polis* by a comically weak modern town (eventually "something technically glittering and gleaming").

"The actual tragic character in the actual comic situation", of which I wrote earlier, seems to me to be a workable working definition for modern tragicomedy. Dürrenmatt's earlier plays postulated a potentially tragic character who was finally prevented from taking the step which would have made his fate a tragic one. The comic situation is common to both types. That type of play can therefore be called a

Komödie since the tragic is not "realised". The comic remains comic, the "darkness" is only a shadow and is never truly threatening as it is in *The Visit of the Old Lady*.[29]

By working as he does with the elements of the comic, Dürrenmatt distances his spectator from the emotions of "pure" tragedy; nevertheless, his Alfred Ill is far removed from being "just another of Dürrenmatt's stoic heroes", as Dr Garten called him. Out of all the characters created by Dürrenmatt, he is still the one who most nearly makes a tragedy out of the comedy. Here Dürrenmatt could indeed say: "We can glean the tragic from the *Komödie*, extract it as one terrible moment, a yawning abyss. . ."

NOTES TO CHAPTER FIVE

DER BESUCH DER ALTEN DAME (THE VISIT OF THE OLD LADY)

1. Bänziger, op.cit., p.180; W. Weber, quoted in A. Arnold, op.cit., p.43. N Tolschenova: *Wie man Gerechtigkeit kauft und verkauft*, Ogonëk, Moscow, 30.1.66; Erich Kühne: *Satire und groteske Dramatik*, Weimarer Beiträge, 12, 1966, pp.539-565, here p.558; J.C. Hortenbach: *Biblical echoes in Dürrenmatt's Der Besuch der alten Dame*, Monatshefte, Vol.LVII, April-May 1965, No.4, pp.145-161, here p.147; F. Buri: *Der Einfall der Gnade in Dürrenmatts dramatischem Werk*, in *Der unbequeme Dürrenmatt*, op.cit., p.55; U. Profitlich: *Dürrenmatt: Der Besuch der alten Dame* in *Die deutsche Komödie*, Bagel, Düsseldorf, 1977, pp.324-341, here p.333; M.W. Askew: *Dürrenmatt's (sic) The Visit of the Old Lady*, Tulane Drama Review, Vol.v, No.4, June 1961, pp.89-105; H. Dittberner: *Dürrenmatt, der Geschichtenerzähler*, *FD I*, op.cit., pp.86-92. (He praises the film version in which he first saw the work!); M.B. Peppard: op.cit., p.62; Max Frisch: *Der Autor und das Theater* in *Öffentlichkeit als Partner*, Suhrkamp 1976, p.77 and G.P. Knapp: *Vorbemerkung* to *Friedrich Dürrenmatt: Studien zu seinem Werk*, op.cit., p.24.

2. The play was translated and "adapted" by Maurice Valency as *The Visit* (New York 1958) and opened the Lunt-Fontanne Theatre in New York (with Alfred Lunt and Lynne Fontanne in the major rôles) on May 5th 1958. It gained the Broadway Critics' Award in 1959; the director was Peter Brook. (Eric Porter played the Mayor!) On this adaptation, see I.C. Loram: *Der Besuch der alten Dame and The Visit*, Monatshefte für den Deutschunterricht, Vol. LIII, 1961, pp.15-21 and H.P. Guth: *The Visit: The play behind the play*, Symposium No. 16, 1962, pp.94-102. Also Alan Brien's scathing comments on the London production in The Spectator (The Visitors) (1.7.60). (It opened the new Royalty Theatre on 23.6.60).

The 1964 film version was even worse. Directed by Darryll F. Zanuck, it starred Ingrid Bergman and Anthony Quinn (as "Serge Miller"!). On this, see Mona Knapp: *Die Verjüngung der alten Dame* in *FD II* (1976), pp.58-66, where we are reminded of Patrick Bowle's much more scholarly translation of *The Visit* (Cape 1962). (The American title was retained "at the publisher's request"). Dürrenmatt liked Wälterlin's 1956 production, but believed that his own (shortened) version (with a cast of 12) in the Atelier Theatre in Berne in 1959 was the best that he had seen. (On this, see D.Fringeli op.cit., and E.Nef: *Der Besuch der alten Dame*, GLL, Vol.XIII, 1959/60, pp.226-227).

3. *K I*, p.343. The play *Der Besuch der alten Dame: Eine tragische Komödie* is in *K I*, pp.249-343 (= *BAD*). The sub-title was originally "Eine Komödie der Hochkonjunktur" (A *Komödie* of the Economic Boom). See too *Randnotizen, alphabetisch geordnet (Marginal Notes, alphabetically arranged)* in the programme of the Schauspielhaus Zürich 1955-1956, pp.7-10, here p.9.

4. cf. *Marginal Notes*, under *Güllen*: ". . . 5056 inhabitants (52 percent Protestant, 45 percent Catholic, 3 percent other . . ." p.11. For this reason, Tiusanen suggests that he be called a "minister", not a "priest". True, but a Lutheran clergyman is hardly a Presbyterian?

5. In the *Physiology of Laughter*, Spencer called this element of the comic "a descending incongruity", ". . . when consciousness is unawares transferred from great things to small". It is the source of much Dürrenmattian comic and is what Emil Staiger called "Fallhöhe" (the height of the fall, i.e. from the sublime to the ridiculous) in *Grundbegriffe der Poetik*, Atlantis, Zürich, 1946, p.212.

6. It is not perhaps surprising that this is one of the most powerful scenes in Gottfried von Einem's opera which had its première in Vienna in May 1971. For views of the première, see H.H.Stuckenschmidt in *FAZ*, 25.5.71 and Kenneth Loveland in The Times, 1.6.71. The opera is more "psychologically" orientated and is more concerned with Claire than with Ill. It was given at Glyndebourne in 1973. (See too William Mann's enthusiastic *Times* review, 5.12.72).

7. For this reason, I agree with Heidsieck's claim that Dürrenmatt is only truly grotesque when he presents "perverted reality", cf. above. Note 52 *EHM*, p.96.

8. He is in fact named as Hahncke on p.264. A small point, but worth making, since commentators have sought to prove that Ill is the only "human being" in the play *because* he is the only true character with a name. That is not the only reason. See inter alia P.J.Breuer in his *Europäische Komödien*, Diesterweg, 1964, pp.214-242, particularly p.239 ff., where he sets Ill, the individual with a name, against the mass, the "collective". But, as we shall see, other characters have names as well.

   The Knapps also fall into this trap saying that "Der Erste, Der Zweite etc." are "incomprehensibly Teutonicized" in Valency's translation. Unsatisfactory though that is, he is correct to call them Hofbauer and Helmsberger (cf *BAD*, p.282 and p.287). (Knapps in *FD II*, p.65).

9. The Doctor's name, Nüsslin (= a little nut) suggests ridicule, but he does go with the Teacher to plead with Claire and he is one of the first to sense Claire's demonic presence: "Jokes like that chill me to the marrow" (p.273).

10. J.L.Styan: *The Dark Comedy*, CUP (2nd edn.) 1968, p.257.

11. L.W. Forster has pointed out however the peculiar paratactic nature of Swiss dialect: ". . . and in the syntax, the lack of subordinating conjunctions causing Swiss syntax to be mainly paratactic and not hypotactic like German or standard English". In *Language in German Switzerland*, GLL, Vol.IV, No.1, October 1939, pp.65-73, here p.67, the point being that Dürrenmatt's style may be more influenced by dialect tradition than by modern *Kontaktarmut* (lack of contacts, ie. alienation etc).

12. E.S.Dick: *Der Besuch der alten Dame*, ZfdPh, Vol.87, Heft 4, 1968, pp.498-509, here p.505. Therese Giehse and Dürrenmatt recorded this scene on Heliodor Cassette 3321 011 (1967/68).
13. See Krättli, op.cit., p.12.
14. See Note 8 above. Ill's wife is Mathilde Blumhard, the Mayor's wife is Annettchen Dummermuth, the Second Man is Helmesberger, the Fourth Man is Kühn, Ill's son is Karl and his daughter Ottilie.
15. J.Scherer: *Der mutige Mensch*, op.cit., p.311.
16. Kühne, op.cit., p.558; J.Kuczynski: *Friedrich Dürrenmatt — Humanist: I* in Neue deutsche Literatur, Vol.12, No.8, 1964, pp.59-89, here p.82.
    R.Kerndl: *Dramatik ohne Blick auf die Zukunft*, Neues Deutschland, 2.8.63; H-G. Werner, op.cit., p.145; Profitlich, *Friedrich Dürrenmatt*, op.cit., p.93; Hortenbach, op.cit., pp.151-152; M.Valency: *The Visit — A modern tragedy*, Theater Arts 42, 1958, here p.17 ff.
17. J.Steiner, *Die Komödie Dürrenmatts*, op.cit., p.84.
18. F.Hebbel: *Sämtliche Werke* (ed. R.M.Werner), Berlin 1904, Band II, p.379. (From the Foreword to his "Tragicomödie" *Ein Trauerspiel in Sizilien* (1851).
19. A milliard is a thousand million in the UK and a billion in the USA. Nowhere is the country of the currency mentioned. Bowles translates it as "a million" (p.35) — but Claire does go on to say: "500 million to the town and 500 million divided among all the families" (p.276).
20. In the Valency adaptation, an attempt is made to "gild the lily" by having Alfred (= Anton Schill) offered and refuse a lift by a truck-driver back to town. This was presumably meant to make Ill's (and Lunt's!) gesture more noble and therefore "tragic". I think it makes it sentimental. Jan Kott saw this as a "great scene from Kafka" in *Theatre Notebook*, op.cit., pp.88-90.
21. H.Mayer: *Friedrich Dürrenmatt*, ZfdPh., 87, 1968, pp.482-498; J.Knopf, op.cit., p.91; K.S.Guthke, *Geschichte und Poetik der deutschen Tragikomödie*, op.cit.
22. See Note 26 (above p.39) to Chapter Two (p.25). Reinhold Grimm, reviewing Heidsieck's book, concluded that the grotesque is an "area of confusion". ("For the time being anyway, we shall all have to find our own answers") in Monatshefte Vol. LXII, No.3, Fall 1970, pp.299-301. See too E.C.Reed: *Dürrenmatt's Besuch der alten Dame: A study in the grotesque*, Monatshefte Vol. LIII, 1961, pp.9.14. In his examination of Brecht's "grotesque", P.C.Giehse comes to this conclusion: "Das Groteske in Dürrenmatt's plays is a clearly-defined manifestation of the Komödie". P.C.Giehse: *Das Gesellschaftlich-Komische: Zu Komik und Komödie am Beispiel der Stücke und Bearbeitungen Brechts*, Metzler, Stuttgart, 1974, pp.47-49.
23. Bienek op.cit. The character was originally meant to be a male in any case. See the interview with Preuss in Literarische Werkstatt, Oldenbourg/München 1972. p.14. Much of the grotesque vanishes in Valency's adaptation where Claire is only 51. In the film, Bergmann's Claire is 47. Neither the author nor the director of the film approved of the change. See H.Dittberner, op.cit., pp.86-92.
24. See the *Marginal Notes*: "Her name is made up from Zacharoff, Onassis, Gulbenkian (last-named buried in Zürich)" (p.10). Her own name "Kläri Wäscher" (= to wash clean) is no doubt symbolic, but whether Ill means "il" (i.e. "he") is doubtful. cf. K.H.Fickert: *Dürrenmatt's The Visit and Job*, Books Abroad, XLI, April 1968, pp.389-392, here p.389. Fickert has extended these remarks in *Wit and Wisdom in Dürrenmatt's names*, Contemporary Literature Vol.II, 1970, pp.382-388, but many conjectures seem far-fetched.

25. Frisch's chorus chants: "Stupidity / never to be extinguished Now / called Fate". Suhrkamp 1958, p.91. Manfred Durzak sees this as the main difference between Brecht's and Dürrenmatt's point of view: "For Brecht is concerned with encouraging reflections which comprehend the state of affairs being presented as changeable and which show possibilities for change": *Dürrenmatt, Frisch, Weiss*, op.cit., p.99.
26. W.Jens: *Antikes und modernes Drama*, in *Statt einer Literaturgeschichte*, Neske, Pfullingen 1957, pp.81-107, here p.88.
27. "The name of the town is to be changed to GOLDEN (*GÜLDEN*) at the request of those entitled to vote" (*Marginal Notes*, op.cit., p.9.).
28. See Hebbel's definition of tragicomedy in his *Sendschreiben an Rötscher*, op.cit., pp.378-380, here p.379. ". . . on one side, the struggling and sinking man, yet, on the other, not the justified moral power, as in tragedy, but a morass of foul relationships . . . which swallows up thousands of victims without deserving a single one of them".
29. This is why Heidsieck calls the play "grotesque" and not "tragicomic", but the grotesque scenes are only part of the play, as he admits (p.39). Breuer tries the middle way and claims that the "tragic comedy is the dramatic form of the grotesque" and says later that the grotesque is only the "most important structural element" (p.218 and p.239). Tiusanen says that the play is a mixture between two tragicomedies. E.Speidel approaches the conclusion from a slightly different angle: "By presenting a tragic development within the framework of a "non-Aristotelian" structure, Dürrenmatt has confronted us with what amounts to a Brechtian "Verfremdung" of the traditional concept of tragedy" (p.23) but nowhere, I think, does Speidel give any indication that this is a "*Komödie*". Indeed, and significantly, Speidel bases his argument on the "tragedy" sentences of Dürrenmatt's famous dictum in *Problems of the Theatre*. See E.Speidel: *Aristotelian and non-Aristotelian elements in Dürrenmatt's Der Besuch der alten Dame*, GLL, Vol. XXVIII, October, 1974, No.1, pp.14-24.

Chapter Six

CONTRA-BRECHT

FRANK DER FÜNFTE *(Frank the Fifth)* (1959)

(ii) DIE PHYSIKER *(The Physicists)* (1962)

"I start from the "Einfall", the "flash of inspiration", the comical aspect, in order to do something quite uncomical, i.e. to put Mankind on the stage. . ." Thus Dürrenmatt defined his *modus operandi* to Horst Bienek in their conversation in 1962. It was the critics' failure to understand his use of *the comic* in his next work that annoyed him:

> . . .I cannot bear plays in which there is nothing to laugh at. So people should laugh at *Frank the Fifth*, despite its wildnesses. It may be a serious play, it certainly isn't a deadly serious one.[1]

Yet, although it is true that some critics dismissed the work on intellectual grounds, the main objections lay elsewhere — they lay in the belief that Dürrenmatt had become a mere Brecht-epigone.[2]

Although one could cite Molière's dictum, "Je prends mon bien où je le trouve" ("I take my themes wherever I find them"), one can nevertheless hardly blame a rather biased German-speaking critic (antipathetic perhaps in any case to Dürrenmatt), from wishing to dismiss *Frank V* as indicative of "a certain Brecht-bondage" among the Swiss. The writer continued: "Switzerland suffers, above all, from acute Brechtitis. The rest of us perform Brecht or we don't — Switzerland is still writing à la Brecht".[3]

There is, however, a good case to be put forward for considering that Dürrenmatt only "used" Brecht as he used Aristophanes, Sophocles, Shakespeare, Strindberg, Goethe and Wedekind, as subjects for parodistic treatment. As Hans Mayer put it: *"Frank V* is a play *against* Brecht but for that reason not a play *without* Brecht".[4] The parodying of great writers of the past has been, as we have seen, one of the features of the work of those contemporary writers who seek thereby to provide a more "relevant" experience for the theatregoer of today.

To begin with, then, the two writers had a fundamentally different approach to the writing of plays; Brecht, in the pre-war works in particular, was concerned with proclaiming a message; he was attempting to prove that Man's only hope for a civilized future was to live in a classless society, a "socialist" society. He believed that, even against the evidence of the Stalinist purges of the 30's and the dissatisfaction of the East German workers in 1953. (He died 14 days before the Hungarian Revolution of 1956). Dürrenmatt, on the other hand, has always held a more pessimistic, but a fundamentally more realistic view of Man's behaviour on earth. In his celebrated *Schiller-Rede* (*Speech on Schiller*) in Mannheim in 1959, Dürrenmatt claimed that Brecht's efforts to reproduce his world on the stage had been in vain since "the old maxim of the revolutionaries that Man can and must change the world has become unrealizable for the individual, it is out of circulation; nowadays it can only be used by the masses as a slogan, as political dynamite . . ."[5] Both Schiller's world of "classical" tragedy with its components guilt, punishment and an idealized freedom, and Brecht's, propounding an equally idealized solution, of Mankind actually *changing the world*, were unattainable, because, Dürrenmatt asserted, the individual is no longer able to control events: "For the individual there is only impotence, the feeling of being ignored . . ." (p.38).

Brecht had taken issue personally with Dürrenmatt only once in his lifetime, in his letter of apology for his absence at the 5th *Darmstädter Gespräch* on theatre in 1955, where he had claimed that today's world *could* be represented on the stage, although, he added, only "when it is described as a world that can be changed" and he went on to say that he was now living in a country (the GDR) "where an enormous effort is being made to change society".[6] Dürrenmatt found this point of view much too naive; in the discussion which followed in Darmstadt he said: "Just writing a drama is so difficult that I have no time to think of the solution of the world's problems when I'm writing it".

Dürrenmatt has always been repelled by those "ideologies that have a solution for everything". For this reason, he has chosen to write his open-ended *Komödie*, presenting insoluble conflicts rather than the more dogmatic Brechtian-type which, Dürrenmatt would claim, by its very didacticism, places a solution before the audience. (Brecht, he was to write later, was more concerned with his ideology than his poetry, an ideology which he declared to be a truth) (*Der Mitmacher Komplex*, p.280).

Brecht saw his solution in the inevitable triumph of Marxist-Leninism; Dürrenmatt distrusts any suggestion of such inevitability; indeed his belief in, and representations of, the forces of Chance, *Zufall*, separate him most distinctly from the German writer. Such a philosophy, that our lives are lived in the daily expectation of some mocking change of fortune which would nullify any rational forward planning, could hardly conceive of a "Communist heaven" where all men shall live together in a planned brotherhood. Yet, as we have seen, Dürrenmatt scourges the unfeeling lack of concern for mankind's freedom, and the love of power, on *both* sides of the Iron Curtain, since his works have been written against a background of Hungary (1956), the Berlin Wall (1961), Czechoslovakia (1968), of de-Stalinization and de-Kruschevization — as well as of Korea, Vietnam — and Watergate.[7]

Dürrenmatt's works do show a curious ambivalence towards Brecht which Professor Hinck summed up rather well: "His attack on a "dogmatic' component in Brecht's playwriting has never been withdrawn. But there is also always the demand for his own theatre to be relevant to society . . ."[8] Both points are illustrated by the Dürrenmatt plays which most closely follow a "Brechtian" pattern: *Frank the Fifth* and *The Physicists*. Dürrenmatt was well aware that *Frank* particularly would "always have to sail under the false flag of the *Threepenny Opera*; that's its fate", as he said to Bienek; but it cannot be thought of as a *copy* of Brecht's work, and I would suggest that it is rather a parody of it, just as Brecht's was a parody of John Gay's *Beggar's Opera* of 1778 (which, in turn, was a parody of the contemporary Handelian operas!)

Yet much of the criticism of the work centred on its similarity to the Brechtian piece: "There were arguments" wrote Joachim Kaiser, "as to whether Dürrenmatt was Brecht's legitimate successor or just — in this *Frank V* — the one who used Brecht's literary estate most effectively!"[9]

★   ★   ★

In his various comments on *Frank V*, Dürrenmatt has stressed that the essence of the *Komödie* lies in the contrast between illusion and reality.[10] Each character finds that the life that he or she had been living has been based on false premisses — the "comedy" arises with the dropping of a mask, the presentation of the character's (human) limitations. Dürrenmatt insists always that comedy has to do with the "insight into human limitations". He presents us, he said to Bienek, with the "story of a gangster bank" which is "modelled on a Royal drama" (e.g. *Henry V*). The conflict here is between those who want to be *free* and those who do not; but the typical paradoxical form of Dürrenmattian comedy lies in his phrase in the *Richtlinien* (*Guidelines*):

"He who would be free, must die", and for this reason, Emil Böckmann's death-scene must be regarded as the key to the whole work.[11]

The scene was the major cause of the controversy after the première, yet the critic of the ultra-conservative *Kirchenbote* (= Church Messenger) claimed (rather remarkably): "I must say that . . . in all the atrocities . . . one could perceive something positive, promising and optimistic . . . the feeling that this was no cynic, no despiser, no misogynist at work. The writer . . . must be a man who loves his fellow-men, despite everything".[12] We think of Bodo's remark in *Mississippi* (see above (p.73). Nevertheless, it was on this scene that Dürrenmatt concentrated when he defended himself before his critics at Munich: "Whoever doesn't understand me in this scene, doesn't understand me at all" (op.cit., p.352).

Böckmann is the spiritual clown of the work, the head-clerk of the Bank ("my best friend", says Frank), who might have been seen to be the "little spiv" or the "shop-assistant" of Dürrenmattian theory, the "victim" which makes classical tragedy an impossibility for our age. It was seen in *Problems of the Theatre* how the comic was employed to bring about a "tragedy for the time being" (above p.102). Does the same situation obtain here?

The scene, No.11: *The woman plunges in the dagger*, which Dürrenmatt has claimed as one of his three best scenes (to Wyrsch, p.38), is introduced by laughter: Egli has just slept with the new employee and has found himself relieved of his gold watch. "You can put the gold watch on your expenses", says Ottilie (p.251). There is therefore a strong dramatic contrast when the second curtain rises to reveal Böckmann's hands clutching the iron bed-head in agony. Frank enters, disguised as a priest, a double comic ploy, since the disguise itself is comic, that of a priest doubly so in this situation. To Böckmann's stifled cries: "The pains", "The fear" and "I'm dying", Frank answers *three* times: "Just have courage", surely a parody of Dürrenmatt's own concept of the "valiant" or "courageous" man, since Frank, the disguised villain, is mocking the inherent "goodness" of the clerk? The repetition is intended to be comical. When Frank tries to show Böckmann that he is disguised out of necessity, Böckmann expresses his disgust at the crimes of the past and insists that men are *free*: "At every hour we could have turned back, at every moment of our lives . . . We were free, false priest, created in Freedom and entrusted to Freedom" (p.252). To prove this, he says, he has sent for the priest to receive the Last Sacraments. Frank's reactions are comically incongruous. He says to his wife: "Wants to confess. But that's just *medieval*" (p.253).

While Ottilie takes over the "nursing", there is a repetition of the "Just have courage" scene with one significant alteration: Instead of "I'm dying", Böckmann cries "I must die" — he longs for a "tragic death", a death which will allow him to atone for his sins by confession — but such a death cannot be granted him, for "confession" would mean betrayal of the firm's secrets. The dying man's wishes are brushed aside and, while Ottilie prepares the fatal syringe, Frank "chants" a grimly comic parody of the absolution:

> It is Night
> Dark night
> Night without end
> Oh, what have I done
> To bring my friend
> almost to the grave?   (pp.254-255)

Böckmann has, of course, committed his share of petty crimes in his time at the Bank and had sung with the others: "If you want to live in luxury / You have to have a racket going for you" (p.211). The same hard, cynical exterior was revealed in Scene 4: *The price of love*: The audience might laugh at his paradoxical summing-up of the situation: "Unfortunately we live in a constitutional state" (p.217); only in Scene 7: *In the shadow of my forefathers* did the picture change and Böckmann become different when it was revealed that he was suffering from stomach cancer. Frank and Ottilie drop their masks to admit to having known about this for two years, but also to having said nothing, lest Böckmann blurt out the Bank's secrets during the operation.

His death is therefore motivated dramatically. Böckmann is aware of the all-corrupting evil of the love of money; his disease is "the wages of sin". He now struggles to become "human", to free himself from the baleful influence which has turned the others into automata. Frank and Ottilie's insistence that all the evil was committed for their childrens' sake is the comic *agens* here; firstly, Böckmann did not even know that they had children and, secondly, it had been his own dream to found a childrens' home. We sense a potential tragedy, yet the situation has comic undertones.

To return to the death-scene: It can now be appreciated what Dürrenmatt was attempting to achieve. The scene is about "Freedom" — as the author has always insisted. The fact that Böckmann does not die "his" death, that he dies without absolution and is actually *murdered* by Ottilie, is meant to indicate that true freedom is impossible in any "gangster-democracy", east or west — the theme of much of Dürrenmatt's later work.[13] To Böckmann's cry about Freedom, Dürrenmatt (in the Munich speech) answered: "Freedom is gained by merit and not by trickery" (p.350). This is the task of humanity and the burden of all Dürrenmatt's writings.

Although no commentator has argued that Böckmann is an Ill, Brock-Sulzer does claim that this scene is one of the "most moral that Dürrenmatt has ever written".[14] This may be so, but for me the scene is a dramatic failure. It presents neither a "tragedy" (since Böckmann was murdered, there is no tragic necessity in his death, it is "death by the hangman" again); nor a tragicomedy (the situation lacks the necessary comic to contrast with any potentially tragic character), nor even a grotesque since the lack of any true comic means that the scene is mere Grand Guignol. Dürrenmatt has overstepped the narrow border-line and has ended up in rather empty melodrama.

Yet from the wreck we can rescue a concept. Böckmann is *meant* to be a "spiritual clown". He had the intention of asserting his humanity by asserting his freedom and betraying the collective. Like all spiritual clowns, he fails to achieve his aim, but, in making his effort, he is an eiron-type who triumphs (albeit only morally here) over the imposter. This is probably what Dürrenmatt meant when he said to his critics: "Frank is destroyed, not Böckmann" (*Munich Speech*, p.352).

★　　★　　★

Dürrenmatt said that "Gottfried Frank only seemed to be the most comical character; he is really the most fearsome . . ."[15] The comic in his character is found mainly in its hypocrisy; we rarely *see* Frank as Frank — he is either the Fifth of a rather comical dynasty (the comic of multiplication), or he is a disguised priest, or he is travelling with Ottilie to their villa on Lake Constance under the disguised name of "Hansen" (p.229). He introduces himself to Päuli and Heini as "Frank the philanthropist" (p.203), but shortly after his "funeral" when he explains to Päuli what had happened to Heini, (he was murdered), he says: "We had urgent need of a male corpse" (p.209).

In Frank's hypocritical assumption of "Bildung" (education or culture), the author seeks to make comic the contrast between the unscrupulous heir to an unscrupulous dynasty, and his attempt to enjoy the intellectual fruits of civilization. In Scene 1, Frank reflects on the murderous past of his forebears: "I'm no bank manager," he groans, "Unfortunately I am a good man through and through" (p.225); they "were bursting with energy", he reads Goethe and Mörike; where they directed gambling-halls, he is "President of a Church Aid Society"; where they created brothels, he organizes literary evenings (p.226). There is a double comic contrast here; the forefathers were barbarous rogues, Frank enjoys the culture of the leisured classes, but he enjoys it on the profits from his own barbarous past.

Yet the fearsomeness and grimness of the character are made ultimately comical when his well-laid plans are foiled. His son and daughter find the diary which reveals all. The upturning of his plans and the comic paradox of their childrens' evildoings, despite Herbert's education in Oxford and Franziska's in Montreux (!), make Frank's end comically absurd.[16] "Values are changed into their opposites", wrote Dürrenmatt about Frank. Raised in the modern world, the son Herbert has nothing but contempt for his father's "weakness"; his desire to be decent (". . . only real rogues can do good", he says, p.273). Frank goes to his death in the vault, an image recalled in *Der Mitmacher* in 1973. The imposter has been driven out.

Richard Egli, the Head of Personnel, is the "miles gloriosus" figure in the work — he is the harsh, boastful, bluff type, a man who sacrifices all and everybody "out of loyalty to the firm"; this is his obsession, his "idée fixe", and he becomes ridiculous by his devotion to it.[17] His unromantic philosophy is revealed in his opening song with its Christmas parodies. Man loses his humanity in this cold brutal business world "surrounded by wolves, snapped at by dogs". In Egli's "loyalty to the firm", Dürrenmatt ridicules the concept of "patriotism". He had noted in *Problems of the Theatre* that "fatherlands" had been replaced nowadays by "firms" which necessitated a sacrifice of the individual. Frieda Fürst, Egli's long-suffering fiancée, is the sacrifice here. There is no doubt — from the evidence of Scene 5: *Early morning before our misdeeds* — that they love each other. Egli has just done his duty to the firm by sleeping with the "millionairess from Milwaukee", Frieda hers by sleeping with the "civil engineer". The comic in this love scene arises out of the banal, inconsequential, inhuman and unemotional dialogue:

> *Frieda*: My sister in Anderthal has had her fifth child. A boy.
> *Egli*:   My brother in Maibrugg has been made Mayor. He's done well.

But this is a "*Komödie* of Freedom", Dürrenmatt told Horst Bienek. When Frieda (like Böckmann) tries to assert her humanity, to break away from the collective, she has transgressed the rules and must be liquidated. "This can't go on", says Ottilie. "Your sentimentality is ruining us" (p.248). Frieda turns to Egli for help, but there is no humanity there. "He who would be free, must die". His heart-pills are a symbol of his inhumanity, just as Claire's artificial limbs were a sign of hers. They are both kept "alive" by inhuman aids.

In some ways, Frieda is "valiant"; she *did* expiate her guilt. Yet the prostitute reformed is a sentimental *topos* and Dürrenmatt fails to avoid bathos — nor are the obscene jokes in the character very funny. Most of them remain obstinately obscene and were the reason for comments like Helene Weigel's: "This pseudo-opera is tasteless, disgusting and antiquated". The function of these "Zoten" in previous works had been to provoke and amuse; here they merely disgust.

★　　　★　　　★

"In *Frank the Fifth*, Chance takes the form of natural phenomena (lightning, the discovery of uranium) which upsets all logical calculations", writes Donald Daviau.[18] Freedom and "its scientific brother" Chance are brought together here to demonstrate that a "gangster democracy" is an impossibility. "Just as Frank the Fifth meets Reason, his personnel manager meets Chance", wrote Dürrenmatt in the *Guidelines* (p.282). The deaths of the three buffoons, Egli, Päuli and Heini, showed that it was logically impossible for a member of the collective to be "free" (cf. their refrain: "For whoever is living on Easy Street is living in a trap / And if you want to get out, the trap shuts tight", (Scene 10)). The interventions of Chance showed that it was logically impossible for a "planner" like Egli to plan, and since none of those involved have been able to achieve their aims, their illusions are shown to be absurd — and comic.

Martin Esslin tells us what Dürrenmatt said about Chance in 1963: "I would call my own theatre a "theatre of paradox" because it is precisely the paradoxical results of strict logic that interest me. Ionesco and Beckett attack language and logic as means of thought and communication. I am concerned with logical thought in its strictest applications, so strict that it sets up its own internal contradictions. But this requires extreme rationality in structure and dialogue, in contrast to the Theatre of Absurd in which language is shown in a state of disintegration".[19]

The Frank children, Herbert and Franziska, might be thought of as the "internal contradictions" of "logical thought". Frank had taken all precautions against their leading a life like his — but it was in "rational" Oxford and Montreux respectively that they learned about the evils of modern civilization. Neither character here is comic in itself — but their *function* is comic. Frank's planning is seen to come to nought and his son (Frank VI) sends him to a farcical death in the vault. The wife's wish for moral regeneration is still-born, for the children's behaviour shows her that "contempt is the true death". Herbert will take over the Bank and will make it even more successful, not by moral methods, but, paradoxically, as any Swiss banker would, by *brutal* efficiency.

★   ★   ★

"Humanity is more than a pretty word: it's a risk and we all need to ensure that this risk doesn't become an act of madness", wrote Dürren-matt in the *Guidelines* of 1964 (p.282). He felt that Man had become a cipher in the teeming business jungle. This was his warning — but the ambience was too much "Grand Guignol" for anyone to take the warn-ing seriously. Böckmann and Frieda did make an attempt to save their humanity, but it needs more than one or two to combat the attitude epitomized by Häberlin's sad comment: "Once I was a human being, now I'm an animal" (p.219).

The work is a failure. All critics were agreed on that, although the reasons differ; for example, Murray Peppard feels that "the figures portrayed are not worthy of either our laughter or our censure", while, for Frau Brock-Sulzer, ever loth to condemn a Dürrenmatt work, the theme was "unimportant . . . not worthy of a tragedy" (p.103).

This failure is very significant. It failed because it was neither "fish nor fowl"; it failed Dürrenmatt's own acid test for a work: "Only internal conviction carries external validity".[20] The work lacks intel-lectual and artistic conviction. When Dürrenmatt's comic touch eludes him, as it does here on the whole, his sense of the tragic is never strong enough to compensate and he falls into Grand Guignol (as in the Böck-mann death-scene) or into bathos (as in the Egli-Fürst love-scene) or — and this would be a judgement on his *oeuvre* as a whole — into melo-drama. Dürrenmatt fails to justify his defence in the *Guidelines* — only if the work's intended comic effects had been generally successful could the piece have been called a *Komödie*. There is no sense of the tragic in the play since the deaths are "hangman's deaths", devoid of tragedy; the situations are not comic enough nor the characters tragic enough for a *Komödie* or tragicomedy to emerge, and, since most authorities on the farce are agreed that the "Zoten" are usually very funny in such a work, it is hardly that either. The work remains a melodrama; what was meant to shock and provoke only amused — and not very much at that![21]

(ii) DIE PHYSIKER (THE PHYSICISTS)

Every man is the centre of his own world and at the same time, he is part of a society. That is Man's major conflict.

(To René Sauter, 19.8.66).

We have already seen that "conflicts" rather than "problems" have traditionally been subjects for comedy, and Dürrenmatt's remark seems to be closely in line with the general thesis of his next play *The Physicists*, an international success, second only to *The Visit of the Old Lady*.[22]

The theme of *The Physicists* is the Brechtian one of the responsibility of the scientist towards the society in, and from which he lives. Since his conception of his responsibilities may not coincide with that of the society, conflict may arise.

The gist of the contents of the play is to be found in Dürrenmatt's 1956 review of Robert Jungk's book *Heller als 1000 Sonnen* (Stuttgart 1956) (*Brighter than 1000 suns*), on the building of the first atom bomb. The review condemns the "international élite" of scientists who had allowed their knowledge to be prostituted by power politicians. Jungk showed how the scientists (Einstein among them) could have prevented this had they acted as an international body. As Dürrenmatt wrote in the review: "There is no possibility of keeping secret what has once been thought".[23] All were against the making of the bomb – but it was made nevertheless. The reader will recall this as a familiar Dürrenmatt theme.

Dürrenmatt had fought the proposal that Switzerland should share in the atomic defence of Europe and it was almost an illustration of a Dürrenmattian paradox that the Swiss should have voted (in April 1962) against his objection, after having applauded his play at the première in Zürich in February, 1962 – a perfect illustration also of *Point* 21 to the play: "A drama can trick the audience into facing reality, but it cannot force them to resist it or even to conquer it", and of his answer to Bienek's question. Can a writer "change the world"? : "He can pacify at best, influence very rarely – but change? Never!"[24]

Dürrenmatt's argument against the bomb was not in its essentials a political one; he was inveighing at this time against Man's inhumanity to Man, and his thesis in *The Physicists* is based primarily on *moral* grounds, in contradistinction to Brecht's in *The Life of Galileo* or

Heinar Kipphardt's in *In der Sache J.Robert Oppenheimer* (In the Case
of J.Robert Oppenheimer) (1964), both of which were more concerned
with political or social issues. Dürrenmatt demonstrates the limitations
of Man himself and not of just one section of the community. "A
plague o' both your houses", he is saying, as he attacks both the western and eastern forms of power politics, which, stupid in themselves,
exploit the weaknesses and stupidities of Man.[25]

In the *21 Points to The Physicists*, the author stressed the para-
doxicality of the plot. It was paradoxical (and not "absurd": *Point* 10),
because physicists, of all people, must be logical planners:

> Men who plan want to reach a particular goal. Chance strikes them
> hardest when it makes them reach the opposite of their goal: What
> they feared, what they sought to avoid (e.g. Oedipus).   (*Point* 9).

Dürrenmatt invites us therefore to laugh at the classical theatre's
attempt to present "Fate" as an "iron necessity". There is no such Fate
nowadays, he had claimed earlier in *The Breakdown*, only Chance
(above, p.30).[26] The mention of "Oedipus" above suggested parody,
and the classical concept of "Fate" is in fact parodied in Dürrenmatt's
concept of "Chance". So, is parody a "comic element" here?

★   ★   ★

The three unities are demanded in the long stage-direction which acts
as an introduction to the book-version. The author's careful description
of beautiful "Nature" outside the asylum "Les Cerisiers" (– one thinks
involuntarily of Swiss *Kirsch*! –), contrasts comically with the one
room of the "ruined" villa. More important still, it contrasts with the
pseudo-classical theory of the Unities because the theory is being
employed only because the action takes place in an asylum: ". . . only
classical form is suitable for a plot which takes place among madmen"
(p.288), a self-parody of Dürrenmatt's by then famous dictum: "Only
the *Komödie* can reach us now" (*TP*, p.48).

We are surely being asked to laugh at this elaborate "classical"
structure which will end, not like the old Oedipus legend, in "tragedy",
but in "comedy".[27]

The unities are certainly observed. The action takes place in one
room, a room in which the chimney is "useless" and the "torn" furni-
ture represents "different ages" (one thinks of the room in *Mississippi*).
The décor here is, again, a visual joke, a visible parody. The comic

conflict is between the idealism of classical order and the realism or reality of our disordered times.

The plot is concentrated on one action, without sub-plots, and is played out in the time that it would take in reality. Yet, just as the "place" is a parody, so too are the "action" and the "time".

When Act II begins, we suddenly realize that we are watching a repeat of the beginning of Act I, but, as it were, through a mirror, a reversal of "the real thing":

Dr von Zahnd: A Havanna?
Inspector: No, thanks.
. . . .
Dr von Zahnd: A brandy?
Inspector: Later. (p.325)

Where in Act I, the matron had asked the Inspector if he would have tea: "I'd prefer a brandy", was his reply. He had had to put his cigar out and his enquiries about the "murderers" and the "murder" were quietly but firmly corrected to "assailant" and "accident" (p.291). In Act II, however, the doctor is similarly corrected by the Inspector (p.236).

The Unity of Time is parodied by placing the action at "shortly after half past four in the afternoon". This means that Act II takes place in "Romantic" darkness rather than in "Classical" daytime — and it will be seen that Act I, rather than Act II, is the "untragic" one. Likewise, the month is carefully given as "November" (p.289), the autumnal month often favoured by Dürrenmatt in his works, and here a dying season for a dying (i.e. unclassical) culture.

The "three Unities" have another significance; it has been pointed out that three objects often have a comic significance. In *The Physicists*, the use of the number itself becomes hyperbolically comical. There are the three unities; there are three scientists, each with "tripartite" names — in one case, doubled; there were three nurses; there are three children, also with "tripartite" names; Fräulein von Zahnd has three ancestors of whom there are three portraits; there are three male attendants; Möbius announces three physical theories; there are three deaths; the play begins three months after the last death; Frau Rose remarried three weeks before the play begins and, at the very end of the play, Möbius repeats the key word to the play, "Solomon", ("Salomo") three times. *And* there are 21 Points, the "magic" 7 times the "holy" 3![28]

In an angry article, Peter Wilker, a physicist, attacked Dürrenmatt for his failure "to go more deeply into these so important questions".

The author had committed, it seemed, the cardinal sin of mentioning the "unitary theory of elementary particles" and the "theory of gravitation" separately; a sin, "for it is the very point of the first theory that it subsumes the second".[29] It seems to have escaped the writer of the article that the three physicists of the play are parodies of the profession. Dürrenmatt has been interested in the natural sciences since childhood and has more than a layman's knowledge of science. These portrayals must therefore be seen as "comic elements", since not only are physicists parodied, but also the whole concept of "classical" physics, of the real Newton's "To every action there is an equal and opposite reaction". The Law of Cause and Effect is parodied, too. This concept depends on an "absolute causality", as Dürrenmatt put it in our conversation. But "Chance is a physical concept which has become very important nowadays, just when the implementation of causality on a world scale is no longer possible", he continued. And it is Chance which predominates in this play. *Point* 15 runs: "The art of the dramatist consists in using Chance as effectively as possible in the plot" — and it is Chance which makes the characters into parodies of physicists — and therefore comical.

                         *   *   *

Walter Kerr wrote in his *Tragedy and Comedy*: "The sign of the ampersand always suggests comedy". Comedy has certainly insisted upon gregariousness. Buffoon characters are rarely alone; short goes with tall, fat with thin. It is too fanciful to see "Einstein" and "Newton" in this light? Are they not a "comic duo"?

All theatre-goers will make a mental association with the names Newton-Einstein. When "Newton" first appears "in a costume of the early 18th century" (p.293), the audience will laugh, because, in Kantian terminology, the "expectation will dissolve into nothing" when his first words are in modern, colloquial German; the costume or "disguise" clashes incongruously with the banal, functional language and the bare functional and modern room.[30]

Our "aural" introduction to "Einstein" is similarly comical. Since curtain-rise, the audience has been listening to an amateur performance of the Beethoven *Kreutzer* sonata for violin and piano played by the "new" murderer, Ernesti, and Dr von Zahnd. When she finally enters, she describes the great physicist: "He threw himself down on the bed and fell asleep. Like a contented kid . . . I was afraid that he was going to insist on playing the Brahms D minor as well".[31] The Inspector had just recalled that, three months previously, Dr von Zahnd had had to calm "Newton" by playing chess with him after *his* murderous attack. A comic ambience has been created.

The scene between the Inspector and Beutler might convince us that the latter was actually mad. Beutler speaks in the illogical, disconnected way associated with the mentally deranged; he asks the Inspector if it would disturb him if he (Beutler) smoked? Inspector Voss pulls out his cigar case to join him. Beutler says: "Only the patients, not the visitors, are allowed to smoke in here. Otherwise the whole room would be contaminated" (p.294). He then asks Voss if it would disturb him if he (Beutler) had a glass of cognac? The stage-direction reads: "Newton fetches a bottle of brandy and one glass from behind the chimney piece". He pours himself out a glass: "Your health". "*Your* health", retorts the Inspector sourly.

The banality of this "asylum-talk" surprisingly disturbed many critics; "superficial and terse" was a Romanian opinion.[32] Surely, however, Dürrenmatt was trying to lure his audience into comedy's "mouse-trap", of which he had written in the *Problems* (*TP*, p.50). The revelation in Act II that the pair are actually scientists, and secret agents to boot, will make all the greater contrast. Secondly, it is a satirical reference to the absurd rôle that these two characters, whether they be Beutler or Ernesti, Kilton or Eisler, have to play in order to carry out their real tasks.

Thus, it will be seen that these characters are professional clowns. They even wear masks, the masks of madness, which, in the style of Pirandello's Enrico IV, they drop, only to find that Life will not permit them to go maskless. Their rôle in Act II is also clownish. After the pantofarcical scene with the revolvers, they are forced to agree to Möbius' terms and they agree to remain masked in madness for ever. Their plans have failed, (although Möbius believes that *he* has triumphed). They are thus made to look doubly foolish when they are unmasked for the second time by Dr von Zahnd and return to their rooms, "mad" but not "wise", "prisoners" and not "free" (p.344).

These are the puppet-like lackeys of the power-politicians of both sides of the Curtain. Science is a question of expediency. Kilton has offered Möbius freedom to work for the defence of his country; Eisler has offered him freedom to work for the benefit of the Party. Möbius mocks both offers of "freedom" by choosing to stay – truly "free" – in an asylum. "It at least gives me the certainty of not being exploited by politicians" (p.341).

Seen from this point of view, Kilton and Eisler are as much lacking in humanity, are as "automatic", as the three attendants who *are* buffoons. *Their* murders are carried out at the command of their political paymasters because their nurses had discovered their secrets. It is therefore doubly comical and ironical when Dr von Zahnd tells the pair at the end that she had "made" the nurses do what they did: "You were as predictable as automata and you murdered like executioners" (p.349). Obsessed by their political affiliations, robbed of their humanity by their murders, they are finally "driven out" of normal human society.

★   ★   ★

The buffoons in the play however are Möbius' family and the three attendants. The former group offers a comic vignette, compounded of farce, wit and satire. Oskar Rose is a comic type — Dürrenmatt's favourite butt, the sanctimonious clergyman in whom there is more than a touch of hypocrisy. There is a comic incongruity between his cloth and his six children and in Frau Rose's ambiguous remarks: "Oskar isn't very robust" . . . and "Oskar is a passionate father"! (p.307).

Frau Rose makes herself a comic figure by her treatment of Möbius; she cuckolds him and then leaves him to his fate, for her excuses sound comically lame (cf. pp.304-307). Her possessive attitude towards her children — evidenced in the ornate, pretentious and eventually comic double-barrelled names (Adolf-Friedrich, Wilfried-Kaspar and Jörg-Lukas) shows a comic sentimentality, as does her constant use of the ridiculous diminutive "Johann Wilhelmlein" for the distinguished physicist. This scene must not be played to gain sympathy for the family — that is why it is comic. They must be made to look ridiculous, the audience must laugh at them, since the dramaturgical point of the scene is to allow Möbius to drive them away (for their own good) by reciting his fearsome psalm "The Song of Solomon to be sung to the cosmonauts" (pp.313/4).[33]

The male attendants are a classical trio of buffoons. Uwe Sievers is the "top clown", the other two carry out his every command, but all three are ruled like puppets by Dr von Zahnd. Their rôle is to provide a comic preparation for von Zahnd's final disclosure. Since, however, there is something fearsome in their sealing-up of the room (p.336), the barking, Gestapo-like style of command, coupled with their enormous size and the silences of Murillo and the negroid McArthur, they could certainly be called "grotesque", since they had a comic function in the pantofarcical scenes (cf. pp.326-327) which, to speak with Arnold Heidsieck, had been "perverted".[34] They are now the Doctor's secret police, the modest beginning of her world-wide network (p.350).

* * *

As protagonist-antagonist, one could compare Möbius-von Zahnd with Alfred Ill-Claire; in both cases, the individualist human being is confronted by an "other-wordly" character. Does the resemblance end there? Is Möbius, like Ill, a tragic rather than a comic character, and is the significance of his rôle such that the play must be termed a tragi-comedy and not a *Komödie*? Or is he, like Romulus, only a *potentially* tragic character placed in an actual comic situation?

Point 3 states: "A story is thought through when it has taken its worst possible turn"; although students of Dürrenmatt had suspected his meaning long before, they really had to wait until the publication of *The Anabaptists* in 1967 for confirmation. There they read: "The worst possible turn that a story can take is the turn towards a *Komödie*" (*Anabaptists*, p.102. See Chapter Nine below). It was from this statement that Hans Mayer in his *Friedrich Dürrenmatt* deduced: "A story is thought through when it has taken a turn towards a *Komödie*"! (p.495). The classical peripeteia is parodied — the whole illustrates again Kant's classical statement on the comic.

Möbius shows a terrifying madness where he recites his psalm — and a sentimental tenderness when speaking to nurse Monika. When she claims to believe that King Solomon does appear to him, he knows that she loves him, since "King Solomon", the "Golden King", is Möbius' "mask". (He has kept his own name and wears no disguise).[35] But he knows, too, that she too must now die, since she has arranged for both of them to leave the asylum. This would mean that the world would demand his "system of all possible inventions" (Kirkup calls it the "principle of universal discovery"), which could destroy mankind if it were to fall into the hands of unscrupulous adventurers.

Thus there is no comic in Möbius' character; he is totally serious in Act I; he has driven his family away and has murdered the only human being who loved him. In the conversation with the Inspector, Möbius therefore tries to have himself arrested. To Möbius's serious demand, however, Dürrenmatt makes a comic response by parodying his own theme of "justice". Since all the murders have been committed by "others" ("Einstein", "Newton" and "King Solomon"), there is no one to arrest, and the Inspector can therefore do nothing. "Justice can take a holiday", he says, "a terrific feeling". He departs, the last contact with the normal world, and thus unwittingly recognizes the supernatural justice of "Les Cerisiers".

The philosophical crux of the play is the unmasking scenes (in two senses) which follow; firstly, Beutler and Ernesti reveal their true identities, and, secondly, Möbius lays bare the truth about his work, that he has discovered his awesome "Principle": ". . .new, unimaginable sources of energy will be released, making possible a technology beyond all human fantasies, if my discoveries fall into other hands" (p.338). The discussion which follows is a serious one, the significance of which is, however, greatly deepened, and the "tragic" alienated, by the farcical scene with the revolvers and the comic duo's regrets at their wasted training as linguist and musician respectively.[36]

Möbius now refuts Dürrenmatt's claim in his review of Jungk's book: "We must take back our knowledge and I have taken it back" (p.342), he says. This is the key passage in the discussion, since it is this statement which wins the others over to his way of thinking. It is also a key passage in Dürrenmatt's works, since his character Möbius is (like Romulus) refusing to "mitmachen", to say Yes to the possibility of evil. The theme of Man's freedom runs like a gold thread through the works up to and including the eponymous *Der Mitmacher (The Man who never said: No!).*

When Möbius then adds that the pair should be treated outside the asylum as murderers, they can only agree to stay with him:

> Either these were sacrificial killings or they were murders. Either we stay in the asylum or the world will become one. Either we eradicate ourselves from the memory of mankind or mankind itself will be eradicated (p.343).,

says Möbius. The play would seem to be proceeding to a rational solution. This "first ending" seems to be a rational, logical solution reached by rational, logically-thinking men. By burning his manuscripts and persuading the only two people left who know his secrets to remain in an asylum with him, Möbius has saved the world from the consequences of his invention. Yet, interestingly enough, just as he said of himself: "I chose the Fool's cap", he now says to the others: "Give us the strength as *madmen* to guard faithfully the secret of our knowledge" (p.344) where, in both cases, the word "Narr" (fool) is used (as Möbius believes) in a literal sense; only when Dr von Zahnd upturns events in the parodistic version of the tragic *anagorisis* does the word become ambiguous and is used in *our* sense of "Fool" — or "clown". It seems to me to justify our line of approach to Dürrenmatt.

This "first ending" is therefore a "Happy Ending" (or "rational solution"); when Einstein is called out of his room by the attendants, he, like the other two, is "transfigured" and mutters blissfully: "The problems are silent, the questions speak no more" (p.346) — we are about to learn however that the "problems" and the "questions" have not been solved or answered — that there is, indeed, *no* solution. . .

★   ★   ★

Before continuing this argument, before indeed looking at the "second ending", I should like to examine the character of Fräulein Dr von Zahnd to see how the author deals with yet another major female rôle.

Von Zahnd is what I should call a typical Dürrenmattian female character, an Anastasia, a Claire, an Ottilie, a dominant personality with a streak of cold-blooded fanaticism. The masculinity in the character may be explained by a remark of Therese Giehse that the rôle was originally a man's.[37] That it was specially rewritten for her does not seem to be true, but her longing to play Richard III may even have decided Dürrenmatt to give the character a hump. (She is ". . .hunchbacked, about 55") (p.298). The deformity has the same function as Claire's artificial limbs — both help to remove the owner from the limitations of the normal world. When the time comes in Act II, the hump lends an air of fearsome strangeness to the character.

Thus von Zahnd becomes, like Claire, a Fate goddess, literally removed from the normal world in her isolated sanatorium and from the living stream by being the last member of her family — her relations have all died in the sanatorium. It is miraculous that she is "relatively normal", she tells the Inspector. Here, the audience may laugh at what seems to be a comic paradox; they are soon to learn the grim meaning behind the words (p.302).

To the Communist world, von Zahnd is of course the "representative of western imperialism" and one of the sources of laughter is indeed the satire on the decadent bourgeoisie of the western world. Her sanatorium caters for "all the mentally disturbed élite of half of the western world" (p.288).[38] Her name would remind Swiss audiences of

the great Bernese patrician families of the past — families which
Dürrenmatt had mocked already in the figure of von Schwendi in
The Judge and His Executioner[39] — and the Doctor's family ancestors
can be seen as a "comic trio" — her grandfather, General Leonidas,[40]
her father, Geheimrat (Councillor) August, an economist, and finally
Uncle Joachim, a politician. One can see that a character with such
forebears must be both despicable and comic in Dürrenmatt's eyes!

Nevertheless, a good deal of the wit comes from the Doctor, in
Act I at any rate. Most of it is "voluntary", that is, the character is
made purely comical. One has, as yet, no reason to suspect ambiguities.
Von Zahnd tells the Inspector that Newton does not really believe that
he is Newton after all. "Are you sure?" asks the Inspector. "*I* decide
who my patients think they are", she replies (p.299), which is to be
significant later, when we learn that she controlled the three men as
if they had been automata (above p.138).[41]

The comic in the character is too pronounced, however, and the
fearsome too melodramatic for the character to be a true grotesque.
It does not ring true, as Claire did, but remains, for me, merely
"ridiculous". Claire gave the watchers the impression of a Clotho, a
Medea, from her very first appearance. This "avenging goddess" *must*
be played as normal however — her "mask" is her normality, and, for
this reason, the elements of the comic in the character are of enormous
importance. Through them, the recognition-scene becomes dramatically
more effective. Deformity is often a sign of comedy — and it might be
so here — but, for the sharp of sight, the hump is the clue to the
criminal in this "criminal *Komödie*".

*   *   *

So let us return now to the "second ending"; Von Zahnd's "unmasking"
as a true madwoman who has photocopied all Möbius' secrets, by
means of which she will now rule the world, makes a fine *coup de
théâtre*;[42] it is also a justification for *Point* 9. These physicists set out
to avoid a fate; Chance has driven them into it. "Everything was
planned", chuckled Dürrenmatt to me over a drink, "and then they
went into the wrong asylum!"[43]

This aspect of the conclusion makes Möbius' description of himself
as a "fool", ambiguous. It now bears my meaning; he has become a
"Fool", a spiritual clown, like Romulus, a victim of Chance. That a

superior intelligence, a man who bears the destiny of the world in his hands, should be outwitted by the mere chance of choosing the wrong sanatorium (of all those available in Switzerland of all countries!) is highly comical. It proves once again the frailty and fallibility of Man.

Can we say, then, that Möbius is one of the "eiron"-figures of our *Komödien*? Can we call him a "valiant man"?

Madler suggests (and Strelka agrees) that he is, although only to a certain degree, while Oberle, on the other hand, can see in this play "no longer any tired, humbled heroes . . . only failures". Here again, Brecht crosses Dürrenmatt's path. There is nothing easier than to claim that *The Physicists* is a borrowing from Brecht. Yet Dürrenmatt's physicists inhabit a world light years removed from Brecht's. They inhabit a world which has seen carnage and destruction on a scale undreamt of by Brecht when he began to write *Galileo* in 1937 and even when he finished the third version in 1947. Dürrenmatt's characters and their fates do not point to a bright new tomorrow where all present wrongs will be righted, but rather view the world realistically, for they cannot envisage a dramatic change in human nature.[44] Like Arthur Koestler, I believe that the "light" has failed too often in the past sixty years, and that Dürrenmatt has interpreted Brecht in particular, and Communist doctrine in general, in eminently realistic terms.

For reasons such as these, I would suggest that the point of the play is to be found in the satirical portrayal of the characters of "Newton" and "Einstein". They are the irresponsible members of the physicists' profession who have sold their birthright, their *freedom*, to the politicians and the corrupting power of money. As Dürrenmatt wrote in the review of the Jungk book: "Knowledge was afraid of Power and therefore gave itself up to 'those in power' ". This is why they are portrayed as clowns, puppets dangling from their political masters' strings. Möbius, however, is a "valiant man", since he has discarded these alazon-characteristics, has tried to remain free, to "stand up and say: No!" It is paradoxically comical that his reason should tell him that the best way to do this is to immure himself in an asylum. Nevertheless, in his "Song of Solomon" and in his last speech, where he foresees the awful consequences of Man's abdication of his responsibilities and of his freedom, Möbius, although a Fool and a clown, represents the "hope" for the human race; in the same way, Beutler/Eisler and Fräulein von Zahnd represent the dangers — the first, the irresponsibility, selfishness and stupidity inherent in us all — the second the warning-made-flesh of the possible consequences of such behaviour.[45]

This is the meaning behind *Points* 17 and 18: "What concerns all of us, can only be solved by all of us", and "Any attempt by the individual to solve for himself what concerns everybody must fail". These are paradoxical comments; Möbius *had* acted as an individual and had failed — the time for heroes was past; and yet, only if all men act like this individual, can we succeed in having the courage to "endure" this world, with all its dangers. Werner has quite misunderstood the play when he suggests that it portrays the *failure* of communal effort — none of Dürrenmatt's plays would give such a definite, unequivocal solution. They present a conflict — the warning is given, but not the solution. That is our concern.[46]

                          ★   ★   ★

Dürrenmatt was not trying to solve a world problem here but to present a human conflict — that conflict was the dilemma of modern science, "that man has not kept step, morally speaking, with the development of his thinking, neither of his scientific nor of his philosophical thinking", as Dürrenmatt put it to Sauter in 1966. By means of such a paradoxical *Komödie*, Dürrenmatt felt that he could "trick the audience into facing reality . . ." (*Point* 21). The elements of the comic in the play are there to provoke and startle the audience into considering the issues presented and to see that the problem is an enduring one which will always be with us and which each succeeding generation must tackle — or fall. It is the privilege and responsibility of being human *and* free.

Möbius' end is "neither tragic nor even just successful", as Hans Mayer phrased it;[47] he is certainly a *potentially* tragic character, but the comic situation around him, both physically comical, (in the panto-farcical scenes), and philosophically comical, (because of the paradoxical workings of Chance[48], make him finally into the comic character of a Dürrenmatt agonistic *Komödie*, just as the outrages of Man against Man make Beutler and Eisler into professional clowns.[49]

Yet, despite the seeming pessimism of the conclusion, Dürrenmatt has justified his statement to Jean-Paul Weber: Having mentioned Ernst Bloch's famous work *The Principle Hope* (*Prinzip Hoffnung*), in which "la réalité et la pensée sont pleines d'espoir", Dürrenmatt said of his theatre: "C'est précisément le théâtre de l'espoir absurde, de l'espérance injustifiable, de l'invincible espoir . . . j'espère contre toute espérance",[50] and, he was to add much later, *that* hope is the "possibility of freedom" (*DMMK*, p.178). How could such a writer be called a nihilist?

NOTES TO CHAPTER SIX

(i) FRANK DER FUNFTE (FRANK THE FIFTH)

1. *Richtlinien der Regie* (*Guidelines to the production*), the note to the text in *KII*, pp.281-282. The first version was produced by Oskar Wälterlin at the Schauspielhaus Zürich on 20.4.59; a slightly altered version received simultaneous premières in Munich and Frankfurt on 10.8.60. This version, with slight alterations, was published as *Frank der Fünfte: Oper einer Privatbank: Musik von Paul Burkhard*: Arche 1960. This is the "Buchausgabe" (Book edition). The "Textbuch" was published by the Musikverlag und Bühnenvertrieb Zürich (with the music) in 1960. The so-called *Bochumer Fassung* (1964): *Eine Komödie mit Musik von Paul Burkhard* is our text, in *KII*, pp.197-282. (= *FV*). cf. "After four weeks of rehearsals, the performance was prevented by Hans Schalla, the Bochum theatre manager", writes the author in *KII*, p.281. This version was never played.
   The British première (in a translation by James Kirkup) was given by the Theatr Yr Ymylon (The Welsh Actors' Company) on 18.10.77 in the Sherman Theatre, Cardiff, during Dürrenmatt's visit to Wales to receive the Welsh Arts Council's International Writers' Prize. It was a "swinging musical on a highly topical theme" said the programme.
   A TV version was shown on West Germany's First Programme on 16.2.67. See FAZ of 18.2.67.

2. cf. H.Rischbieter: *Dürrenmatts dünnstes Stück*: Theater Heute 1, No.3, 1960, pp.8-12, and J.Kaiser: *Friedrich Dürrenmatts singende Mörder*, SDZ, 21/23.3.59.

3. H.Weigel: *Dürrenmatts "Frank V"*: illustrierte Kronenzeitung, Wien, 28.1.62.

4. H.Mayer: *Brecht und die Folgen* in *Bertolt Brecht und die Tradition*, dtv, 1965, p.119. Elsewhere he wrote that *Frank V* was "a new functioning of the Brecht theme". cf *Friedrich Dürrenmatt*, op.cit., p.488.

5. *Friedrich Schiller: Eine Rede*, Arche 1960, p.8. In my conversations with him, he said; "In '43 when I started to write, Brecht wasn't all that important. I was too far on for his influence to be so great", while in his conversation with Fringeli in 1977 he claimed that he met Brecht twice and spoke to him at great length — about cigars! On Dürrenmatt and Brecht, see too E.Diller: *Human dignity in a materialistic society; Friedrich Dürrenmatt and Bertolt Brecht*, MLQ, Vol.25, 1964, pp.451-460.

6. E.Vietta (ed.): *5. Darmstädter Gespräche — Theater, 1955*, Neue Darmstädter Verlagsanstalt, 1955, pp.276-277. Brecht's letter is the foreword to the abbreviated edition of his *Schriften zum Theater*, Suhrkamp, 1957, Band 41. Dürrenmatt's view has always been that *human nature* and not the *institutions* will have to change — or be changed. Still, he added later, changing the institutions would help (*Gespräch 1971* in *TSR II*, p.276). See too: "Of course, the world can be changed. That's a platitude — the world changes itself!" (In *GHLA*, p.77). In the Düsseldorf *Note to the Portrait of a Planet* (1971), he wrote: "There will be no change in human society without a change in mankind" and repeated this in *Der Mitmacher-Komplex* in 1976 (p.141).

7. See too his criticism of the USA in *Sätze aus Amerika* (*Sentences from America*), Arche 1970, and on the USSR system of government in his short Novelle *Der Sturz* (*The Downfall*), Arche 1971. During Dürrenmatt's visit to the USSR in June 1974, Professor Samarin, in a speech, compared Dürrenmatt with Brecht: Dürrenmatt was a "critic of capitalist society indeed, but where Dürrenmatt came from a world full of danger and was therefore pessimistic — though not a nihilist since he believed in Man — Bertolt Brecht comes from a world of security and therefore could believe in the future". (Die Tat, 24.4.64).

8. W.Hinck: *Von Brecht zu Handke*, Universitas, Vol.24, 1969, pp.689-702, here p.695. Dürrenmatt's later remarks on Brecht in *Aspects of dramaturgical thinking* in *TSR II* seem to agree with Hinck's analysis.
9. J.Kaiser: *Freud und Leid des mordenden Managers*, SDZ, 20.10.60. The Burkhard songs are likewise very much in the Weill or Dessau manner. Therese Giehse (who played Ottilie) has recorded two of them on a cassette *Therese Giehse spricht Dürrenmatt und Brecht*, Heliodor 3321 011 (1967/68). The songs are far removed from Burkhard's great "hit" "O mein Papa" from his *Feuerwerk* (1950)! Dürrenmatt had praised Burkhard's music as early as 1952 in a review *Kleine Niederdorfer Oper* (Weltwoche 11.1.52).
10. Dürrenmatt turned on his critics in his *Münchner Rede 1963 (An Stelle eines Nachworts: An die Kritiker Frank des Fünften)* (*In place of an epilogue: To the critics of FV*) in *TSR I*, pp.347-352.
11. Or as he put it later in *Der Mitmacher*: "He who dies no longer needs to say Yes!" (Wer stirbt, macht nicht länger mit) (*DMM*, p.167).
12. Review of 1.6.59. cf. too J.Keller-Senn: *Friedrich Dürrenmatt: Ein christlicher Dichter*? Neue Zürcher Nachrichten 20.11.59. Dürrenmatt "puts all the pseudo-powers in the pillories in his *Komödien*". R.Stickelberger in *Frank V: Dürrenmatts jüngstes Stück* in Reformatio, VII Jg, Heft 4, April 1959, pp.239-242, reminds that the Zürich première took place on Palm Sunday!
13. Were it not for the evidence of Dürrenmatt's 30 years of happy marriage, with three children, Peter, Ruth and Barbara, one would take him for a misogynist. Think of: Julia (*RDG*), Anastasia (*EHM*), Claire (*BAD*), Ottilie (*FV*), von Zahnd (*DP*), Auguste (*DM*), Blanka/Konstanze (*KJ*), Alice (*PS*), Tamora (*TA*), the four harpies (*PEP*), and the whole ghastly "woman's lib." concept of *The Waiting Period* (1977)!
14. E.Brock-Sulzer: *FD*, op.cit., p.104 and J.Müller: *Max Frisch und Friedrich Dürrenmatt*, op.cit., p.737. H.Rischbieter thought it quite tactless, op.cit., p.8.
15. *Münchner Rede*, p.351. The name Frank, although common enough in Switzerland, adds to the hypocritical nature of the character with a possible double meaning of frank = free and Swiss Frank = money. It is possibly also no coincidence that *Gottfried* Frank dies in a Swiss *Keller* (= cellar). Gottfried Keller (1819-1890) is one of the "mandarin" Swiss authors.
16. For Dürrenmatt, Oxford represents a doubtful bourgeois culture. Remember that Mississippi and Diego were educated there, too!
17. *Guidelines*, p.281 and also: "The job of illustration has been given to this pair (Egli and Frieda) and so they carry the burden of the comic in the play", NZZ 30.3.59. Throughout the work, Egli is seen as the dominating figure over the buffoons, the three clerks. These three buffoons are joined from time to time by Gaston, the "automaton" waiter – they supply the pantofarcical scenes. Egli therefore becomes the "top clown", as seen in the circus.
18. D.Daviau: *The rôle of Zufall in the writings of Friedrich Dürrenmatt*, op.cit., p.285.
19. M.Esslin: *Dürrenmatt – merciless observer*, op.cit., p.15. See also J-P.Weber: *Friedrich Dürrenmatt ou la quête de l'absurde*, where he calls the absurd "le moment poétique et cruel de notre existence", that is, the moment of rupture where logic and reality part company. In our conversation, he called the absurd "a superficial catch-phrase". Weber's article appeared in French in Le figaro littéraire on 10.9.60. (p.3).
20. *Note* to *EKB* in *KI*, p.248.
21. In his *Dramaturgie des Publikums (Dramaturgy of the audience)*, Dürrenmatt mentions that *Frank* was "tested out" in Paris before an audience of schoolteachers who sat "with stony faces" listening for the "exact pronunciation and the correct usage of grammar" rather than to the play. (*TSR II*, p.143).

(ii) DIE PHYSIKER (THE PHYSICISTS)

22. It was by far the most successful play of the 1962-1963 German season, with 1598 performances in 59 theatres. See the review of *German Drama 1945-1970* in Theater Heute, October 1970, pp.52-53, and M.Patterson: *German Theatre Today* Pitman 1976, pp.114-117. Joachim Kaiser in *Die Welt als Irrenhaus* pointed out that an "atom-drama" has no solution! (Theater Heute 4, April 1962, pp.5-7.)
23. *Gefährliches Denken*, Weltwoche 7.12.56 and in *TSR I*, pp. 272-276.
24. *Die Physiker* in *KII*, pp.283-355 (= *DP*). *21 Punkte* pp.353-355. (James Kirkup's translation was published by Samuel French. It is also in *Four Plays*, 1957-1962 Cape 1964). The première took place in the Zürich Schauspielhaus on 20.2.62 with Giehse as Von Zahnd, Blech as Möbius, Ling as Einstein and Knuth as Newton. Kurt Horwitz directed. Peter Brook's Aldwych production (RSC) with Cyril Cusack as Möbius and Irene Worth as von Zahnd on 9.1.63 was called a "splendid evening's entertainment" by Harold Hobson in the Sunday Times of 13.1.63. Levin went lyrical in the Daily Mail: (*"This* is the way the world ends, not with a whimper but a bang!"*) 10.1.63, while Tynan saw Dürrenmatt as a "Hitchcock turned prophet" (Observer 13.1.63). It opened in New York in October 1964.
25. Manfred Durzak discussed the point and concludes: "The view of the future given in Brecht's *Galileo*, that the objective future development of science is guaranteed, yields in Dürrenmatt to a feeling of complete hopelessness" (op.cit., p.17). Yet he, like other commentators, fails to appreciate Dürrenmatt's point – this is *not* a factual account – it is a "model". It is a warning of what *might* happen if mankind does not awaken to its responsibilities.
26. See too Dürrenmatt's remarks in *Sentences on the theatre* (No.34): "Chance is that which cannot be foreseen. In classical times, that was *Fate*" (p.13).
27. In the *DMMK*, however, Dürrenmatt shows how classical *Fate* could have been *Chance* and how the legend of Oedipus could have become a *Komödie*! (pp.236-274).
28. See P.Dickinson: *Chance, Luck and Destiny*, Gollancz 1975, pp.117-120.
29. P.Wilker: *Bemerkungen zu Dürrenmatts Physikern*, NZZ, 24.3.63. (He adds: "Is the clever remark more important than the thesis? "!) See to E.Brüche: *Die Physiker*, Physikalische Blätter 18, 1962, pp.169-172, particularly p.170. He likewise took umbrage!
30. W.Muschg is of course correct to point out that the costume is in fact a hint that Beutler is *not* mad, since schizophrenics do not need a disguise. In *Dürrenmatt und die Physiker*, Programme of the Schauspielhaus Zürich 1961-1962, pp.5-10. The *21 Points* (dated 13.2.62) were on pp.3-4.
31. The Kirkup translation has "the G major Sonata", but that is surely No.1 (op.78)? No.3 is in D minor (op.108). Dürrenmatt is particularly fond of Brahms.
32. Biberi in Gazeta literara, Bucharest 11.11.65, quoted in Bänziger, op.cit., p.260. Muschg remarked that asylums had never been so popular – either in fiction or reality! (cf the programme, op.cit.). Manfred Haiduk's book on Weiss reminds us too that this is because madmen, (like clowns), can speak the truth because *their* truth is not practicable, an interesting view from an East German academic: *Der Dramatiker Peter Weiss,* Henschelverlag, Berlin, 1977, p.83.

33. E.Brock-Sulzer, *FD*, p.116. The wonderfully comic pantofarcical scene where the children play their recorders is the climax to the comic portrayal of bourgeois complacency of the cuckolding Lina and the smug hypocritical Oskar, yet another Dürrenmatt attack on established religious institutions. Lehnert sees the scene differently however. For him, it is a "play of euphemisms" which pervades the whole play. In his desire to explain the device "philosophically", I believe that he misses the comic of this "possibility of the theatre". H. Lehnert: *Fiktionale Struktur und physikalische Realität*, Rice University Studies, Vol.55, No.3, 1968, pp.115-130, here pp.121-122.
34. For this reason I cannot agree with Muschg's comment that "the purely comic element appears in the attendants' scenes only" (p.10). They represent that "bruce force and ruthlessness" behind so many 20th century political decisions. See A.Taylor in *Die Physiker*, Macmillan 1966, p.101.
35. The real August Ferdinand Möbius (1790-1868) was a German astronomer. Children in our schools still play with "Möbius rings", a twisted ring with peculiar "paradoxical" qualities.
36. cf Newton: To think, for this I had to strangle a nurse and learn German.
     Einstein: While I had to learn the violin, Hell for a completely unmusical person like me (p.340).
37. cf. Giehse to Peter Wyrsch: "As a joke I offered to play Doctor Zahnd. The next day he (Dürrenmatt) had thought it over. He changed the doctor into a woman; he discovered a lot more possibilities of characterization" (Wyrsch, op.cit. 23.3.63). Dürrenmatt told Urs Jenny that this "nice anecdote" was untrue. "The change gave a decided contrast, a tension that I had been looking for for a long time") (See *Lazarus der Fürchterliche* in Theater Heute 2, February 1966, pp.10-12). The play is nevertheless dedicated to Giehse, who of course also created Ottilie, Claire and Frau Nomsen in *Der Meteor*.
38. cf Kuczynski, op.cit., p.69. See too: "They are nothing but fragments of human fates, unworthy representations of the relationships between the sexes and the denial of any sort of healthy mentality": R.J.N.Furceva of the Ministry of Culture, USSR, June 1963, quoted in F.Phillipp, op.cit. The play was not performed in the USSR again until Dürrenmatt's visit in 1964 (cf NZZ, 24.6.64).
39. Der Spiegel remarked: "Not unintentionally, the name sounds like an abbreviation of the filthy rich, bloodthirsty Zachanassian" (28.2.62, pp.65-67). The writer is far out, as I have shown. L.W.Forster adds interesting comments on the Swiss use of "von" in *DRH*, Harrap 1962 (p.133).
40. Leonidas, King of Lacedaemon (a "hero"), opposed Xerxes and his "five million men" at Thermopylae. "General" is the title used by the C-in-C of the Swiss Army, but only in times of *war*.
41. Dürrenmatt would know the remark of the virulently anti-semitic Mayor of Vienna, Karl Lueger: "Wer Jude ist, bestimme *ich*" (*I* decide who is a Jew!)
42. Indeed, Dürrenmatt was attacked for this by among others, J.Chiari in *Landmarks of Contemporary Theatre*, Jenkins, 1965, p.188.
43. Siegfried Melchinger said that Dürrenmatt had found John F.Kennedy's assassination a perfect illustration of his "thesis": Theater Heute, September 1968 (*Theater ist Theater*). Tiusanen is, of course, perfectly justified to ask: "How far does chance introduced on the stage remain chance?" (p. 282). My answer is that chance will always remain chance whether on the stage or elsewhere. (Dürrenmatt repeated this remark to H.L.Arnold in March 1975 and connected it this time with Oedipus, "going the wrong way" (p.25).)

44. Madler, op.cit., p.48. Strelka, op.cit., p.152. Brock-Sulzer hesitatingly suggests that the "valiant man" concept is cancelled out here (p.114). Oberle op.cit., p.21. See too H.Mayer in *Dürrenmatt und Brecht oder die Zurücknahme*, op.cit.; Also K.S.Weimar: *The scientist and society*, MLQ 17, 1966, pp.431-438 and U. von Massberg: *Der gespaltene Mensch*, Deutschunterricht 17, Heft 6, 1965, pp.56-74. Profitlich continually draws the distinction between the two writers: "Where Brecht's audience is continually made to reflect on the basic concrete situation but also on the social order which makes sacrifice, self-denial, even heroism necessary, the Dürrenmatt spectator concentrates his attention rather on the mentality of those who are the immediate cause of the catastrophe . . ." in *Friedrich Dürrenmatt . . .* op. cit., p.47. Werner Mittenzwei, on the other hand, sees Dürrenmatt's view as "certainly humanistic but, in the last analysis, really idealistic", in *Gestaltung und Gestalten*, Aufbau Verlag, Berlin 1969, p.269.

45. See Peter Hacks: "The contradiction between human dignity and inhuman behaviour, that is the "un-freedom" of mankind, is the main object of his satire", in *Das realistische Theaterstück*, Neue deutsche Literatur 5, 1957, Heft 10, pp.90-104, here p.97. Dürrenmatt picks up the Möbius theme of freedom again in *DMMK* describing his visit to the atomic physics centre in Geneva (CERN) in February 1974 (pp. 94-103).

46 H.G.Werner: *Friedrich Dürrenmatt — Der Moralist und die Komödie*, op.cit., p.148.

47. *Dürrenmatt und Brecht*, op.cit., p.114.

48. cf. "So not every misfortune is tragic, but only a misfortune which robs man of his support, his last all-important goal in such a way that he will stumble from now on and lose his senses. Thus the well-known remark that Chance is not tragic, that a tragic happening must have a certain inevitability". Emil Staiger: *Grundbegriffe der Poetik*, op.cit., p.201.

    Murdoch, on the other hand, seeks to prove that Dürrenmatt's thesis in *TP* ("Tragedy presupposes guilt . . ." etc) is proved by Möbius' fate and that *DP* is in the line of *tragic* tradition. I can only disagree. (B.Murdoch: *Dürrenmatt's Physicists and the tragic tradition*: Modern Drama, 14, 3, December 1970, pp.270-275).

49. Peppard writes that it has been "sometimes overlooked in discussions of the "message" of the play . . . that the sub-title is 'A comedy in two acts' " (p.70). That indeed is the reason for the present book!

50. See too D.Daviau: "In a broader way, *Zufall* by ridding man of his own blindness which has allowed him to fall prey to materialism, may ultimately prove to be the operative principle that will produce beneficial results for mankind as a whole" (op.cit., p.293).

Chapter Seven

AN HELVETIC INTERLUDE

HERKULES UND DER STALL DES AUGIAS
(Hercules and the Augean Stables) (1963)

In my conversation with Dürrenmatt, he was ready to admit that, of all his works to date, "probably *Hercules* is the most satirical". He added that "the setting doesn't need to be Switzerland", but that "I was thinking of Switzerland". It was certainly this "purposive comic", the elements of satire in the work, which caused active commentators on the writer's work (such as Siegfried Melchinger) to call him "our Helvetic Aristophanes", and Frau Brock-Sulzer to write: "This work above all showed Dürrenmatt how difficult it is today to be a country's Aristophanes – and not only in Switzerland".[1]

The *weakness* of the satire and the comic, on the other hand, was one of the reasons for the play's rejections by many critics. Dürrenmatt told me: ". . .Now *Hercules*. . .the Swiss didn't like that very much". One of the most savage Swiss critics was Philipp Wolff-Windegg in the *Basler Nachrichten* who began by calling the play "an uncommonly stupid play", and went on: "If stones could blush, then the fact that this play was premièred within its not uncelebrated walls should make the Zürich Schaupielhaus glow like a tomato".[2] Indeed, the adjective "stupid" summed up most of the hostile criticisms of the work: This was Dürrenmatt's most "unintellectual" play to date. It intensified the strife between critics who demanded a "message" and a writer whose prime purpose, with this work above all, was to create a "festival play". Relations between Dürrenmatt and some Swiss critics have been very strained since *Hercules*.

The germ of the *Komödie* is to be found in the so-called *Ur-Herkules* ("First" Hercules) which was the plan for the radio-play of 1954 and which in turn was widely performed by amateur companies throughout Switzerland, the author told me. He had also broadcast a Swiss-German version and recorded a (Bernese-accented) shortened version of the radio-play. The *Komödie* had its première in Zürich on 20-22 March, 1963; Hercules was played by Knuth and Augias by Schröder. The much-discussed set of "brown brocade", symbolizing the dung, was by

Dürrenmatt's favourite designer, Teo Otto. The play was produced by Leonhard Steckel.[3]

Why was the critical reception so hostile? One reason was advanced above: Frau Brock-Sulzer felt that the predominantly urban audience at the première was disturbed by the "country air" in the work and since the normally anti-Dürrenmatt *Bund* of Berne found it a "very funny play", perhaps one could suggest that a closer acquaintance with the ubiquitous "dung heaps" of the Emmental is indeed necessary to appreciate this *Komödie?!*

My own belief, however, is that Dürrenmatt annoyed his Swiss critics with his provocative use of the satirical elements; true satire hurts. It is one of Meredith's "powers of laughter" which drive into the "quivering sensibilities" and is a source of laughter only for the non-involved. Swift's assessment of the English as "the most pernicious race of little odious vermin that nature ever suffered to crawl upon the surface of the earth" is particularly amusing to non-Englishmen — just as Dürrenmatt's assessment of Switzerland: "There you lie, my country, ridiculous, and we can cross you with two or three strides" — is particularly amusing to non-Swiss.[4]

*   *   *

The Dürrenmattian Hercules is an "unheroic failure"; the first four "labours" set by Eurystheus found him wanting, and he undertakes the cleansing of the Augean stables only because Augias mistakenly believes that Hercules' title, "the Cleanser of Greece", refers to physical cleansing, whereas it refers, of course, to his moral outlook. The première version ended with Augias showing his son Phyleus how to make humus out of the dung which had engulfed them and Elis and thus create a world worth living in. Wolff-Windegg found this ending "a little gratuitous self-edification", while Voser called it "school-masterly didacticism" (NZZ 22.3.63). Dürrenmatt answered such criticisms with one of his favourite ploys, a "second ending", where Phyleus rejects his father's "Voltairean" solution and sets off, sword in hand, to meet, and, we know, to be killed by Hercules.[5]

Dürrenmatt's admiration for Aristophanes has been frequently mentioned in this study. With the possible exception of *Angel*, no work is more Aristophanic than *Hercules*. As we have seen, all of Dürrenmatt's plays have contained elements of the Attic Old Comedy;

the characters have resembled the types; the structural elements have
harked back to the farcical effects of the *mimus* or the later *commedia
dell'arte*, and the language has been full of the typical Aristophanic
pun, paradox and irony.

Like so many of Aristophanes' works, *Hercules*, too, is intended
to be an agonistic comedy, a conflict of characters. Hercules, the
powerful interloping antagonist, faces Augias, the mild, self-deprecating
protagonist. The conflict never develops, however, since Augias' rôle
is too insignificant, compared with that of Hercules, who, as
Dürrenmatt once said of himself, is a "child of nature".[6] He is the
swaggering alazon-type, who comes in from afar, upsets the community
and is driven out.

From Scene 2 on, it becomes obvious that this is not the heroic
Hercules of Greek mythology, but rather the lampooned Hercules of
later ages.[7] The immediate comic is in the parody of the labours of
Hercules; Polybius, Hercules' secretary, tells us of his master's misfortunes as he tried to carry out the labours:

> The Nemean Lion whose weight decided the fee turned out to be
> a dwarf Balkan mountain-lion, the giant Hydra sank into the
> Lernaean swamps and the Ceryneian Hind streaked away, never to
> be seen again. . .

This Hercules, plagued with "chance" misfortunes, does not carry
out Eurystheus' twelve labours to achieve god-hood, but to pay off his
debts to his banker Eurystheus (in legend, Hercules' bitter rival), his
pawnbroker Epaminondas (the "frugal" hero of Thebes), his
architect Aias (= Ajax!) and his tailor Leonidas (the "hero" of Thermopylae), all names with classical "heroic" associations, here comically
"reduced".

At the outset, Hercules, the "great", along with the concept of the
"hero", are similarly reduced in a classically comic way. All these
comic types have had an obsession, an *idée fixe*, the vain pursuance
of which has made them look ridiculous. So too Hercules; his
obsession, his dominating characteristic, is his desire to use his fabulous
strength — but he is always frustrated. His plans to divert the two
streams, Alpheus and Peneus, and thus to "cleanse" the kingdom
come to nought because of the refusal of the various authorities to
give him permission; his renowned sexual exploits are shown never to
have taken place. The slave Cambyses (in legend, the King of Persia!)
has to satisfy the women of Elis who creep to Hercules' tent every
night.

The hyperbolical comic is used to ridicule the heroic; where a hero is expected to do the impossible, Hercules is baffled:

> I stumped through fearful swamps, I crossed dreadful passes,
> between heaven-storming peaks, clambered over gigantic cow-
> pats, chasing away millions of clucking hens, dung-beetles in my
> beard and my body covered with flies. . .

These hyperboles suggest a being out of control, a lack of balance,
which, given the untragic ambience, makes the character comic. There
is a clownish quality here. Indeed, in the play, Hercules is literally
reduced from hero to clown. In the *Ur-Herkules*, Dürrenmatt wrote:
"The productive force, capable of civilizing the country, was degraded
to a clown" (op.cit. p.7). Tantalus, the circus-director, a "miles
gloriosus" figure, engages the out-of-work Hercules as a weight-lifter
in the belief "that circus life as well as hero-worship has reached its
nadir" (p.402); when Tantalus makes off "in night and fog" (p.421)
with the takings, leaving them all in deepest penury, Hercules is seen
to have been duped as well. His life's failures, measured in parody
against the successes of the mythical hero, make him ridiculous.

It seems that the love of two women might nevertheless save this
character from complete absurdity. When Iole declares her love for
him, Hercules in turn mocks the myth of heroism: "I am a monster
like those saurians that I dispose of in the swamps. Their time has
gone and so has mine — I only rarely succeed in being a human being..."
(p.410). What separates him from other men is the cause of his
obsession; his desire to be strong, or, in other, more modern terms, to
"have power". Thus, Hercules *and* the heroic myth are anachronisms.

His plans for the two women in his life go comically awry as well.
Iole follows him to the end and her action precipitates the "tragedy"
which will follow this "satyr play". Deianira, Hercules' wife, will be
consumed with jealousy and, in attempting to regain Hercules' love,
will give him the poisoned tunic of Nessus which, paradoxically, will
bring about his death.

When Dürrenmatt attempts to make the audience laugh out of a
feeling of superiority over this absurd character and uses it as a butt
of his attack on the concept of the hero, he is following Aristophanes
in his reducing of the great. In *The Birds*, Aristophanes' Heracles has
"the build of a wrestler and an appetite to match". William Arrowsmith,
the American translator of Aristophanes, wrote: "Herakles, it should
be noted, does *not* in the original speak a dialect at all, but his hungry
lowbrow character seemed to me to require conventional treatment,
and I accordingly arranged it". When one listens to Dürrenmatt's
"Bernese" version of the radio-play, one realizes that the Swiss author

is striving after the same effect.

Is Hercules a *true* comic alazon-character however? Is he an impostor unable to carry out his promises? I believe so. The "proof" might be found in the conversation with Augias in the milking-shed (Scene 9), when the latter reminds Hercules that it was he who accepted the commission to cleanse Elis. The audience know that the "hero" was obliged to accept the commission, not because he was a hero, but to pay off his growing debts, unheroically accumulated. Yet even a hero is unable to combat the strangling power of bureaucracy. Hercules therefore fails – for the fifth time – and is in this sense an "impostor".

Pestalozzi saw Hercules (with Kurrubi) as examples of the Biblical verse: "And the light shineth in the darkness and the darkness comprehendeth it not".[8] That is valid as a "Christian" interpretation, but it seems to me to miss the point of the *comic* characterization of Hercules. Indeed, the citizens do fail to seize the opportunity of having their country cleansed of "dung" – but the author is trying to show that the heroic use of individual strength is no longer the way to solve these problems – *all* will have to participate and *all* work together in order to reshape the country. The great Leader, whether he be a "Führer" or an Imperial general, is outmoded.

*   *   *

If Dürrenmatt's Hercules is the impostor, then Augias is the man who triumphs, in his self-deprecating way. The comic plot is motivated by Augias' initial and innocent misunderstanding of Hercules' title, the "Cleanser of Greece". "Cleansing and dung-clearing are the same", Augias tells the Council (p.375) – a superb Dürrenmattian "Einfall"! (Swiss audiences would no doubt recognize in Augias' peasant-like manner and contrasting social position the only lightly-concealed figure of the wealthy farmer, Minger, who worked his way up to the office of Federal President).

Augias' innocence throughout the work makes him appear a "fool", but Dürrenmatt is careful to present him as a "holy fool", one of those who do good silently and inconspicuously, even though they may suffer for it, for, although Augias seems to be presented to us as the leader of the buffoons, (the "Chorus of Parliamentarians"), it is he who tries to bring reason into their irrationalities. It is he who shows that the

"Chief Cleansers", those Führer-characters who "clear the dung away radically", can become a danger to society: "History teaches us that it's the Chief Cleansers who remain", he says (p.374).

Nevertheless, Augias' physical limitations are symbolized by the acceptance of the inevitable consequences of human blindness and folly at the end of the farcical debate (Scene 12): "The dung is growing, we've come too late" (p.415). He does however suggest a rational solution to his son, Phyleus: "It is a bad time in which one can do so little for the world, but this little we should all do – our own thing..." (p.248). In the context of the play, it means turning dung into humus, and Phyleus is told to do this "not as someone contented, but someone discontented, who spreads his discontent and so changes things in time..." Augias' words mark him out as a "valiant man" who knows that his words may go unheeded, but who continues to hope that, one day, someone will listen. Voltaire's *Candide* has a not dissimilar ending: "Puisqu'on ne peut espérer vaincre le mal universel, la seule sagesse est de cultiver notre jardin".

The "second ending" betrays Dürrenmatt's belief that the world is not yet ready to receive an unconditional message of hope; the young pair, Phyleus and Iole, will not learn; both will come to grief in their vain search for their ideal. Thus, Augias' triumph, though a hollow one, is certainly in the comic tradition – the alazon has been driven out and "unmasked" by the eiron. "The most unheroic job imaginable appears as the heroism of our age: the little gesture that costs the great self-sacrifice", writes Werner.[9] It can therefore be seen from this example how the comic tradition has been adapted into the German *Komödie*; no longer does a comedy end "with a marriage" and a "Happy Ending". In these self-conscious days, the tragic looms not far away – the comic is no longer a "poetry of escapism", but rather, as Enid Welsford wrote, "a foretaste of the truth, the fool is wiser than the humanist; and clownage is less frivolous than the deification of Humanity".[10]

*   *   *

If we might now look briefly at the "minor characters", we see that Deianira, Hercules' wife, is presented as a serious incarnation of the Greek spirit, but "according to Dürrenmatt", since she, like his other Greek beauty, Chloë, in his "prose *Komödie*", *Once a Greek*, is a former prostitute. She is an ideal, a "human being", against whom the other characters are measured and, in so far as they are found wanting, are made comical.

Polybius, Hercules' secretary, is just such a comic type, the alazon, the pedant who fails to come to terms with his world.[11] Like Dürrenmatt himself, he is an academic manqué: "I had bad luck in my exams, in Athens *and* in Rhodes" (p.368); his situation is made clown-like by the repetitive and hyperbolical comic of the disasters arising from his conflict with the physical reality of Hercules. He is a symbol of that Aristophanic tradition of the comic "slave" who is beaten and kicked. This tradition is also seen in the genuine comic "chorus", the buffoons of the play, the "Chorus of Parliamentarians" (reduced here certainly from 24 to 10). They are comic puppets who speak chorically:

Fifth Man:	But we're covered in dung.
Sixth Man:	Up to the neck. And over.
Seventh Man:	Full of filth and shit.
Eighth Man:	Drowned and stinking.
All:	Stinking . . .
. . .	
Ninth Man:	Yet we're healthy.
The Others:	But covered in dung nevertheless.
Tenth Man:	That's why we go to the temple.
The Others:	But covered in dung nevertheless.
Ninth Man:	Yet we're Greece's oldest democracy.
The Others:	But covered in dung nevertheless.
Tenth Man:	The freest people in the world.
The Others:	But covered in dung nevertheless.
Ninth Man:	We are the original Greeks.
The Others:	But covered in dung nevertheless. (pp.372-373)

"Satire is not only the commonest form of political literature, but in so far as it tries to influence public behaviour, it is the most political part of all literature", wrote Matthew Hodgart.[12] Here, Dürrenmatt is attacking those Swiss qualities formerly regarded as desirable — cleanliness, piety, respect for tradition and so on — but now regarded by some as representative rather of complacent provincial conservatism. In our conversation, Dürrenmatt said that their comic names (Pentheus von Säuliboden, Kadmos von Käsingen, Sisyphos von Milchiwil) were a "poetic marriage of the Greek and the Swiss", but the satire bites deep when we note the "inelasticity" of their characters. The "agon" in Scene 12 turns on their hypocritical and uncritical attachment to the past. The whole scene satirizes the automatic reaction, the stock response, the cliché-forming of local government officials. They are not "human", since there is no ratiocination involved in their decisions. "Thus is, was and ever shall be", is their motto, too: ":In Elisian politics/

It is never too late yet always too early" — with the final stage-direction: "Silence" (p.415).

When talking to me, Dürrenmatt called *Hercules* a "sort of description of Swiss customs", and it is certain that he meant to make a good deal out of those elements in the production which would settle the play firmly in Switzerland. For all these elements are the mechanics of the *Volkstheater*, a comic for the groundlings. In many ways, this play is Dürrenmatt's *Midsummer-Night's Dream* — the myth has replaced the fairy-tale, the Chorus of Parliamentarians the rude mechanicals, while the modern comic realism, concluding in open-ended disillusionment, has replaced the airy escapism of Shakespeare's play which ends in a marriage as befits a classical comedy.

The symbolical dung in the pantofarcical scenes with the Parliamentarians made the play what Urs Jenny suggested it should be: a child's play for adults.[13] The critic who is not prepared to share this naivety will be disappointed.

*   *   *

Was this why the play failed? Or was the reason to be found in the remark that Dürrenmatt made to that meeting of foreign authors in Zürich in 1961 — to be Swiss you need a virtue, "which we normally don't possess: namely, the ability to laugh at ourselves" (*TSR I*, p.67)? It is true that Switzerland comes off badly on all counts in the work: Augias describes Elis' weather: "The winters often unfortunately a bit harsh and a warm wind from the mountains often makes you want to sleep . . ." (p.370), a reference to the notorious Swiss *Föhn*; each prized Swiss institution, health, democracy, freedom, is mocked at the Councillors' meeting and all their proud boasts are answered by: "But we are covered in dung (i.e. useless traditions) nevertheless".

The people of Elis can only count up to three and tend to shoddy business deals and practices. The picture is of a country given over to the dubious acquisition of wealth at the expense of culture and sensitivity. When Deianira quotes Sophocles (in Friedrich Hölderlin's German translation) to Phyleus, he answers sadly: "We don't know any poetry; we only use language to barter cattle" (p.399). By *not* parodying Hölderlin here, the author presents a picture of what Man could achieve — the parody would show what Man has achieved.

It seems to me however that the real cause of the failure was that the audience found little to laugh at in the theatre. (A comparison of the

radio-play with the *Komödie* will show how much of the sharpness of
wit was lost in the transition, it should be added.)[14] Above all, however,
the comic of the visual elements foundered on the disgust provoked by
the central element — the dung. Perhaps Dürrenmatt should have asked
of the theatre audience what he asked of his radio listeners: to conjure
up a "world of filth" in its imagination?! But then the point of trans-
ferring the play to the theatre would have been lost — to show the
stifling effects of bureaucratic "dung" on a people who "felt that
cleanliness was needed, fresh air",[15] but who could not throw off the
weight of old habits and traditions. The underlying theme warned
bureaucrats not to dehumanize a world which Dürrenmatt insisted is
still beautiful. The "dung", all the excrescences of useless bureaucracy,
if not used properly, that is, as "humus", for and by human beings,
will finally engulf us.

I must take issue with Arnim Arnold who asks why Hercules was
called in when Augias had found a solution for himself — the point is
that it *is* only a solution for himself — only if all the people of Elis do
as he has done, will a better world be created.[16] Until the clowns and
buffoons of the world can use these traditions and values in a more
fruitful way, their world will become as Dürrenmatt painted it, firstly,
in his little poem *To my Fatherland*:

> a stony waste, hill upon hill,
> heaped up like a moonscape.

and then *a fortiori* in *Portrait of a Planet* in 1970.

Whatever the viewpoint, Dürrenmatt's attempt to write a play in
the manner of the Attic Old Comedy with its earthy themes and comic
was no great success; the sexual licence of the Old Comedy had been
accepted by 1963 — it would seem that *physical* filth was too much for
a modern Swiss audience. Perhaps this said something about modern
Swiss culture? At any rate, I hold it to be one of Dürrenmatt's wittiest
creations and well worth a revival.

NOTES TO CHAPTER SEVEN

HERKULES UND DER STALL DES AUGIAS
(HERCULES AND THE AUGEAN STABLES)

1. Melchinger quoted in Der Spiegel, 27.3.63. E.Brock-Sulzer: *Dürrenmatt
   und die Quellen*, in *Der unbequeme Dürrenmatt*, op.cit., p.134. The Guardian wrote of the première: "It is a political satire with strong Aristophanic
   affinities", (28.3.63). See too the chapter Dürrenmatt und die Schweiz in
   T.Lengborn, op.cit., pp.255-258 for Dürrenmatt's criticisms of Swiss society.

2. Basler Nachrichten, 21.3.63. Jacobi, in Die Zeit, was similarly severe. Risch-bieter, on the other hand, was (surprisingly) "pleasantly entertained", Theater Heute 4, No.5, 1963, pp.36-37.

3. The programme note of the première suggested that the *Ur-Herkules* was written "ten years ago". Wyrsch tell us that Dürrenmatt had had the idea for a sketch at the Cabaret Cornichon (Wyrsch, 1.4.63, p.24). The radio-play was broadcast by Radio Beromünster. The record is DGG 43013 (1957). The "Ur-Herkules" is now in *Lesebuch* (Arche 1978) pp.95-99.

4. G.Meredith: *Essay on comedy and the uses of the comic spirit*, Constable, 1897, p.80. J.Swift: *Gulliver's Travels*, Oxford 1959, p.132. Dürrenmatt's poem *An mein Vaterland*, in hortulus, op.cit., See too A.A.Häsler: *Gespräch zum 1. August mit Friedrich Dürrenmatt*, Ex libris 21, 1966, No.8, pp.9-21 for some pungent remarks on Swiss "democracy". He quotes his *Hercules*.

5. This is the edition of our text: *Herkules und der Stall des Augias: Eine Komödie*, in KII, pp.359-429. It is dedicated "To Lotti (his wife), 4.9.62". Jauslin, whose book finishes with the première version, claims that this is the first Dürrenmatt work with a solution and adds: "Whether he has taken a completely new path remains to be seen". My remaining chapters answer the question, I hope.

6. See the *Note* to *The Visit*: "I . . . prefer to be taken as a rather confused child of nature with a defective sense of form" (*KI*, p.342). Hercules bears a marked resemblance to Korbes in *Evening Hour in late Autumn* and with Schwitter in *The Meteor*. The later Dürrenmatt would like to deny this. He told Dieter Fringèli in 1977 that he now sees himself as introverted rather than extroverted.

7. cf. "He is held out by the ancients as a true pattern of virtue and piety and as his whole life has been employed for the common benefit of mankind, he was deservedly rewarded with immortality" (*Lemprière's Classical Diction-ary*, Routledge and Kegan Paul, 1949 edn. p.270). Although the Middle Ages saw him as a "Christian Knight", he was also portrayed as a gluttonous buff-oon (as he was in *The Birds*). In Dürrenmatt's radio-play, he complains that he is regarded as "an eternally drunken roughneck" (GH, p.159). Walter Sokel thought that Dürrenmatt's Hercules was the nearest to the Euripidean version of the eight that he had examined.

8. K.Pestalozzi, op.cit., p.396. Similarly in the programme of the première, Schauspielhaus Zürich, 1962-1963, pp.8-10.

9. Werner, op.cit., p.148. He naturally goes on to compare Augias with Romulus.

10. E.Welsford: *The Fool*, op.cit., p.323.

11. According to the opening lines of the radio-play, Polybius is to be taken as a parody of Gustav Schwab (1792-1850) the author of *Die schönsten Sagen des klassischen Altertums*, 3 vols., 1838-1840. A new edition was published in 1948. The historical Polybius was a First Century historian from Samos, famed for his learned digressions. In his first speech, Polybius keeps saying "Zur Sache" (A nos moutons!), cf. p.361.

12. M.Hodgart: Satire, op.cit., p.33.

13. Jenny, op.cit., p.89. See too the Basler Nachrichten: "You may find dung in itself and as such side-splittingly comical and laugh yourself silly at every dung-heap on a walk through a village. I cannot". (21.3.63.).

14. Peppard felt that the satire of the radio-play became "overlaid with didactic speeches". Perhaps. I find many of them "side-splittingly funny".

15. *Ur-Herkules*, op.cit., p.3.

16. A.Arnold, op.cit., p.83.

Chapter Eight

"DEATH ISN'T A PROBLEM!"

DER METEOR *(The Meteor)* (1966)

It would be a legitimate exercise to compare *The Meteor* (1966) with Dürrenmatt's later play *Die Wiedertäufer* (*The Anabaptists*) (1967); in both cases, an old theme is taken up again, for the first time since the early works, an overtly Christian theme, that of Faith.

Secondly, the *Dramaturgische Überlegungen* (*Dramaturgical Considerations*) appended to the later work, refer in part directly to *The Meteor* and can (and should be) considered as valuable addenda to the writer's earlier theoretical writings.

The connection between *The Meteor* and *The Anabaptists* is of some importance for this study and for the understanding of both works. The 7th *Consideration: The Theater of Non-identification* is devoted to a discussion of the "clown" whom Dürrenmatt calls "the isolated man", the man objectified by the audience, alienated by "distance", by their lack of sympathy with him. "With me," adds the author, "the character which corresponds most closely to the "isolated man": Schwitter".

In *Point* 14 to *The Meteor*, Dürrenmatt claims that Schwitter isolates himself from society by "not believing": "Not believing means isolating oneself" while, in *Point* 16, he says that Schwitter isolates himself twice, "by not believing, and by believing that he is dying".

The book version of *Der Meteor: Eine Komödie in zwei Akten* was dedicated to Dürrenmatt's great friend, Leonard Steckel, after the latter's 50th performance as Schwitter. (Steckel died in a train crash in 1971); the three "premières" on 20th-22nd January 1966 at the Schauspielhaus Zürich also had Gustav Knuth as Muheim and were produced by Leopold Lindtberg.[1] The Zürcher Woche reported that the booers in the audience were protesting about the "comfortable philistine ... who was making fun of a society in which he himself was quite happy". The play was repeated three weeks later in Hamburg with Giehse and Hasse where it was called a "crude farce". From the remarks made by the cast of the work, however, one can see that

Dürrenmatt had once again pleased his fellow-professionals in the theatre, annoyed (some) critics and confused his audiences.[2]

Hugo Loetscher says that the theme of the play is taken from the short story *Pilatus* of 1946 where there is shown that the only "agreement" between God and Man is Death.[3] It seems much more likely however that it derives from Dürrenmatt's unfailing interest in physical phenomena evinced right up to his play "about" supernovae, *Portrait of a Planet* (1971). He himself has said that the title is metaphorical: "A meteor is an elementary natural happening like Schwitter, who of course sees himself as a falling object. A meteor is something that "occurs" (the German word is "einfällt" which also means "to fall in"), like a play".[4] To this physical "Einfall", there then came the "supernatural" one of the miracle. In a 1959 essay on miracles, Dürrenmatt had written:

> That is why a miracle must either *not* be motivated as something incomprehensible in itself, or the meaning of the miracle must be worked out most precisely, particularly, naturally, when it happens twice. In the theatre, God has to show his cards.

When the mass media publicize it, however,

> the miracle loses its credibility with people. It gets worn out. Man prevents Man from believing . . . The Church is forced to distance itself from a miracle that has become a blasphemy.[5]

It can be seen how the two ideas fuse together into the conception of the man who was not only miraculously resurrected — but who could not die; a typical Dürrenmattian paradox: "Schwitter is a Lazarus of our age", he said to Urs Jenny.[6] It would appear that this theme required a tragic treatment, but it is my view — and we have already seen that it was Dürrenmatt's also (see *Note* 2) — that it was the treatment of the theme rather than the theme itself which caused a good deal of the critical resentment.[7]

★　　　★　　　★

Like Romulus (or Goethe's Egmont), Schwitter is the character around whom the other characters revolve and from whom they have their *raison d'être*, since, in one way or another, he brings about their ultimate fate. Hugo Nyffenschwander, the painter, is presented as a comic pedant: "My art is holy to me", he claims. "Art is only holy to botchers", retorts Schwitter. "You are mad on theory, because you can't *do* any-thing" (p.46). The comic in this character lies in the contradictory coupling of Nyffenschwander's desire to "experience" "Life" (this is his "illusion") and his pitiful attempts to achieve it — by painting nude studies of his wife, August (his "reality"). The natural and comic consequence is that he is cuckolded and then destroyed by Schwitter.

Der grosse Muheim ("The great Muheim") is another comic charac-ter-type — the "miles gloriosus", a rumbustious 80-year-old who is comically broken by Schwitter's assertion that he, too, was cuckolded. (The parallel with Boss in *Der Mitmacher* is interesting). The bullying magnate is "reduced" to whimpering obsequiousness by Schwitter's disclosures that Muheim's wife slept with him whenever he went to pay the rent. As Muheim himself says, this makes him a "comic number" (p.48) — particularly when we hear that Schwitter cannot remember the name of the woman with whom he slept! *Was* it Muheim's wife? In this agony of ignorance, Muheim is arrested for killing Nyffen-schwander — and Schwitter admits to having invented the story because Muheim had interfered with his dying. The "fortuitous" meeting has ruined the "great man": "I'm ruined, washed-up, trampled-on, ridiculed, contaminated!" (p.48) — in a word, "brought down". The alazon is driven out, his "simulation" unmasked.

Dürrenmatt opposes this "tragic" figure (i.e. "not comic") with the Doctor. "The comedy of the play lies in the doctor", he once said. (To Ketels, p.105). Professor Schlatter, the comic "dottore", as the *commedia dell'arte* would have known him, is the learned pedant who is duped time and time again by Schwitter's inability to die. (Perhaps it is Dürrenmatt's illness which makes him so savagely critical of doctors. The theme recurs in *Die Frist* of 1977). Here the sources of the comic lie in the paradoxes which befall the character:

> The scientific world is as convinced of my ridiculousness as the theo-logical is of your resurrection. Heavens above, *that's* the catastrophe. The one lot think I'm a fool, the others think that God has made me one. Either way, I look an ass (p.60).

Schwitter's refusal to die "drives" Schlatter out, presumably to take his own life (p.62). His great learning is made comically nought when confronted with the paradox: How can one save the life of a man who cannot die?

The same problem confronts the parson, Emanuel Lutz.[8] Is he just another comic type, the "funny clergyman"? Frau Brock-Sulzer thinks not. She finds in him a serious cleric who has seen a miracle and then dies: "Only a parson who *didn't* believe that a miracle could happen, would be ridiculous".[9] There is, of course, some truth in that remark, but surely Lutz's mannerisms and his vocabulary: "Minütchen, Sekündchen, Momentchen" — rather childish German diminutives, are meant as comic incongruities? He may not be as ridiculous as Utnapischtim in *Angel*, but, nevertheless, the fact that a clergyman should *die* as the result of witnessing what, after all, should be the ultimate proof of his Christian faith, is comic — and Dürrenmatt's intentions seem underlined by the pantofarcical (and Shakespearean) "lugging out of the guts" on to the landing (p.24). That his death was caused by an excess of *human* emotion suggests that we should see something of the spiritual clown in Lutz. Like Bodo, he is ridiculous, yet he dies with hope on his lips. If the character is not quite developed enough to call him a "holy fool", then he certainly belongs to this group in Dürrenmatt's *oeuvre*. Dürrenmatt said to Ketels that "the minister (her translation) is not a comic, but rather a genuinely moving figure".

Olga, the fifth character to be considered, is Schwitter's fourth wife (the "comic of repetition"). There is however nothing remotely comic in anything she says or does — that lies in what she is — a former prostitute who has brought Schwitter undemanding sexual happiness; the seeming incongruity between their professions is made comical when the audience is given to understand that her work is more honest than his. Olga, too, is the innocent sufferer of a "natural catastrophe": "Her demise is a catastrophe nobody wanted", Dürrenmatt said to Jenny and he went on: "Like all catastrophes, like everything". She becomes the plaything of Chance, and if not directly "comic", then certainly "untragic": "Life is cruel, blind and ephemeral," says Schwitter. "It all depends on Chance. An illness at the right time and I would never have met Olga. We had bad luck with one another, that's all" (p.68).[10]

Frau Nomsen, Olga's mother, and the toilet attendant, is one of the "lower-class" characters dear to both Brecht and Dürrenmatt. With them, they can "épater le bourgeois" and create comedy by comparing and contrasting two worlds. Much of the comic here arises from the direct or indirect use of the mention of pimps, prostitutes, toilets and natural body-functions — a source of laughter which Monro in *The Argument of Laughter* called the "mention of the unmentionable" and with which Freud naturally made great play in *Der Witz*.

Mrs Nomsen serves both a comic and a serious purpose. As Olga's mother and therefore Schwitter's mother-in-law, the character is comic as an incongruity, but she also allows Schwitter to show his real self and the author to underline the point that he is making. She

has the realistic common-sense which (in this play) is absent in "Lit.Crit.";
Schwitter gradually begins to realize that she is the only true "human
being" around him, one who sees Life as he does, in terms of "business"
and not of "art": "You sold flesh for money, an honest trade . . . You
worked at whoring, I've just worked at literature" (p.67). *She* is the
true reality: "Reality can't be grasped at a writing-desk, Mrs Nomsen,
it only appears in your blue-tiled underworld" (p.68). Yet the journey
from this "underworld" has killed the old woman; the news of her
daughter's death and the journey to inform Schwitter were too much
for her heart. That she should die Dürrenmatt's "favourite" modern
death is appropriate since one could say that she, too, dies of excess of
emotion — as did her daughter: "We're mourning my child. Do you
know why? Because Olga allowed herself feelings, I was always warning
her about that . . ." (p.67). Her remaining two children, Inge, a stripper,
now in America, and Waldemar, already a criminal, will be brought up
without illusions or pretensions. Money will be their one goal, inhuman-
ly gained from prostitution of the flesh — Waldemar will take over the
brothel.

Mrs Nomsen could therefore be grouped with Lutz and Olga as an
innocent victim of the natural catastrophe, the "meteor"; these types
are clowns, in that they are forced into ridiculous and/or inappropriate
chance deaths, yet there is some sympathy for them, since their good
intentions are foiled by Schwitter's egotistical inhumanity. They were
genuine.[11] Schlatter, Nyffenschwander and Muheim, on the other hand,
are "brought down" when they are shown to be impostors; the first
two are comic pedants, the third a "braggadocio"-, "miles gloriosus"-
figure.

It is true that all six are ruined in one way or another by contact
with Schwitter. It could be argued that the fact of Schwitter's resurrection does not really affect some of the confrontations. Nyffenschwander
and Muheim, for example, would have been ruined whether he was a
"resurrected miracle" or not. Yet, all six *had* expressed human
emotions of some sort. "You, as a writer, did you ever allow yourself
feelings in your profession?" Mrs Nomsen asks Schwitter (p.67). The
distinction must be made, however, between "honest" deep feelings
such as the first group have and the "dishonest" and consequently
inhuman feelings of the second.

Auguste Nyffenschwander and Jochen, Schwitter's son, show no
feelings whatever and yet they "escape" at the end. Why? Auguste
takes Schwitter sexually because he is — paradoxically and comically —
a "living" man beside her dessicated husband. A "nice lay", as
Schwitter calls her, she is the "Zote" dramatized, a comic butt for

Schwitter. Jochen (the parodies of the Goethean "Johann" and "Wolf-gang" were no doubt intentional) is made comical by the Kantian evaporation of his expectations on learning that Schwitter had burned one and a half millions worth of notes. He is ruined, but he knows that his father is ruined also, since Schwitter's books are already forgotten in the bookshops.

Both characters are hard, cynical and selfish − and it would seem that this type of character wins the day, but closer examination suggests that this is not the case. These characters are the warning in the play, the warning against the inhumanity of the world. The characters who died or who were socially discredited, had lost their belief in something or someone − but Dürrenmatt's point is that they *had* a belief. Auguste and Jochen had none. In the context of this study, they are soulless buffoons, without human feelings. The alazon-types are credited with human feelings, but are mocked for abusing them.

When the play is looked at in this light, it becomes what Dürrenmatt claimed it was − before the premières: a play about lack of respect for human law, a play about inhumanity and its consequences, a play whose *theme* is nihilism.[12]

The final comic character to be considered will lead us to Schwitter himself. At first sight, Major Friedli of the Salvation Army would seem to be a typical comic buffoon − her parodistic name, her over-enthusi-astic Swiss reforming zeal and, one is sorry to have to add, the popular comic associations of the "Army", give a standard comic type. She is also a religious fanatic and has that *idée fixe* common to our alazon types.[13] The figure is therefore undeniably comic and causes laughter, but Dürrenmatt also makes his "tragic" statement through this figure: "Thou wert dealt with according to thy Faith", she says to Schwitter (p.70). Schwitter has no faith, no feelings, and therefore his resurrection has become his punishment; where Christ's miracles were to lead to eternal life in Heaven for all, Schwitter's will lead to eternal life − or "Hell" on earth, "like the Wandering Jew, the Flying Dutchman or, as with Swift in Gulliver's Travels, a whole race".[14] The final hymn, *Morgenglanz der Ewigkeit* (*Jesus, Sun of Righteousness*), is therefore no parody, but a serious quotation, an indictment of Schwitter:

> Lead us all our days and years
> In Thy straight and narrow way,
> Lead us through the vale of tears
> To the land of perfect day,
> Where Thy people, fully blest,
> Safely rest.

Since there is here a genuine mixture of the ludicrous and the demonic, the ridiculous Major confronting a man doomed, one may call it a "grotesque dissonance".[15]

★   ★   ★

"Long considered portents of dire catastrophe, the appearance of comets blazing their fiery paths across the skies used to fill man's hearts with terror".[16] Since meteors are the blazing remnants of comets, it is quite certain that Dürrenmatt had this destructive effect in mind when he titled his play. All the characters, bar one, stand in just such a fearful relationship to Schwitter and all are chance victims of this physical phenomenon. Dramaturgically speaking, this is inevitable, since Schwitter is on stage from his entrance a minute or so after curtain-rise. It is therefore from their reactions to the resurrected Schwitter that, as we have seen, the comic is evoked. Schwitter's manner and appearances have led to much conjecture about his relationship to the author.[17] Both men are successful playwrights, although Dürrenmatt has yet to win a Nobel Prize for Literature; Schwitter was formerly a painter too (p.11); both suffered from shortage of money in their early days as artists and lived with their young wives in a garret. (See above p.16). Schwitter's narrative technique bears a resemblance to Dürrenmatt's (cf. his story on page 20); and their attitudes to "art" and to critics have much in common — although Dürrenmatt did remark to Violet Ketels that he hadn't had four wives!

Dürrenmatt's love of food and wine is also very much part of Schwitter's personality. His publisher, Koppe, says: "Schwitter never despaired. You only needed to put a cutlet and a decent drop of wine in front of him and he was happy" (p.42). Those who have seen Dürrenmatt's generous physical proportions often assume that these are the result of over-indulgence. They forget, or do not know, that he has suffered for nearly thirty years from diabetes; Renate Usmiani makes the interesting suggestion that his recoveries from periodical bouts of diabetic comas may have given him some personal experience of Schwitter's condition. It would certainly be a very Dürrenmattian source of humour and it does reappear both in *Play Strindberg* (1969) and in *Die Frist* (1977).

I believe, with those who were present at Dürrenmatt's fiftieth birthday celebrations in the Zürich Schauspielhaus in 1971[18], that the character *was* modelled on the author as he then was, and that certain consequences for this study follow: Dürrnematt wants us to accept Schwitter as a "clown": he is the "individual", the man who is objectified by "distance" from the audience by his comic behaviour: "Our laughter is the force that drives the comic object away from us" (*7th Consideration*, p.105 of *The Anabaptists*). If we translate Dürrenmatt's vocabulary into that of my study, Schwitter would be a professional clown at whose behaviour we laugh because it is both inapt and inept, in a word, comic.

Schwitter possesses many of the characteristics of the alazon-type; he is one of the "miles gloriosus" braggarts: "My illness is world-famous, my death is public property" (p.9). He has been an impostor; as success came to him, he adopted a false style of living: "I filed my nails and my style", (a comic zeugma) (p.37). He is very much the "unwanted guest" who bursts in on the "community" and insults his host — and, lastly, he has a comic obsession — to die. His last words are: "When will I kick the bucket?" (p.71).

Thus the character is conceived in terms of comedy. Indeed, the author admitted that Schwitter should have had a "counterpart" who would almost certainly have been an "eiron"-type, as Bockelson had his Knipperdollinck.[19] Dürrenmatt viewed the character much as he viewed himself in 1960: "I'm just such a joke in the world of literary appearances, and, I know, for many I'm a bad joke, and for others, a doubtful one".[20] Schwitter chortles to the parson: "Resurrected! Me! From the dead! What a joke!" (p.18) and when Nyffenschwander attempts to take pity on him, Schwitter answers: "Dying isn't tragic", (p.10).[21]

In other words, Schwitter is an "impossible" figure for our times; the great individual, the "hero", is now a clown-figure, made comic by his very attempts to assert his egotistical individuality, as was Hercules. He refuses to accept the "miracle" which has befallen him and becomes, as *Point* 8 says, a "double annoyance"; Schwitter is a scandal as a resurrected man and he is a scandal as an unbeliever. Indeed, one of the main comic ideas is that the miracle should have struck an unbeliever.[22] Yet I cannot accept that the total comic effect of the play rests in the fact that Schwitter is a religious unbeliever. Surely, Dürrenmatt, albeit unwittingly, has extended his play to embrace "unbelief" in general, and I would suggest that Schwitter has something of the "spiritual clown" in him because of this. He is "distanced" from us, certainly, by his comical brutality and rudeness to Nyffenschwander, by his uncontrolled sexual appetite for Auguste and by his callous treatment of Olga and Muheim; but, in the scenes with Parson Lutz and Mrs Nomsen, and in Georgen's necrologue, we see another side of his character, a side for which we can have some sympathy and which lends the final scene a typical Dürrenmattian ambivalence. The comic in these scenes helps to achieve this effect.

It is no coincidence that all three scenes concern themselves with Schwitter's "unbelief" in the value of "literature": there might be grounds for taking Schwitter's approach as an illustration of the closing sentence of *Problems of the Theatre*: Schwitter, too, would like literature to weigh nothing on the scales of today's literary criticism. Then it might become "weighty" again. Schwitter would certainly rather have written detective stories.

In each of these three key-scenes, it is not religious faith, nor unbelief, nor the fact of the resurrection that is Schwitter's concern. He — and Dürrenmatt — are concerned to stress the unworthiness of the modern "culture industry", as it has been termed in West Germany — the audience is meant to laugh at this washing of dirty linen in public.[23] We note how Lutz's attempts to discuss Schwitter's resurrection are dismissed time and again with a remark intended to cause laughter: "Praised be the Lord of Sabaoth!" says Lutz as he enters Schwitter's room. "I don't need any slogans", is Schwitter's crushing reply (p.14). This leads to Lutz's disclosure of the 'resurrection": "Don't be tasteless," retorts Schwitter and tells him how his life as a successful author has robbed him of any "belief" in such miracles that he may have had: "Just you try writing a play a year and you'll quickly give up your inner life" (p.18).

This is the first sign of the corrupting influence of literary success; the disparagement of the literacy world seems to be of more importance to Dürrenmatt here than the miracle. Schwitter says: "I want to die honestly, without fiction and without literature" (p.18); so the phrase includes *all* "unbeliefs".

The comic should arise from the contrast between the clergyman's naive acceptance of the miracle, (which is deepened by his incongruous death), and Schwitter's rough, realistic, "shocking" refusal of it. The result is rather like laughing in church — what Freud called the "satisfaction of an impulse. . .against a barring hindrance" — but the reason for the religious unbelief lies in Schwitter's literary experiences.

Friedrich Georgen, "the star critic", delivers the necrologue at the beginning of Act II and is (possibly) a satire on the Berlin critic, Friedrich Luft, who had been a severe critic of Dürrenmatt and his work, but who said of this play: ". . .of all his plays, the most attractively repugnant, the funniest and the best. . ."[24] Georgen is a composite of all those critics who have bemoaned the lack of intellectual substance in Dürrenmatt's work or who have dismissed him as a nihilistic bogeyman or an Helvetic joker.

Georgen says that Schwitter was "the last despairing man of his age who set out to overcome despair". He was "a moralist born of nihilism"; all his works showed an inner "lack of hope" — "His theatre, not reality, is grotesque". In sum, Schwitter is dismissed as a savage satirist whose despairing pen failed to see the beauty of what Georgen would no doubt have called (after Emil Staiger) the "sane world". Although a German-speaking audience, usually *au fait* with literary controversy, would have laughed at the satire, it is significant that the author thought it worthwhile to emphasize the point by having Schwitter's publisher, Carl Conrad Koppe, mock Georgen by saying: "All honour to your profundity, Georgen, but, really, your speech was balderdash" (p.42). The scene is no "throwaway", but closely relevant to the play's central intention. More understanding has been gained for the view finally expressed in the scene with Mrs Nomsen.

She represents reality and honesty; only she awakes a chord in Schwitter. She too is lonely in her "blue-tiled underworld" (p.68), but her profession, female pimp, embraces the true reality of living. The laughter here might be less certain than elsewhere, partly because the theme is "doubtful", but also because a genuine seriousness has come over the play.

The "mention of the unmentionable" is the source of much of the laughter. Mrs Nomsen's bad back is blamed on "sitting all day long, the draughts, the damp — of course, down there in Bellevue (!) everything is insulated, but in time any hygienic installation gets wet with the constant flushing". (Foreign audiences would have to understand that Swiss/German toilets are controlled by elderly women!). She tells Schwitter that he will not remember the name of her second child (Inge) but only her "superb breasts. Inge is a stripper with an international reputation". While Mrs Nomsen then seems to be listening, Schwitter unburdens himself of his distaste for *his* world, the false world of "literature" in which he has been living: "I surrounded myself with invented creatures because I could make nothing of real ones" (p.68).

He has discovered the truth about himself: "My life wasn't worth living". This situation suddenly becomes comic when it is seen that Mrs Nomsen has died while he was speaking — the one person whose views seem to coincide with Schwitter's, and Schwitter, the great man, cannot even die. By his egoism, Schwitter has removed himself from the world of human beings: non-human, he cannot share the fate of humans. He has made himself "a monster . . . he wants to die, he needs it as an excuse for his brutal egoism", Dürrenmatt told Jenny.

Until this *volte face*, Schwitter might have been seen as one of the spiritual clowns of my study, an eiron-type figure who was honestly trying to stand up to "evil" or the stupid inhumanities of this world and to give an example, in his own way, of how to combat them. By his inability to die, however, he is presented as a professional clown, a mechanical comic figure endlessly repeating the action of dying.[25] It becomes a "running gag". Many critics have overlooked his remark to Olga: *"For a year now*, I'm always being saved at the last minute", (my emphasis) (p.29). The punishment for his inhumanity and his lack of human feelings is "the eternal dying" (*Point* 18), which prevents him from attaining "the only reality", Death (p.68). This is the "worst possible turn" and, since non-dying is, as has been seen, a standard ingredient of comedy, this is the final "turn towards the *Komödie*".[26]

★　　　★　　　★

Structurally, the play is a series of "revue-sketches", eight in Act I and eleven in Act II, all set in a room with one door — a *sine qua non* of the classical farce — out of which the characters make not only their exit, but usually their exitus.[27] The contents of the room, the bed, the armchair, the easel (with nude studies), the nappies, the curtains, the candles, the stool, the chest of drawers and the Spanish wall are all part of the *Komödie*. For example: the bed is a comic contrast between the possible beginning of a life and the certain end of one; the easel with its nude studies offers a contrast between Nyffenschwander's hypocritical desire for "Life" and Schwitter's genuine longing for Death, and so on. As the candles are lit and extinguished, the curtains pulled and drawn back, the stove continually tended, we are witnessing that age-old comic device of "repetition", the "running gag", mentioned above. A good director will use these devices to bring out the comedy in the play. Without that, it will not be a Dürrenmatt *Komödie*.

It is noticeable too that Dürrenmatt's stage language has become tauter and more colloquial as his style has matured. In *Meteor*, Schwitter's manner and mannerisms demand a short, sharp, laconic and colloquial dialogue. Only in Olga's, and, later, in Schwitter's speeches (cf. "A writer who is taken to the bosom of our present society is corrupted for all time") and in the last scene with Mrs Nomsen do we hear elevated language. (The "star" critic's elevated speech is a parody, of course).

For me, then, Wolfgang Schwitter is a singular character at this stage of Dürrenmatt's career, for he combines my two main types of comic figure, the spiritual and the professional clown: on the one hand, he is trying to stand up honestly to "evil", as he sees it, what, in Schwitter's case, could be called his "unbeliefs", the evils of "literature-making"; yet, on the other hand, he is a braggart and a bully, who, bursting in on this community from the outside, upsets them and creates havoc for all. An inhuman character, this, whose "dying" becomes comical, mechanical repetition which shows him to be, at the end, impotent. Do we then praise or condemn Schwitter, take him as a model or as a warning?

The truth is that he is both, and is made clear by Points 10 and 11 to *The Meteor*. These follow *Points* 10 and 11 to *The Physicists* strangely enough, where, after discussing those plots which present "people who plan" and who fail to reach their goal, Dürrenmatt concludes: "Such a story is of course grotesque but not absurd (contradictory)" . . . "It is paradoxical" (*Point* 11).

Schwitter is also paradoxical in a slightly different way. *Point* 11 to *The Meteor* says: "A paradoxical human being is a comical character in a more elevated sense, a character who is both comical and tragic at the same time". Schwitter is a parody, because he is "the risen man who doesn't believe in his resurrection" (*Point* 14), and Dürrenmatt added, "*The Meteor* is a play about not being able to believe".

But, surely, this play is not about "resurrection"? *That* is not the dramatist's major concern?[28] Surely the play is about the "great individual", the "hero" in an end-situation in the modern world where he has rapidly become as anachronistic as the dinosaur, here given a chance to review his life as a dying man who cannot die, in roughly the position of Max Frisch's Kürmann in his *Biografie* (Suhrkamp 1967)? More important than this even is the fact that Schwitter is a great writer; Dürrenmatt was attacking the (to him) unreal world of "belles lettres" and the whole "Lit.Crit." industry, of theatre as "a doctoral dissertation", as he was to say later. He said to Jenny: "Here in *The Meteor*, literature is an anti-world, quite simply that which isn't real, and Schwitter's case shows that literature becomes irrelevant as soon as it becomes a matter of life and death. The reality of death eradicates all the protective inventions with which Schwitter has surrounded himself", and, in the discussion in Zürich, he added: "The human situation is very sad. Man has turned his world practically into a hell. You'll only find consolation nowadays from a theologian or a philosopher — not from a writer". (*Die Tat*, 22.2.66).

Surely the key to the work is Schwitter's final conversation with Mrs Nomsen — here, says Dürrenmatt, "the two worlds collide". Anyone who has had the sad opportunity of talking to a distinguished author faced with a domestic tragedy of great dimensions will know what Dürrenmatt is writing about here. "Literature" is of very little importance at such times when it does indeed become a mere shadow of reality. Scholarship becomes insubstantial, fiction almost an obscenity. This faces Schwitter; given the unique opportunity to review his life, he becomes aware of its uselessness. The loss of belief in life causes him to destroy those with whom he comes into contact. He thus becomes "the great individual", but also "the great lonely one"; a potentially tragic character made untragic by the elements of the comic in the situation and in the characters around him: "a character who is both comical and tragic at the same time".[29]

One cannot deny that a producer could turn this play into a farce, but I believe that this examination has shown that it is, by intention, a *Komödie*, and that it should be played as such.[30]

NOTES TO CHAPTER EIGHT

DEATH ISN'T A PROBLEM!

DER METEOR (THE METEOR)

1. *Der Meteor*: Arche 1966 (= DM) and in *K III* (Arche 1972). Translated as *The Meteor* by James Kirkup, Cape 1973. The *20 Points* were read out later in a discussion at the Zürich Kunsthaussaal on 25.2.66. See *Friedrich Dürrenmatt über seine Komödie Der Meteor* (NZZ, 28.2.66). They are now in *TSR II*, pp.156-161. In his *Der Mitmacher: Ein Komplex*, Dürrenmatt reminds us that *The Physicists* and *The Meteor* were both conceived in 1959 on a visit to New York. *The Meteor* was written in 1965 after Dürrenmatt and his wife had been to the USSR for the 150th anniversary of the death of Shevchenko. See *Meine Russlandreise*, Zürcher Woche, July 1964.
2. Zürcher Woche, 28.1.66. See too Melchinger's article on the same theme: *Wie schreibt man böse, wenn man gut lebt?* Theater Heute, September 1968. On the Hamburg production, see K.Wagner: *Ein Todsüchtiger am Mittsommertag*, FAZ, 11.2.66. For the remarks of the cast, see P.Wyrsch: *Ein Meteor erhitzt die Gemüter*, Schweizer Illustrierte, January 1966, pp.12-13. Dürrenmatt felt that the play had been properly produced in Zürich: "... we brought out the characters in a style that was almost comedian-like, not at all solemn, and that made people mad. And everywhere that it was played, solemnly, it left the audience unmoved". (To Ketels, op.cit.) See too my conclusion above.
3. H.Loetscher: *Von der Unmöglichkeit zu sterben*, programme of the première, Schauspielhaus Zürich, 1965-1966, pp.1-4, here p.1. Dürrenmatt told Heinz Ludwig Arnold that he took the story from Lessing's remarks on miracles in his *Hamburgische Dramaturgie*. (*GHLA*, p.39).
4. See U.Jenny: *Lazarus der Fürchterliche*, Theater Heute 2, February 1966, pp.10-12.

5. *Untersuchung über den Film 'Das Wunder des Malachias'* (1965): In *TSR I*, pp.283-288, here p.283, and p.285. One might recall here Utnapischtim's remark that Kurrubi should "paraphrase the miraculous for a public who regard the extraordinary as a crude sensation", (*EKB, KI*, p.238), and Möbius' remark to Monika: "There is nothing more indecent in the realm of science than a miracle" (*DP, KII*, p.317).
6. To Jenny, op.cit., p.11. Dürrenmatt chose the St John version (Chaps. XI and XII) rather than that in St Luke (Chap. XVI, v.20 ff.); the John story is "merely a scandal" and shows the *absurd* side of the episode: "Lord, by this time he stinketh", v.39. See too Hans Mayer in an interview in the programme of the première and to Schumacher, op.cit., pp.773-774. Violet Ketels' interview at Temple University gives a good idea of what Dürrenmatt was looking for. *Meteor* was performed there after the award of an honorary degree to the author.
7. cf. H.Karasek: "It was not the theme which shocked, but the way it was peddled at greatly reduced prices", Stuttgarter Zeitung, 24.1.66. cf. Hübner: "Dürrenmatt is trying to see how long readers and audiences, boxed about the ears and sold down the river by prominent authors, will let themselves be maltreated", Rheinische Post, 28.1.66, while Harold Hobson predictably summed up Dürrenmatt's views thus: "Life is odious, so foetid and so disgusting that no one but a lavatory attendant could find it tolerable", Sunday Times, 31.7.66. The Aldwych production (26.7.66) was directed by Clifford Williams, with Patrick Magee as Schwitter, and Patience Collier as Mrs Nomsen.
8. The name was satirized in the character of the magistrate in *DRH*. See L.W.Forster: "The Lutz family has been settled in Bern (sic) since the sixteenth century", *DRH*, op.cit., p.128. Spycher plays the name-game again: *Emanuel* = God with us – *Lutz* = lux = light (!), (op.cit., p.169).
9. F.Brock-Sulzer: *Dürrenmatt in unserer Zeit*, op.cit., p.45. It was the vehement views about Lutz expressed in the Zürich *Kirchenbote* by Pastors Sturzenegger and Vogelsanger which led to the public discussion on the play. See *Aufstand des Publikums*, FAZ, 4.3.66 and Die Tat, 27.2.66. Nevertheless, Dürrenmatt did assure Vogelsanger: "I tell you, *Meteor* really is a Christian play". P.Vogelsanger: *Dürrenmatt und die Auferstehung*, Kirchenbote, 1.4.66. Dürrenmatt has always been concerned that no-one has considered the question of faith which is raised, viz.: "Can an unbeliever be made to believe?", and he quotes Barth's "Belief is grace" – but we must also recall his remark later to Dieter Fringeli (1977) that "grace is connected to chance, for if anything is incalculable, it is grace"!
10. Ulrich Profitlich's footnote on Chance points out that the "bad luck" was *not* that the unusual happened, (i.e. the illness), but that the *usual* (i.e. his normal health) prevailed. (op.cit., pp.117-118), footnote 125.)
11. See H. and E.Franz: *Zu Dürrenmatts Komödie Der Meteor*, ZfdPh, Vol.87, 1968, pp.660-661, for a suggestion that they all die because they show human feelings. See too Dürrenmatt to Ketels: "She (Mrs Nomsen) can speak to him (Schwitter) because she has absolutely no illusions" (p.101). I disagree with Melchinger that Lutz's death is the only one directly caused by Schwitter. (See *Dürrenmatts Salto mortale*, Theater Heute, March 1966, p.18).
12. In an interview with J-P. Lenoir, Dürrenmatt said that it was not a nihilistic play, but rather a play about nihilism. (Quoted in Peppard, p.142).
13. The Zürich painter Varlin painted the satirical picture of the Salvation Army which hung opposite the French window in Dürrenmatt's study when I visited him in Neuchâtel.
14. H.J.Weitz: *Meteorologisches*, programme of the première, p.9.

15. See M.Wehrli: *Wie der Meteor einschlug*, Theater Heute, March 1966, p.17. The words of the hymn are by Christian Knorr von Rosenroth, the melody can be found in Freylinghausens Gesangbuch (1704). This translation, *Jesus, Sun of righteousness* is by J.L.Borthwick (1813-1897). Dürrenmatt saw a "Billy Graham" side to his Salvation Army: "They are the Christians and they accept the miracle of Schwitter's rising from the dead without question as being the great salvation" (Ketels, p.91).

16. W.Bergamini: *The Universe*, Time-Life 1964, p.82. See too Bockelson to the Anabaptists: "I shall fall through your nights like a gleaming meteor" (*ESG*, *KI*, p.23) and Schwefel in *DB*: "A comet means something bad . . . The war will take a bad turn towards peace" (*KI*, p.138). I noted an imposing array of globes, telescopes and charts in Dürrenmatt's house. See too *Dokument* in *TSR I*, pp.30-37 for more proof of his interests in heavenly bodies.

17. Peppard suggests that the name could derive from "schwitzen" = to sweat, or "Zwitter" = a mixture of things. The name may also be intended to suggest "Schwyzer" = Swiss, is his final guess (op.cit., p.81). The name is however quite common in the Basle area. It has, of course, parodistic connections, strengthened by the parodistic Goethean Christian name. (See H.Siefkin: *Dürrenmatt and comedy: Der Meteor*, Trivium 17, 1977, pp.1-16, here p.5). R.Usmiani: *Friedrich Dürrenmatt as Wolfgang Schwitter*, Modern Drama, Vol.11, 2, September 1968, pp.143-150, usefully details some of the resemblances. Talking to Jenny, Dürrenmatt agreed that "Schwitter shared many of my views . . . but you can't call it a self-portrait" (*Lazarus der Fürchterliche*, op.cit., p.12). Ernst Scheidegger claimed that Maximilian Korbes was originally called Schnitter! (See *Malende Dichter - dichtende Maler*, Zürich 1957, p.xxii, quoted in P.Spycher: *Friedrich Dürrenmatts Meteor: Analyse und Dokumentation* in *Friedrich Dürrenmatt: Studien zu seinem Werk* (1976) op.cit., pp.145-187, here p.150, footnote 19).

18. The final speech from *Meteor* was given by Werner Wollenberger and Andreas Wirth because of its "strongly autobiographical content", (NZZ, 20.1.71).

19. See H.Mayer: *Komödie, Trauerspiel, deutsche Misere*, Theater Heute, March 1966, pp.23-26, here p.23.

20. *Der Rest ist Dank*, 4.12.60 in *TSR I*, p.72.

21. When I told Dürrenmatt of a thesis on him entitled "The Problem of Death in the Works of Friedrich Dürrenmatt", he chortled and said: "Death isn't a problem"!

22. Dürrenmatt told Hans Mayer that the resurrection was to be taken as a "shocking story" as it was in the Bible. (In the programme of the première). He expanded on this thought in No.30 of his *Sentences on the theatre* and told H.L.Arnold that "the inner dramaturgical meaning of the miracle in *The Meteor* is that a miracle is useless to the unbeliever" (*GHLA*, p.40).

23. It is interesting to note that Dürrenmatt always uses the same braggadocio type to do this: cf. Korbes, Tantalus, Tiphys (in *The Trial of the Donkey's Shadow*). He told Ketels that "Schwitter is a dying Hemingway". See too Scheidegger in *Note* 17.

24. Die Welt, 23.1.66. After Georgen departs in Act II, the comic caretaker, Glauser, says: "Das wäre vorbei. Luft!", (lit.) "Now that's over. Fresh air!" The name would seem to be formed from Stefan *George* and his hagiographer, *Friedrich* Gundolf, (who, incidentally, was Joseph Goebbels' "Doktorvater"!).

25. The theme reappears in *Die Frist* (The Waiting Period) (1977), where we wait for the death of the Generalissimo throughout the play.

26. Bänziger neatly points out the superb theatricality of "dying" in the theatre, "where every evening a curious change occurs and, after their demise, people

get up and go on stage again . . ." (op.cit., p.210). Melchinger sees in stage deaths "a motif that is as immortal as, so to speak, Death" (op.cit. p.18). No commentator seems to have noticed the similarity between the end of a Dürrenmatt *Komödie* and what Frye called "the point of ritual death" in a comedy. (In *Anatomy of Comedy*, op.cit., p.179). Profitlich misses the point of the recurring deaths and calls them "a purely contextual amassing of deaths" (op.cit., p.130).

27. Jan Kott takes issue with Brock-Sulzer's claim that the play is built up on the classical unities in *Theatrum mundi, FD I*, pp.30-40, p.36. I do too, but see it as a *parody* of the unities, as occurred in *The Physicists*.

28. cf. "The catchword *Lazarus* is a bait for public and reviewers" (Bänziger op.cit., p.210. Tiusanen disagrees and criticizes the "holes" in the thought behind *The Meteor* severely (pp.303-308). My view is supported, I feel, by Dürrenmatt's comments in No.30 of his *Sentences on the theatre:* "In Schwitter's 'madness to death', the (great) individual is taken ad absurdum" (p.11).

29. cf "The motif of Death is transformed so decisively from the very beginning into the motif of Non-Death that there is no room for an express reversal of the tragic aspect to the comic. The play's construction points to a pure *Komödie*". B.Allemann: *Die Struktur der Komödie bei Frisch und Dürrenmatt* in *Das deutsche Lustspiel* II, Kleine Vandenhoeck Reihe 1969, pp.200-217, here p.215.

30. cf. K.Wagner, FAZ, 11.2.66. and A.Schulze-Vellinghausen in Theater Heute, March 1966, p.17: "A farce . . . about last things". Hinrich Siefkin finds it "an extraordinary combination of essentially comic features with basic issues like truth, illusion, justice, fear, reality, fiction, disorder and perfection"! (op.cit., p.11).

Chapter Nine

*"REVERSIONS"

(i) DIE WIEDERTÄUFER (*The Anabaptists*) (1967)
(ii) KÖNIG JOHANN (*King John*) (1968)
(iii) PLAY STRINDBERG (*Play Strindberg*) (1969)
(iv) TITUS ANDRONICUS (*Titus Andronicus*) (1970)

The Anabaptists represents a retake, now as a *Komödie*, of an experiment I undertook in 1946 . . . (It) represents a confrontation of my present with my early theatrical style. I was tempted to work the old theme again, this time with more awareness.[1]

Although one must have sympathy with Hugo Loetscher's telling thrust that it looked "as if this scoffer of Germanisten wanted to give these very Germanisten some work for their philological seminars", I believe that the real reason for this new version of *It is Written* lay in Dürrenmatt's changed attitude to the theme of the earlier play.[2] His growing disenchantment with institutionalized religion has been fully documented in this study so far and demonstrated in the comic portrayals of representatives of the church. In *Zusammenhänge* (*Connections*) (1976) Dürrenmatt was to write: "I am myself a Christian, more exactly a Protestant, more exactly still, a very strange Protestant, one who rejects every visible Church, one who regards his faith as something subjective, as a faith which is falsified by any attempt to express it objectively; I am a man to whom subjective thinking is more important than objective thinking" (p.35).

Likewise, it has been shown that his works since 1960-1961, say, since the film version of *The Marriage of Mr Mississippi*, perhaps, have been concerned more and more with political matters. "Everything that I write," he said to me in 1969, "is more or less political".

The critics reacted favourably, on the whole, to the new version at the première in the Schauspielhaus Zürich on 16 March, 1967. Where *It is Written* had been described as the "still pretty chaotic and undisciplined pubescent fever" of a young son of the manse, *The Anabaptists* was greeted as "quite simply superb theatre, scene after scene full of characters teeming with life . . ." Loetscher's suggestion: "The

---

* (The "reversion" – i.e. the re-working of old plays, was a common practice in Shakespeare's day).

parallel reading ... is, firstly, an excellent lesson for playwrights, how one makes theatre from a text written for the theatre ..." seems to be a good one, for this is how one should consider *The Anabaptists*: as an almost casual attempt to put an old wine into a new bottle.[3] "I was like those painters," said Dürrenmatt, "who fall so much in love with, or get so involved in a theme, that they paint it again and again".[4]

It was seen in Chapter Three above that the première of *It is written* was an "adventure".[5] There, I claimed, the "scandal" was caused by the provocative use of the comic elements in the work. Dürrenmatt now appends twelve *Dramaturgische Überlegungen* (*Dramaturgical Considerations*) which explain the metamorphosis of the *Drama* to the *Komödie* and which justify our study.

★   ★   ★

The major point is made at the close of No.1: "The worst possible turn that a story can take is the turn towards *Komödie*" (p.102), and this accurately describes the difference between the two versions before us. The 1947 *Drama* has become the 1967 *Komödie*, the main character of the *Drama* has vanished to be replaced by the "negatively tragic hero", Bockelson — but we see that this is, in fact, a standard *comic* character: "He becomes a comic character and thus a special case", that is, Bockelson becomes, like Schwitter in *The meteor*, "the isolated man", i.e. the clown figure (p.107). Dürrenmatt compares him to his picture of the archetypal, modern "hero", Robert Falcon Scott, ready to boldly go where no man has gone before, to the Pole, but seen perishing to a ridiculous death in a refrigerator in a room a few yards from a busy city street. He is man become comical through his (ridiculous) "Fate". Bockelson, too, becomes "comical", Dürrenmatt claims, because, where one would expect him to end on the wheel as Knipperdollinck does, (and as he himself did in the first version), he becomes rather the beloved of Princes and the epitome of the picaresque "comic hero", of "poneria", that "ability to get the advantage of somebody or some situation by virtue of an unscrupulous but thoroughly enjoyable exercise of craft", as Whitman wrote of the Aristophanic comic hero.[6]

"If the *Komödie* becomes a *theatrum mundi*, then", writes Dürrenmatt, "only the plot need be "comical", the characters in contrast to the plot are not only 'not comical', but tragic", (p.106), which, it will be recalled, was my definition of a "tragicomedy", rather than of a *Komödie*. We learned from the *Points* to both *The Physicists* and

The Meteor that "comic" and "paradoxical" can be near synonyms for
Dürrenmatt: "A paradoxical human being is a comical character in a
more elevated sense . . ." (*Point* 11, *The Meteor*), and that the action
which leads to the opposite of the intended goal is, in Dürrenmatt's
terminology, "paradoxical" (*Point* 11, *The Physicists*). Bockelson,
refused an engagement as an actor by the Bishop of Münster, takes
over the town and defends it against the Princes. The "worst possible
turn", the "turn" which makes the play into a *Komödie*, occurs when
the Cardinal engages him for his theatre ("at three times the top salary")
and escorts him off-stage in a sedan chair (*DWT*, p.93).

Bockelson, who, in *It is Written*, was simply "member of a drama
club", is now an experienced actor and writer who has played "the
great heroic rôles of world literature" (pp.14-15). He is still an alazon-
type, the braggart and liar of the first version, demonstrated here by his
frequent "quotations" from classical writers, particularly from Seneca.[7]
Yet the character has shed some of its rumbustiousness. Where the
comic in the first version lay in its braggadocio, outrageous hyperboles
and obscenities, it now lies in its cynical wit. Bockelson is the comic
philanderer, the picaresque adventurer with all the tricks of the experienced actor. He acts a "rôle" and wears a "mask" throughout the play.

At the beginning of the work, he leads the chorus of Anabaptists'
jubilations with insincere interpolations. His "Rejoice!" "Sing!" and
"Praise!" (p.12) are negated by his address from the "dung-cart" to the
people of Münster and his hyperbolic description (also in the first
version) of his arrival to the "rustics" gathered around. (See p.44
above).

He is much more eloquent about women in the first version and
more concerned there with the sexual aspect of the relationship; Dürrenmatt now makes these scenes comic by turning Bockelson into a
producer (a rôle in which Dürrenmatt had, of course, had recent
experience in Basle). In the earlier work, Bockelson lolled among his
women admiring their breasts; now he has "the eleven women" parade
before him like probationary chorus girls. They must act like comic
automata: "In single file . . . always two by two . . .", he shouts, and
they become examples of the comic of multiplication, several people
acting like machines, like one. Bockelson sums up the situation with a
Dürrenmattian comic epigram: "Polygamy is a director's problem"!
(p.71).

The adventurer has become a "Komödiant" (a *comédien*), a comic
player, a clown. Rejected by the bishop, he takes over the leadership
of the Anabaptists from the ridiculous Jan Matthison and encourages
the citizenry to repel the besiegers. All his encouragements are presented

comically in "theatrical" vocabulary which "reduces" the grandeur and the seriousness of the bloody struggle. In this holy war he says: "Production is waged (as it were) against production"; the Anabaptists support the Holy Ghost "with our skill as directors"; when the battle goes against them, then "we have to put up with it, brethren, like actors when the whistles screech and the rotten eggs rain down on us" (p.72). Such "heroic"-sounding speeches make the audience believe that the adventurer is genuinely for the cause of the besieged. Only at the end of the play is the full "comedy" revealed, when Bockelson "drops his mask" and admits that he thought as little of the people as the Princes did:

> I step before you
> I played a King
> And recited like a comedian a farcical text,
> Spiced with Biblical quotations and with dreams
> Of a better world
> That the masses love to dream of . . .   (p.92)

Having duped the people, he delivers them up to the Princes, who have also been duped, since they believed that Bockelson, too, was seeking political power. He shows them that their search for power was as vain as the Anabaptists' search for the Holy City. He, Bockelson, had "produced" the whole war: "The game is over, you matchless Princes / I just wore your mask, I was never like you" (pp.92-93). The whole charade had been produced as his revenge on the Bishop who had not engaged him.

Thus, Bockelson, "playing the fool", has turned history into a charade, but a charade in which innocent lives are lost at the whim of a few powerful men. He has become (like Schwitter) "a fiction": "It is not lust for power that drives him on — it is the comedian's wish to make fullest use of theatrical means that no power can do without" (10. *Consideration*). By taking this historical figure whose bloody career ended in the cage on the tower of the Lambertikirche in Münster and turning him into an actor *manqué* who makes the world a theatre and the other characters mere puppets, Dürrenmatt makes Bockelson a "comical character", but, as Frau Brock-Sulzer rightly says, "Bockelson is and remains a comic character and because he is a comic character, he escapes once again", that is, he escapes in the tradition of comedy.[8] Bockelson is a demonic Akki, indestructible like him, yet demonic like the realist Diego who wins the day at the end of *Mississippi*. Two themes converge here: The comic hero who never dies, who lives on "to fight another day", and the triumph of the "artful politician who counts on the weakness of the masses", as I described Diego (see above, p.75).

★   ★   ★

To decide whether Bockelson triumphs or not, we must look at the protagonist of the work, the Bishop of Münster.

"A theme is joined by a countertheme etc. (Don Quixote is joined by Sancho Panza)", wrote Dürrenmatt in *Consideration* No.11. This is the classical comic situation: ". . . there is a contrapuntal development", added Dürrenmatt, as if he were quoting from Heinz Kindermann's definitive work on the Comedy and who regarded Aristophanes' comedies as the *contrapunctum* to the *cantus firmus* of the tragedy-giving *polis*.

The Bishop is an even weaker figure here than in *It is Written*. Not only has he the knowledge of the impotence of the Church on his conscience, he knows, too, how weak his position is *vis-à-vis* the Princes with whom he is in league. Yet, in his very weakness lies his strength; I suggested at the end of Chapter Three that it was the Bishop who best filled the rôle of Dürrenmatt's "valiant man". It was he who had faced up bravely to the obvious evils of the world and had seen what had to be done, with a realistic eye and without the impracticable idealism of a Knipperdollinck. Here as there, the Bishop is made a comic figure, both theoretically and physically, but, at the same time, it is he who, at the close, represents the world of *potential* good, who recognizes and deplores the inhumanity around him:

> This inhuman world must become more human. / But how? But how? (p.95).

He recognizes, too, the impotence of institutionalized religion and religious institutions like the Church by trampling his cross into the ground. Dürrenmatt gives here the most obvious proof of the weakening hold of orthodox Christianity upon him; the Bishop's disgust with the attitude of the Church is symbolized by his rising from the impotence of his wheel chair to which he has been shackled all his life. Like Dürrenmatt himself, he has become a "doubter".[9] Such doubting makes the Bishop a sympathetic, yet comic character; he is doomed to be a "watcher", a "spectator", an "outsider":

A fellow-player in reality, enmeshed in guilt, an accessory to crime,
We need the illusion of carefree hours just to be a spectator (p.19).

His rôle, like Knipperdollinck's, is a passive one, it is a "wearisome
stumbling on the flight from the truth and the search for it", a more
resigned view of life than in the earlier version.[10] The attitude of his
servant, Heinrich Gresbeck, and of the Emperor: "Roll the Bishop into
the corner" (p.59), underlines the comic pathos in the character.

Scene 12 does, however, restore some status and theatrical dignity
to Bishop Waldeck and motivates the pathos of the final scene. The
childish stupidity of the "Mächtigen" (those in power), their *Real-
politik* and lack of feeling for the people are all opposed by the humanity (albeit impotent) of the Bishop. The Cardinal calls the Anabaptists
"harmless little people" whose opposition to Martin Luther and to the
beheading of political enemies is not consistent with Catholic beliefs
and behaviour. Hesse, the Protestant, and the Electoral Prince see only
profit for themselves in the Anabaptists' Rising. The Bishop's plea:
"Think of the people!" is rejected with derision by the Count's "Waldeck, now you're getting embarrassing" and the Cardinal's shocked,
"Bishop, I really must say: what sort of people do you go around
with?" (p.62), a remark which brought down the house at the early
performances.[11]

The Bishop is a spiritual clown, a Fool who recognizes what misery
is brought upon the ordinary people by the rulers of the world. Weak
though he is, he is the one character to whom one could look for that
"espoir absurde" (absurd hope) of which we heard Dürrenmatt talk
earlier (see above p.144). Such "hope" is shown in the scene which
best demonstrates Dürrenmatt's "paradoxical comic": the Bishop's
contemplating Matthison's severed head. Mayer called this "the princip-
al scene in the new *Komödie*". The Bishop realizes that Matthison's
folly is his (Brechtian) obsession to "change the world"; *his* way is
different, though, he is well aware, equally impotent:

I, on the other hand, didn't want to change the world like you.
I wanted to remain sensible in the midst of senselessness.
Now I'll just have to keep patching up a rotten social order
A fool, a diplomat who has lost hope . . . (p.52)

The Bishop is, literally, a "holy fool", but, in his final pathetic speech,
as he contemplates Knipperdollinck on the wheel, he represents
Dürrenmatt's attack on the dehumanization of the world. Although —
at 99 years of age — there is little that he can do, he makes the
attempt to "stand up and say: No!" to inhumanity: "This inhuman
world must become more human. But how? But how?"

As Hugo Loetscher puts it, the Bishop has learned two things: "Firstly, that it is impossible to remain a spectator in a farce, and, on the other hand, that he is condemned to remain just a spectator", the perfect paradox. His rhetorical question at the end must be answered, like Shaw's Joan of Arc's, by the audience. "What concerns all of us can only be solved by all of us", was *Point* 17 to *The Physicists*.

This is indeed Dürrenmatt's paradoxical comic, but he sees the Bishop as a positive figure whose belief that Reason alone cannot save the world is realistic – and hopeful.[12] He is the eiron-figure of the *Komödie*, the spiritual clown to the blustering professional clown, Bockelson. Out of this comic contrast comes the comic and the tragic in the work, *because* they are paradoxical characters. (Cf. *Point* 11 to *The Meteor*).

The character of Knipperdollinck has radically changed from the first version's where it was of major importance. Here he is a relatively minor character. He is a sufferer, an absurd character who has lost his humanity: "Am I so sinful that I am no longer a human being?" he asks the Bishop (p.22). He is dismissed in the *Considerations* as "the religious man who is driven to the wheel, who suffers the world: Knipperdollinck etc" (No. 11). There is just not enough in this character to sense the comic of the man with the *ideé fixe* (the alazon type) or the fundamentalist with the literal belief in the Word which we met in the earlier version. Only in *The Dance* (Scene 18) does the author try to recreate the comic in the character. Knipperdollinck describes himself as "the poorest of your subjects" and is treated as such by Bockelson throughout the scene, his serio-comical remarks being met by Bockelson's comically inappropriate rejoinders, but, where, in the first version, the obscenely comical dance was a "Dance of Death" on a hyperbolical "roof" and which led them both to the wheel, this one takes place on an ordinary stage and resembles a music-hall comic patter duet which ends "midst thunderous applause". It is only real for the victim who loses his God: Bockelson, the comic victor, calls it "our own staging of the end of the world" (p.91). Knipperdollinck's death becomes a parody of his death in *It is Written*; there he had the last word; here, he is only one of many representatives of the suffering "masses", the victims of inhumanity, mourned (again) only by the Bishop.

With the exception of Judith and Matthison,[13] all the other characters are, to a greater or lesser degree, buffoons and clowns. The Princes, the representatives of secular and religious authority, are made comic by "reduction". They are shown to be interested only in their own political chicaneries and are made comic by being made to look stupid. In his *Problems of the Theatre*, Dürrenmatt wrote that "man's freedom is manifested in his laughter" (meaning, in his *freedom* to laugh) and added that writers *could* attack the "tyrants of this planet" for, "they only fear one thing: ridicule" (TP, p.55). These buffoons are therefore types of inhuman rulers mocked by Dürrenmatt as Chaplin mocked Hitler and Mussolini in *The Great Dictator*. Spectators of this *theatrum mundi* like the Bishop, they are only "cynical" where he was "despairing" (*Consideration* No. 11).

The ordinary people are likewise portrayed as "buffoons" – but because they are *willing* sufferers and victims. Their rôle is a more cynical one than in the first version. The comic Catholic-Protestant duo (which mirrors the absurdities of their masters) of von Mengerssen-von Büren is the liaison between the two groups. The result of their defeat in the siege – a scene of comic hyperbole – betrays the flimsiness of their faith, since both now want to convert to the other's religion (pp.49-50). In *It is written*, these were true clowns, whose knockabout pantofarce represented one of the oldest traditions of the *mimus*, an integral part of the Dürrenmattian *Komödie*, as we have seen. Here, they can be taken as more typical of the dramatist's tauter stage technique. Much of the automatism has vanished; the comic laughter must now arise mainly from the language and the usual Dürrenmattian satire of religious beliefs, now more explicit than implicit. This is why Reinhold Stumm had to remark: "That tree which was always producing new blossoms, the tree of puns and situation comedy, has been pruned", but he added ". . . so that we can now see the thin branches"![14]

*   *   *

The absence of the Master of Ceremonies, the "Chronometric Turk", the two automated wives of the Count, the three introductory Anabaptists, the drummer and the parodying executioner, has naturally robbed the early work of much of its Aristophanic exuberance. In *The Anabaptists*, the 49 scenes have been reduced to 20 and, although many of these are still like revue-sketches, the inner structure, the links between the scenes, is tighter. Each scene has a more definite purpose: this can be noted in the Brechtian titles: e.g. Scene 1: *Münster in Westphalia is converted*. The result is, or should be, a faster-moving, more effective piece of stagecraft. But not all critics found the change to their liking.

I am as sceptical as Dürrenmatt about the immediate reaction of "journalist-critics" on first nights, writing against a dead-line, and I agreed readily with him when he dismissed première reviews as "fly-by-nights". That is why Frau Brock-Sulzer's perceptive comment is worth noting: "It is almost comical to see how many of these audiences attacked the second version for the lack of precisely those characteristics which were so violently attacked in the first version". By "audiences" she meant, of course, the journalists.[15]

I believe that this "reduction" in pantofarcical scenes heralded a new type of dramaturgy for Dürrenmatt. When I visited him in 1969, and came to talk of his reasons for re-writing Strindberg's *Dance of Death*, he said: "I wanted to get rid of the trappings" – but the deeper dramaturgical reasons lay in his increasing interest in the technical details of play production. To adapt his own Bockelson, Dürrenmatt might say: "Important as an author, I'm a genius as a director!" The "reversions", his insistence on his works being thought of as "scores" and not as "literature" – "A play never 'is' – it's always 'becoming' " – his attendance at all rehearsals of his plays, his description of his profession as "tailors" and certainly not as "poets", on writing "with the stage" and not just for it, his additions of scenes for favourite actors and so on – all this adds up to a deep concern for dramaturgical possibilities.

Thus *The Anabaptists* removed the "trappings" from the earlier work and became a more practical possibility for producer and actor. But what significance had this new style for this study of Dürrenmatt's development as a dramatist?

Clearly, much less emphasis is now placed on pantofarcical scenes; his great comic scenes have often depended on the comic of multiplication, of disguise and farcical business, linguistic as well as dramaturgical. (For example, there is only one pun in the whole of *The Anabaptists*). But the real importance lies in the use of the comic to change the balance of the work which, in turn, demonstrated the change in the author's *Weltanschauung* since 1947. Bockelson is now a "Komödiant" (which he was, of course, historically, as Ranke testifies). He is therefore now both a *comédien* and a comedian, that is, an actor and a "clown". The consequence is that the comic elements in his character make him a true comic figure, where, in the first version, though "untragic", his death did bring an earnestness into the work which the 26-year-old author tried to justify by his sub-title, "Ein Drama".

Now, however, the comic elements in the plot make this a *Komödie*. Bockelson, as a "special case", is a comic character – he carries the day over the Bishop who refused to engage him for his troupe. Since Bockelson is clearly meant to be a clown, our laughter must be "purposive" laughter, at the end — we are meant to "distance" ourselves from him, to laugh *at* him, therefore, and not with him. Bockelson must be seen not as the triumph of cynicism and nihilism, but as the warning which has been presented before to us in Dürrenmatt's works. He might be seen as a Hitler who, refused by the Viennese Academy, was swept into power by the well-meaning enthusiasts around Hugenberg, or even as an example of that "pseudo-ness", the modern obsession with the reproduction at the expense of the original. However we see him, the Bishop's lone cry at the close is the proof that Bockelson represents *not* the triumph of evil, but the tragic condition of the modern world, that such a liar can win the day. The Bishop's cry shows, too, that we must do more than laugh at Bockelson and his like. It shows that we must *all* stand up and attempt to throw off our shackles — otherwise, it will be the story heard before in *An Angel comes to Babylon*: "All are against the Tower and yet it is *still* built". The Bishop is Dürrenmatt's "absurd hope".

The pendulum has swung from the religious drama of 1947; the presence of the comic elements in both works shows however where his concern has always lain — not in transcendental philosophy, but in the world of today, the *hic et nunc* of the comic writer. Dürrenmatt the realist, has long believed that Man is a *zoon politicon*: ". . . and the political cage in which he lives . . . conditions him too".[16] His concern is with humanity and particularly with modern humanity, crushed under the burden of an anonymous state and a technological society. Man must be made to accept his responsibilities and not be allowed to slip easily into error.[17]

"Humanity is more than a pretty word — it's a risk and we all need to ensure that this risk doesn't become an act of madness". Inhumanity will be branded by his comic. This is the real significance of the comic in his plays, for, as he said in the *Conversation 1971*, he didn't like being called a "pessimist". He is a *realist* distrusting the optimist who sets out from what *should be* instead of what *is*. Humour is the answer: it overcomes pessimism and allows us to use optimism sensibly. (*TSR* II, p.280).

(ii) KÖNIG JOHANN (KING JOHN)

In her *Friedrich Dürrenmatt* (4th edn., 1973), Professor Elisabeth Brock-Sulzer writes:

> But even if the Shakespearean original itself did not prohibit it, this play, despite its many comic highlights, could not be called a *Komödie*, like most of Dürrenmatt's other dramas.   (p.180).

Shakespeare's *King John* is certainly no comedy; on the other hand, Dürrenmatt's researches into the original proved that it had nevertheless contained a good deal of comic writing. Dürrenmatt recalled how Shakespeare had rewritten the play "in great haste" to present it as a rival to a *King John* play already running.[18] He admitted to Hans Linder: "I was confronted by a confusion of historical facts and a peculiarly composed plot which suddenly treated the last two acts quite differently from the first three".[19]

C.H.Herford had pointed out as long ago as 1899 that the *King John* play, the "Troublesome Raigne", contained a good deal of "horseplay and burlesque", particularly in the character of the Bastard, who (in Shakespeare) "foreshadows the historical conqueror of Agincourt" and "opens the cycle of Histories founded upon humour and heroism".[20]

One cannot deny the humour in Shakespeare's *King John* — one need think only of the Bastard's famous exposure of "commodity" at Pandulph's expense: "That smooth-faced gentleman, tickling Commodity" (II, i, 573) while the heroism is possibly the only part of the play still familiar to British audiences:

> Come the three corners of the world in arms, And we shall shock them. Nought shall make us rue, If England to itself do rest but true.
>   (V, vii, 116-119).

Dürrenmatt might well have been attracted by these two ingredients, humour and heroism; the first in a positive, the second in a negative way. His satire has been mainly directed, as has been seen, towards mocking useless heroism — such is his goal here too.

A third factor must be mentioned however. Dürrenmatt had long had an idea for a play called *Kaiser und Eunuch* (*Emperor and Eunuch*), on a Byzantine theme. The Emperor was Justinian, his "great genius" was his eunuch, Narses, "who got his own back for having been made a eunuch". Eunuchs had power, but could never attain the highest positions, because they could always be exploited. One recalls Shaw's famous remark!

Such, thought Dürrenmatt, was the Bastard's quandary in *King John*: He was "outsider . . . and patriot", whose one aim was to make England great — through war. The author was obviously unhappy about the Bastard's warlike plans — he compares him to Carl Zuckmayer's *The Devil's General*, and it is very likely that he intended to make *King John* an anti-war play directed against the inhumanities of the Vietnam War still raging in South-East Asia in 1968. (The German ZDF TV version of 20 January 1971 certainly gave this impression, since Göring and Hitler appeared in the introduction).

To return however to Frau Brock-Sulzer's point that the adaptation cannot be called a *Komödie*. In the notes to the text, Dürrenmatt wrote: "A dramatic chronicle becomes an allegory: The *Komödie* of politics, of a particular political situation",[21] while shortly after the première in the Basler Theater on 18 September, 1968, he had posed the question: Might there not be two dramaturgies? "Is there a drama-turgical method of showing those in power, and one for showing the *victims* of those in power?" If an old man, he went on, in an old people's home, and Walter Ulbricht (the then most powerful man in the GDR) were both asked the question: "Are you happy?" — the old man's answer (viz. he was alone and helpless) would be *tragic*; Ul-bricht's, on the other hand, ("he was a happy man") would be *comic*: "The private lives of victims appear tragic because they have nothing but this private life, they only have themselves; the private lives of those in power appear comical because the effects of their policies make their private cares insignificant . . ." Following this slightly gnomic utterance, Dürrenmatt continued a theme familiar to this study: "The tragic is what is human, the comic what is inhuman (or *non*-human)". We can see therefore that his "reversion" of *King John* *does* make it a *Komödie* in his (and in my) terminology: "Yet it is precisely those in power who are the clowns among men, albeit, the terrifying clowns".

Why should this be so? "Men laugh at their fellow-man when he appears as a clown; the clown is the man disguised from other men, the inhuman human being". So, have we not returned to our *point de départ*, to Henri Bergson who believed that Man was comical when he acted as a "non-human", as a machine? (See above, p.22). By turning Shakespeare's characters into clowns, Dürrenmatt makes *his King John* a *Komödie*. The Bergsonian conclusion to this essay puts the issue beyond doubt, I feel:

> The victims are "comical", too, because it is inhuman to have to be
> a victim, since the victims, *because* they are victims, are separated

from what they could be: human beings. Therefore there is perhaps
only one possible dramaturgical method nowadays: the *Komödie*.
Unfortunately.[22]

★   ★   ★

Basle had been thought of for some time as (to use a Dürrenmattian
term) "the deepest provinces". In an attempt to revive its theatrical
fortunes, Werner Düggelin, the new *Intendant*, invited Dürrenmatt to
join the theatre as "Advisory Member of the Directorate" in the autumn
of 1968. (The combination became affectionately known as "Dü-Dü"!)
Dürrenmatt's task was to participate in "team-work", he said to Rainer
Litten: "I think I've had, as a writer, as a writer for the theatre, certain
experiences in directing as well as in writing, so I could make myself
useful in this team as a sort of control factor . . ."[23] He hoped to be
able to produce his own works, to write new ones or to make "alterations or attempts at alterations of authors or re-workings of old texts",
he told Litten. He did all of these during his short span of activity at
the Basle Theatre, a period full of tension, anyway, after the May 1968
"événements" in France and the Rudi-Dutschke-led students' revolts
in West Germany.

   Dürrenmatt told me: "*King John* was an occasional work for the
theatre. It had been an age-long dream to do it", even though he
thought little of Shakespeare's play: "Just variations on the theme of
weeping"! The political implications for our own day obviously attracted him: Shakespeare had been "the aristocrats' poet", he said. "The
strange thing with Shakespeare is the absence of the people. That was a
condition of his times. Shakespeare has the nobility and the rabble".
Shakespeare's aim, Dürrenmatt believed, had been to strengthen the
"aristocratic feeling" of the nobility, a thought which is repeated in his
notes to *Titus Andronicus* (See *TSR II*, p.189).

   I have been stressing how the elements of the comic in Dürrenmatt's
later works are directed towards revealing the inhumanity in the political structures of the world, in the relationship of man to man and,
particularly, of ruler to ruled. Joseph Scherer had noted this emphasis
as far back as 1961; it was now becoming a "dramaturgy of the victim".[24] In the *Prinzipien der Bearbeitung* (*Principles of the Revision*),
Dürrenmatt wrote:

An old play, actually only revised, but with the old style retained. Thus the possibility of relating it to our times becomes all the more terrifying. That *King John* is still relevant for us, shows the extent of our problems.

Such a burning interest in human relationships, as expressed in political structures, is emphasized in his *Gigantic Lecture on Justice and the Law* (1969) based on the Hobbesian "thesis", *homo homini lupus*, or, in the Plautinian original, *lupus est homo homini* (*Asin*. 495). This witty exposition of the "Wolf-game" (the capitalist system) and the "Good-Shepherd-game" (the communist system) was well summed up by Friedrich Luft: "He regards both concepts with something less than sympathy", since both lacked *humanity*.[25]

★   ★   ★

Dürrenmatt likened the changes that he had made in his reversion to a changing of the points on a railway track. Eventually the train goes off in a completely different direction.[26] The main change that altered the direction of this "train" was in the relationship of the Bastard to King John. Of the Bastard (who, in *King John*, is "Philip the Bastard") Dürrenmatt said to me: "I find that this Bastard as played today . . . is a very dangerous figure. A man who remains loyal to the State despite everything is rather suspicious". The new direction seems to give the Bastard a Bockelson-like ambivalence, with traces of both the professional and the spiritual clown. His obsession with patriotism and his blind faith in the power of "Reason" would seem to be *idées fixes*, an alazon characteristic; his concern for the future of the "people" and his hatred of the hypocritical inhumanity of the ruling classes, is an eiron characteristic.

The key to his character lies in Dürrenmatt's comment:

> My Bastard is neither an ideologue nor a moralist, for him the Kings are those in power and the people are the victims of those in power. All that he demands from Kings is that they rule rationally, he tries to make John a rational man.   (*Principles*, p.101).

The abysmal failure of his attempt to do this makes the Bastard into a paradoxical comic character and the play into a bitter modern "*Komödie* of politics".

The Bastard is introduced in a classically comic way: as the product of an illegal sexual relationship between Richard the Lionheart and Queen Eleonore. Richard is (for the Bastard) "the hero of far-off wars and foreign marriage beds . . ." (p.11), while the Bastard himself is presented by Eleonore (in comically Helvetic terms) as "covered in dung, uncultured, unknown . . ." (p.14); when he is granted the name Sir Richard Plantagenet by John to serve, on the one hand, as cannon-fodder, and, on the other, as a stallion to Blanka von Kastilien (Blanche of Spain in Shakespeare), John's niece, we see that he accepts the position as a hypocritical "game":

> Thus shamming so as not to lie to myself,
> I remain so true to myself by lying to the world,
> And so by deeds of bravery I climb
> The hen-ladder of honour, covered in muck,   (p.16)

where the "rural" vocabulary is obviously intended to be Helvetically humorous.

The Bastard's cynical acceptance that the "game" is played by opportunists establishes the mood of Dürrenmatt's reversion; no mood of great tragedy broods over this work — all is opportunism and chance. From the Bastard's fortuitous "engagement", unforeseen consequences will ensue.

He is made the voice of conventional Reason imploring the English John and the French Philip not to wage war and he tries to make them allow the citizens of Angers to decide which King they will choose. (Philip makes the suggestion in Shakespeare, II, i, 197-200). When Pembroke bursts in to announce that the Swiss (under Leopold of Austria) have broken the armistice and have attacked the *rear* of John's army, the cause of Reason suffers its first set-back. The important Act II, Scene I, therefore closes with the Bastard realizing that war cannot be prevented by Reason, but *can* be caused by stupidity. The laughter here is *with* the Bastard *at* the buffoonish stupidity of the rulers — he represents the defence of the "humans", the people.

When the battle has been waged and the Bastard tries for the second time to make the two kings see "reason", their inhumanity is symbolized by the decision to lay Angers waste because of the citizens' inability to decide which king they should support. Nowhere is the difference between the two concepts of the theme clearer than here, since it is the Bastard in Shakespeare who proposes the *sack* of the town: "By heaven, these scroyles of Angiers flout you, kings . . . (II, i, 373).

In Dürrenmatt's version, however, the kings' decision implies that the Bastard's plea for rational thinking is flouted for the second time. "Philip wants to carry out this madness simply for a whim . . ." says John to the Bastard during the pantofarcical shaving scene which (as

Dürrenmatt points out) is meant to make the Bastard — and us — aware of his lowly position (See *Theaterarbeit. Anderungen* (*Theatre work. Alterations*) pp.95-98, here p.97, No.5).

A rational voice he may be, but John is King and "in power", so the Bastard is treated as a comic menial like the eunuch mentioned above.[27] Nevertheless, John accepts that the Bastard is his only hope in his present dilemma, the only person in England whom he can trust. The fall of Angers is therefore the immediate stage symbol of the fall of Reason. The Bastard has become a "Fool".

The Bastard's third attempt to make John act rationally is foiled by Chance: John is to announce to the world that Arthur is dead and then to produce him, safe and sound, when accused of his murder. But Arthur commits suicide and is presented as an "unfortunate" corpse to the nobles who turn in disgust to support the Dauphin. (Since Hubert de Burgh is significantly omitted from this version, Arthur's suicide is therefore presented as "Chance". Incidentally, Dürrenmatt's Arthur is 8, Shakespeare's, 15).

But, even now, John is prepared to accept the Bastard's last counsel: to submit to the Church and receive England back as a fief, an England which the Bastard is teaching John to love. Dürrenmatt's Bastard defends Shakespeare's "rabble":

> *King John*: The people!
> They live in apathy, uneducated,
> Lie down in the same straw to copulate and
> To die, only vegetate, a rabble.
>
> *Bastard*: Rabble? Sir, they represent the majority.   (pp.75-76)

Each suggestion of the Bastard's has been nullified, either by the inhumanity of man or by the incalculabilities of Chance. The "worst-possible turn" which finally makes the Bastard a truly comic figure is the news of the poisoning by Pembroke. Although John is ready to grant the people their rights: "What we call rabble owns the land / What we call "commodity" is paid for by the people" (p.91), he nevertheless accuses the Bastard of duping him and, on John's death, the Bastard has to recognize the futility, the comic futility of his struggle against a double foe:

> With the world of those in power I mingled,
> Tried to guide them to a better goal,
> But stupidity drew the carriage of Fate.
> And Chance . . .   (pp.93-94).

His return to his former life as a cow-herd will enable him to create
a race of bastards endowed with the strength of "lions": "Only thus is
this England to be helped" (p.94) — a far cry indeed from the Shakespearean Bastard's patriotic cry:

> This England never did, nor never shall,
> Lie at the proud foot of a conqueror . . .   (V, vii, 112-113).[28]

Dürrenmatt's Bastard is a true comic character, a spiritual clown,
because he too is a victim of the "system". Pembroke's closing words
show us that the *status quo* will be undisturbed by such "holy fools":

> Let's off then to state business,
> To cart this country through our age
> In the old ways, untroubled by fools.   (p.94).

The victim is a clown because the unheroic futility of his actions
prevents our sympathy going out to him; it also prevents his fate from
appearing tragic.

Thus, again, we have a Bockelson-like figure, an ambivalent comic
figure, but where the alazon-traits dominated in the Anabaptist and his
end was just a warning to the world, I see the Bastard as a more positive
character; a spiritual clown, on the whole, of good intentions, defeated
by inhumanity and Chance, but ready to fight another day; the hope
for the future lies with him and his like. He will remain a watcher of
this "game" from the sidelines, (like the Bishop of Münster), but his
fate turns the end of the play into what H.Beil called "a terrible warning vision of Un-Reason".[29]

                          ★   ★   ★

King John is likewise a somewhat ambivalent character. Dürrenmatt
believed that he appeared in Shakespeare as "a stage villain with neither
glamour nor fortune" and admitted to Linder that Churchill's picture
of John had influenced his own portrayal. Churchill, it might be remembered, wrote: "Moreover, when the long tally is added, it will be
seen that the British nation and the English-speaking world owe far
more to the vices of John than to the labours of virtuous sovereigns".[30]
Thus: "I revalued him", wrote Dürrenmatt in the *Principles* (p.100).

The comic-grotesque variant on the French theatre's *trois coups* —
the three executions with which the Dürrenmatt play opens — show
King John to be as insensitive to human misery and suffering as King

Philip. (Indeed they are presented for much of the time as a comic duo, as I shall show). John is likewise as hypocritical; knowing full well that war with France will serve to keep his nobles patriotically together, he builds up his system of government on two pillars of faith — cruelty to the people and expediency with the nobles. (The programme of the première quoted Machiavelli's *Il Principe*: "Therefore a Prince must learn to rule like an animal as well as a human being"). Their expression in the play leads to comedy. John is soon established as a blustering alazon-type, comic in his impostoring, in his hypocritical double-dealings and in his political chicanery. The comic lies in Bergson's "transposition of the ancient to the modern", in the anachronistic 20th century colloquial speech contrasting comically with the 13th century armorial trappings.

The eiron-image appears only slowly; firstly, when John allows himself to listen to the Bastard and then when he takes his advice and allows the citizens of Angers their choice of king. John's seduction by Reason has been traced above; at each stage, he appears less inhuman and more sympathetic as he follows the Bastard's advice. This places John firmly between the Bastard and Philip in the comic spectrum; a spiritual clown in that he (albeit dimly) perceives the way out of the "system", but cannot follow it, an alazon-type when he blindly curses the Bastard's rational planning and realizes that Chance (in the form of Isabella's unexpected son) has driven him to a "ridiculous death" (p.92). Although Dürrenmatt pointed out that John's "ability to follow rational advice must earn our respect" (*Principles*, p.100), and therefore suggested *one* way of considering John, the pantofarce of the later acts (possibly borrowed from *The Troublesome Raigne*) swings the pendulum in the other direction. When John, in his scanty penitent's robe (and a "comic" crown on his head) shuffles about with Pandulpho on the floor and is finally invited to jump into bed with the Papal Legate, all kingly dignity is sacrificed to pantofarce (pp.80-84). The "reduction" of the pair makes a mockery not only of the solemn dignity of the Shakespearean original, but also of the "system" of feudal government and, by analogy, of all unenlightened political structures nowadays. As Schwab-Felisch rightly pointed out: "It is clear, not only that the thrice-revealed impossibility of enforcing Reason within an irrational system must lead to the decision to change the system. It is also clear that this system is dependent on its ideological superstructure".[31]

Although Dürrenmatt makes of John a King who tried to "see justice" by introducing the Magna Carta (the "limiting of my royal power", p.91), with some dignity, John's hysterical rejection of the Bastard must display the truer side of his character and lead us to think of him more as a professional, than as a spiritual clown. His true motive force was "commodity" (self-interest), and not humanity.

"Commodity" is the lowest common denominator of all the other leading male characters. Philip sums this up in his remarks to Austria:

> To resolve our differences in battle
> There are our people, the two armies;
> Yet we, oppressing each other hard,
> Are separated only by "commodity", not by hatred . . .   (p.20)

The consequent lack of sympathy for others, the inhumanity of "those in power", distances them from us, and they become clowns. They are made comic, too, in the physical sense by their actions, as when Philip and John, now a comic duo, "two sinister buffoons", as Hilde Spiel called them, behave like Bergsonian automata at the beginning of Act II, sitting down, standing up, sitting down again in unison as they negotiate their cynical formula for peace (p.27).[32]

The scene with Louis and Philip fulfils the same function; serious, indeed tragic, matters of state affecting the destinies of thousands, are discussed against a farcical background; here, Louis and Philip in their bath-tubs take the momentous decision to leave England, since Pandulpho's announcement that England now belongs to the Pope has "made fools" of them. Thus, this bath-tub scene, with its emphasis on Louis' cuckolding, serves to make the whole a comic allegory of what Dürrenmatt called the "formulation of their treaties and their misfortunes" (p.101, where "their" means, "of those in power").

Dover Wilson remarks that the moral of Shakespeare's play was "that for his day and for his England, the supreme need was national unity";[33] "national unity" and "patriotism" (of the senseless sort) are mocked by Dürrenmatt in his pantofarcical portrayal of the aristocracy, the three Lords, Salisbury, Essex and Bigot, a comic buffoon trio. The fortuitous storm which soaked them also makes them look ridiculous:

> King John: You are dripping wet, my Lords, yet
>   Under the canopy it was quite dry.
> Salisbury: It pissed down only on your subjects . . .   (p.69).

Having established them as comic characters physically, Dürrenmatt demonstrates how they share the inhumanity of the other "ruling" characters by their hypocritical treatment of the "people"; they seem to sympathize with the people in their struggle against the King – but then Salisbury savagely strikes down a locksmith who acts clumsily in undoing his armour (p.69).[34]

But the major buffoon in the play is Leopold, Duke of Austria (whom Shakespeare calls Lymoges).[35] He is a lickspittle, a double-dealer and a firebrand, all in one; by making him the Bastard's sole opponent, the author satirizes him above all as the voice of self-interest and doltish inhumanity. When the Bastard seems to have found a formula for peace between England and France, Austria mutters: "There's a smell of rotten peace here. I must act", and he steals away unnoticed (p.28). Dürrenmatt had early established the comic in the character in the Bastard's speech denouncing Austria as a cuckold. He now makes Austria into a comic glutton (p.42), a well-tried source of comic laughter on the stage, since it shows a lack of control and therefore marries well with a lack of "reason".[36] He is completely ignored by the others during the discussion on whether Philip will side with the Pope or with John, and when the French King ends the parley with John with "I must obey the Pope and the Pope / Has decided: We are at war!" the cynicism of "commodity", the *"Komödie* of politics", is stressed by the buffoonish behaviour of the go-between clown, Leopold: *"Stage direction*: All rise, except Austria, who goes on eating" (p.49). This character contains the well-tried and traditional ploys of the old comic theatre; "reduction" of the great, the inappropriate, the mocking of the cuckold, whose end is as absurd as his life. The significance of these elements is that Leopold personifies "those in power" and the opposition to the Bastard's voice of "Reason".

Since, as Dürrenmatt notes, the two dynasties, the Plantagenets and the Capets, have a metaphysical *raison d'être*, the Church must be regarded as part of the "system". In 1975, Dürrenmatt was still saying (to Heinz Ludwig Arnold) that he was still "totally against the Church", and here too Pandulpho, the Papal Legate, is painted as another comic clergyman. The satire is mainly contained in the self-portrait in Act V, Scene II, but also in the pantofarcical scene with John mentioned above. Pandulpho was once "of the people", his mother a favourite of the Prince who was wont to fetch her into his bed, "and me too, if it suited him" (p.89), adds the Legate.

His inhumanity is revealed in the cynicism with which he greets John's new reforming zeal;[37] he feigns delight, but sends secret orders to Pembroke to have John poisoned. When the deed is done, Pandulpho is ready to offer the new King, Henry III, the Church's protection and help, but this is much more of a threat than a promise (p.93).

Thus, Pandulpho is one of those "terrifying clowns . . . distanced from mankind and thus from their victims, apart, inhuman . . ." His blessings and prayers are empty, almost comical gestures, his words are double-talk at the best, and lies at the worst.[38]

★   ★   ★

The Life and Death of King John, a "tragedy . . . with a very pleasing interchange of incidents and characters", as Dr. Johnson described it, has become a *"Komödie* of politics" at Dürrenmatt's hands. (He told Linder that it could have been called *The Politicians*). It is the game of politics, analogue to the game of chess, but a "game among murderers", another *"Komödie* of the *theatrum mundi"*. The elements of the comic have prevented any of the characters from being "tragic", since they are either ludicrous in themselves or because their potentially tragic fates lack the inner necessity or logic that would make them tragic.[39] The only possible tragic figures cannot be called tragic because their fates are never shown to us — Arthur's suicide occurs off-stage and thus the audience cannot show sympathy for him, and the "people" never appear. When they *are* mentioned, they are mere numbers, ten thousand here, fifteen thousand there, mere cannon-fodder, pawns in the great "game". Their fates *might* be tragic, but only in private, like the old man's in *Two Dramaturgies*? (see p.187 above). On the stage, however, we see a *Komödie*.

Professor Arrigo Subiotto claims: "It is not difficult to find in this adaptation. . .a pessimistic philosophy of political motive and action . . ." (op.cit., p.145). I wonder if he has sufficiently appreciated Dürrenmatt's obvious sympathy with the absent "people" throughout the play? Indeed, the elements of the comic, by pointing out the weaknesses and fallibilities of the "great" underline the unreasonableness of the fates of the "small". Nor does he mention the hope displayed in the Bastard's final return to the people. The play mocks the tyrants by its use of the comic elements and demonstrates in the ambivalent character of the Bastard Dürrenmatt's determination to show Man's "possibility of freedom".[40]

(iii) PLAY STRINDBERG (PLAY STRINDBERG)

Dürrenmatt's third major "reversion" was an "arrangement" of *Dödsdansen* (*Dance of Death*) (1900) by the Swedish author, August Strindberg (1848-1912). It is always misleading to attempt to see a "pattern" in an author's work. Dürrenmatt said to me when asked why he had chosen any particular subject: "You just pick up what lies nearest to hand", and this is probably true of most dramatists. Nevertheless, the composition, production and direction of *Play Strindberg* seems to confirm many of the statements that I have made about Dürrenmatt's dramaturgical method.

He first read Strindberg's play in 1948; he assured me that Strindberg had had no influence on his dramaturgy otherwise, but that the adaptation grew out of one of his first tasks as adviser to the Basle theatre; the directors had decided to produce the *Dance of Death* in Emil Schering's German translation: "We played it" — he said to me — "and the actors protested and were all very depressed. So I said: I'll do it for you and wrote it straightaway . . . It was as with *John* — practical theatre . . ." It was to be an "examination" of an old play, he said.[41]

For Dürrenmatt, Strindberg was a "great philistine", to be compared with Wagner. What he saw in the *Dance of Death* was a "Beckett-situation". ". . .I wanted to get rid of all the trappings and give an old work back to our modern age. . . and leave all the fustian out. . ." he told me. It is therefore important to bear in mind from the outset that we are dealing here with a production fashioned for a particular group of artists in a particular theatre at a particular time — when Dürrenmatt was *a fortiori* the "man of the theatre". Thus, when dealing with *Play Strindberg*, future scholars might bear in mind Wolfgang Kayser's timely warning: ". . .the literary historian who does not know the contemporary theatre of the drama he is considering can easily go astray".[42] *Play Strindberg* should therefore not be taken as a profound exposition of Dürrenmattian "philosophy". It is a piece of theatrical craftsmanship. Strindberg's *Dance of Death*, on the other hand, *is* biographical. His tragic relationships with women, with Siri von Essen, Marie David, Frida Uhl and Harriet Bosse, must be mirrored in the misogynist captain Edgar's relationship with Alice, while the background to the work was certainly his stay in 1899 with his sister Anna and her husband, Hugo Philp, who had been married for 25 years. (Anna, we learn, was a fine pianist, whose favourite piece, Saint-Saëns' *La danse macabre* (op.40), lay behind the original conception of Strindberg's play).[43]

But this is certainly not the case with Dürrenmatt's "arrangement". Horrified with Strindberg's work, he constructed an "anti-Strindberg" play; out of a "domestic marital tragedy" he made a "*Komödie* on domestic marital tragedies".[44] He said to me: ". . .for me it's a phenomenon that this play is still performed. It's *so* bad".

Not all critics agreed after the première on 8 February, 1969; some, indeed, criticized his adaptation for lacking just the depth and intensity of the original. The *National Zeitung*, Basle, for example wrote: "Because the play nowhere affords insights into the depths, the 'battle' becomes uninteresting". Certainly, few literary critics could deny the insights into the human soul which Strindberg's plays afford; it is believed by some that a good deal of the knowledge about complexes stems from the interest shown by Viennese psychologists like Adler in Strindberg's work, and Werner Mittenzwei gives him the credit for being the "progenitor of the psychological drama" in which the battle of the sexes was "only the poetic expression for the absolute alienation of the individual".[45] Dürrenmatt, too, was certainly prepared to grant Strindberg's importance for modern drama and his influence on writers like Albee, and he was well aware that the theme of *Dance of Death* had a contemporary relevance which would attract audiences. Nevertheless, I feel that the theme was much less important for him *at that time* than the experimental technique through which the theme was presented. "To allow a theme to become a plot — and nothing else" was how he had expressed this approach to Frau Brock-Sulzer as long ago as 1961. The "new" Dürrenmatt was at hand.[46]

★   ★   ★

Play Strindberg became what we should like to call — following Strindbergian terminology — a "chamber *Komödie*". Indeed, the reversions of *It is written, King John, Dödsdansen* and *Titus Andronicus* are clearly, in retrospect, examples of the new Dürrenmatt technique. The verbiage and fustian both of language and set, are removed, leaving the bare essential details behind. ". . .a stage play (lit. an actor's play) becomes a play for actors" (*Bericht*) (*Report*). But *Play Strindberg* also became a play for "clowns", since the actors had to move and speak like "inhuman human beings". Dürrenmatt was able to demand this technique since he was portraying man's inhumanity to man in an "end-game"; hatred between two people condemned to live together. Their inhumanity is presented in the comic of their speech and actions which vividly recall those Bergsonian precepts examined earlier. The audience will punish the characters for the "defects that are ridiculous" and their "mechanical inelasticity". "That inelasticity is the comic and laughter is its corrective", wrote Bergson in *Le Rire* (p.16). Throughout this play, we laugh at the "something mechanical encrusted on something living", the mechanical in the language and in the actions. The comic is derived from the lack of humanity shown on the stage.

> The attitudes, gestures and movements of the human body are laughable in exact proportion as that body reminds us of a mere machine.   (pp.22-23).

Through the comic situation, the author can present a trio of potentially tragic characters whose "ridiculed frailty" constitutes the theme of this *Komödie* (see above, pp.21-22).

Dürrenmatt adopted the characters from the original story with only a few adjustments: for example, Olaf, the son, in Part II was called Allan, after Edgar Allan Poe, in the original. His Edgar has much in common with the alazon-types we have met in his other works. He is a braggart and an impostor who lives in a make-believe world, shut off, both literally and metaphorically, from reality. Edgar's "Don't let's talk about it anymore", becomes the comic symbol of their isolation and alienation; repeated on five occasions, it prevents the invasion of reality into his illusions. Each time he says the words, Edgar attempts to brush away an unfortunate or unwanted memory with the same phrase whose repetition in the situation represents his "weakness" and becomes that "inelasticity" in his character of which Bergson wrote.

Edgar's obsession with his health is also an *idée fixe* which the audience will castigate with its laughter. Edgar's jealousy of the doctor and his parties is in Strindberg: Dürrenmatt retains the "Einfall", but the doctor is now made responsible for Edgar's illnesses and is called an "idiot" (p.10), and then, three times, "a weakminded quack" (pp.19, 33 and 35). Closely connected with his opinion of the doctor is his own diagnosis of his condition. Where the doctor believes that Edgar has not long to live, Edgar repeats four times: "I'm as fit as a fiddle" (pp. 10, 25, 32 and 44) and when he hears of his promotion to Major, and decides that it has come too late, since he will soon be dead, he has the phrase sarcastically hurled back at him by Alice (p.53).

The comic effect of repetition is seen in a typical Dürrenmattian linguistic device. In Willi Reich's version, Edgar says: "Illness? I have never been ill, only once unwell. And I shall still be living twenty years from now". Dürrenmatt parodies the phrase by giving it a triadic structure and then repeating it: "I'm not ill, I've never been ill and I shall never be ill" (pp. 10, 32 and 42). The comic effect is heightened when the same structure is repeated with "lonely": cf. *Edgar*: "I'm lonely, I've always been lonely and I shall always be lonely" (p.11), with "crawl" (p.14) and finally when Alice taunts him in the same way with "cowardly" (p.16). The laughter is at the braggart, the whistler-in-the-wind whose illusions fall so palpably short of his achievements.[47]

With *Play Strindberg*, one has to be on one's guard against accepting what Dürrenmatt has written as a representation of his own "philosophy" — indeed, the play gives a good example of that "ambiguity" that the author is always demanding from the stage. Nothing here is what it seems to be: Strindberg's Edgar is one of those men who might say or think: "To be able to live one's life, one must do ill to others, by the very fact that one crosses their path". Dürrenmatt's realistic view of life would not have permitted him to write such a sentence. His opinion of Strindberg, as expressed to me at any rate, made it clear that we must regard such utterances as suspect. For this reason, too, we should regard Edgar's linguistic repetitions as parodies of what Dürrenmatt called Strindberg's "soul-studies" (in *Report*).

The captain can be mocked, too, as an example of outdated heroism, of "sabre-rattling" as Dürrenmatt's grandfather would have called it. This is to be found in Strindberg as well, of course. His Edgar says: "I'll die with my boots on without pain". Dürrenmatt's Edgar says: "I'll die with my boots on like an old soldier" (p.10) — but he repeats the phrase on pages 26 and 33, the first time immediately after one of his "attacks" of unconsciousness, and the second time, just after a pantofarcical scene with Kurt. In both cases, the words occur in an incongruous context and the original comic effect is made doubly comical by (intentional) parody.

Edgar's "I shall still be living twenty years from now" is changed to "I shall live another twenty years" and then parodied. It is heard firstly in context with the phrases above, then it is repeated on pages 11, 13, 33, 44 and 61, while Alice taunts Edgar with it on page 53.

Thus Edgar's life is built up on comic illusions; he pretends that his out-of-date textbook on ballistics has made him a "world-famous military author" (pp. 13, 15 and 19) and that he is rich as a result: "I spend money like water", (pages 19 and 24). Finally, he believes that his Colonel will soon promote him: "The Colonel knows my worth" (pages 11, 16, 31, 41 and 43; again Alice taunts him finally with the phrase on page 61). In each case, the bubble is eventually pricked to reveal the "impostor".

This is the "involuntary comic"; Edgar is an alazon type whose personality and idiosyncrasies make him appear comical. The "grotesqueries" of his "fits" must be seen in this way also. They are mocked as situations with tragic implications. They can therefore legitimately be thought of as being related to the "comic deaths" discussed earlier. By repeating these "ritual deaths", Dürrenmatt compounds the comic they take place on pages 26, 34, 35, 36 and 59. The "attack" in "Round Six" demonstrates the author's love of "ambiguity", since this is an "acted" "ritual death"! Edgar's attack is feigned to allow him to spy on Alice's adultery with Kurt. As they go off to bed together, the stage-direction reads: "Edgar watches them, grinning, then he dances off left. Gong" (p.49).

One can see the different intentions of the two playwrights in their attitudes to Edgar's attacks. Strindberg's Edgar is a "wolf", a "vampire" who sucks the life out of those who surround him by his constant demands on them. (Strindberg had intended to have Edgar die in Part I, and live on as a vampire in Part II). His self-pity is supposed to be genuine: "It is finished. All that is left can be put on a wheelbarrow and be taken out to the flower-bed . . ." and again, ". . . when one's mechanism fails, then one is only a wheelbarrow used for carrying the earth out to the flower-bed" (TT, pages 7 and 20). Dürrenmatt, however, creates laughter out of the phrase firstly by making it (Helvetically!) Dürrenmattian: "All that is left of us is a wheelbarrow *full of dung* for the flower-bed" (my emphasis) (p.9) and then by repeating it exactly on page 22 and having Alice use it on pages 22 and 66, on the last occasion reporting to Kurt what the now paralysed Edgar is trying to say.[48] In Dürrenmatt's version, it has become, not a serious expression of self-pitying philosophizing, but yet another of Edgar's comic obsessive banalities, what Alice calls his "eternal clichés" (p.41).

Three pantofarcical traits in Edgar's character might be finally mentioned. His vain attempt to prove that he is not ageing is expressed in his death-dance to the "Entry of the Boyars" (the music by the Norwegian Johan Halvorsen (1864-1935); when he suggests to Alice that he should dance it for her, she laughs: "*You're* too old for it" (p.16). In Kurt's presence he does dance it however − and collapses. A subtle change from the Strindbergian original tragic concept makes the scene comical, as will be seen.

Food is mentioned in the original to show how the fortunes of the couple have sunk. The wine-cellar is empty, mackerels are the only delicacy left. The captain recalls nostalgically a meal in the America Bar in Copenhagen: "Nimb's navarin aux pommes"; Dürrenmatt uses the meal for the same dramatic reason, but, when *his* Edgar goes into town (*Round Four*) he claims on his return that he has managed to find the meal, and, since we are not told how he was able to buy it, we must assume that he is again posturing. While Alice and Kurt are committing adultery in Edgar's bed, Edgar's "desires" are satisfied with a "huge dish of cold meat and a bottle of wine" (p.50). When Alice and Kurt reappear (*Round Seven*), Edgar is still eating − "an hour later". The scene, with its very Dürrenmattian emphasis on the pleasures of the table, develops thus:

> *Kurt*:   You're eating?
> *Edgar*:   It tastes good.
>   (Edgar goes on eating.);
> *Edgar*:   It tastes wonderful.
>   (Edgar goes on eating.)
> *Alice*:   Have you been eating a long time?
> *Edgar*:   Long — and well.
>   (Edgar goes on eating.)   (p.51).

This is now the example of "comic irony", since we, the audience, know what Alice and Kurt do not yet know, namely, that Edgar's "attack" in Round Six was feigned (p.47). The comic lies in Alice's dawning suspicion: "Have you been eating a long time?"

Edgar's position as a redundant officer is satirized by his "mechanical" behaviour. He dons a "comic disguise" (cap and sword) to carry out a patently ludicrous task — the inspection of the (non-existent) guard. As Alice and Kurt look at the photo-album and recall bygone days, Edgar is seen "outside": "Stage direction: Edgar, on the props-bench, plays the commander". The direction is repeated throughout the small scene six times (pp. 28-29). The combination of the automatism in his behaviour and the ridiculous futility of the manoeuvre makes for a richly comical scene.

Why does Dürrenmatt present Edgar in this way? F.L.Lucas, in his bitter diatribe against Strindberg, writes that the Swedish author is popular with modern audiences because this is an age "dizzily attracted by madness and morbidly avid of uncivilized irreticences" (op.cit., p.314).

He is horrified by Strindberg's misogyny: "The mind that does not pity Strindberg is hard; but the mind that does not also find him horrible, is either blind or crude" (p.324), and he says of the characters of *The Dance of Death*: "They would be atrocious, were they not ridiculous" (p.387). Even though he sees the characters as "cardboard monsters", he finds the work *tragic*: "The play's real theme is that this Life is a Hell in which we are doomed to torture one another" (p.388). A less hysterical and less "English", and more balanced critic, Elizabeth Sprigge, while treating the play as a "tragedy", saw in it what we must presume Dürrenmatt did. She writes: "Part I is a masterpiece of horror, a caricature of tragedy", and compares it with Ionesco's "grotesque and wildly funny tragedies", which seems to suggest that she had not looked carefully enough at the *modern* genres of "comedy" and "tragedy".[49]

Melchinger points out, too, that the town in Strindberg's island (called *Little Hell* by the locals) is different from Sartre's *Huis clos* only "that he shows Hell not surrealistically but realistically" (*TT*, p.125).

Strindberg's "Fustian x Infinity" (*Report*) seems to have affected Dürrenmatt considerably. He recognized however that the basic "idea" was a good one and from this came the decision to write a parody of *Dance of Death*, for, as Gilbert Highet wrote, you are watching a parody "if you admire the original a little less".[50]

A second reason was one mentioned by Siegfried Melchinger in a review of the Dürrenmatt version, but not associated by him with parody. He noted that Dürrenmatt's characters have "humour": "The true genesis of *Play Strindberg* is seen in the way he (Dürrenmatt) handles Death. It lies in humour. In that blackest of humour from which *The Meteor* came. Strindberg has no humour at all, as far as I can see, in any of his plays".[51]

This is certainly the case in Strindberg's work; what humour one finds is heavy, truly grotesque, ludicrous, demonic and fearsome. Edgar and Alice hate each other; their feelings are genuine. Each time that Dürrenmatt takes over a scene more or less in its entirety from the Swede, however, the result is dark comedy at the most. Two examples might suffice:

In the dance-scene in *Dance of Death*, Alice says: "Shall we repeat it?" and then turns round to find Edgar on the floor. She says: "Jesus!" (Stage-direction: "She stands still, her arms crossed on her breast and groans — seemingly with gratitude and joy"). Her gesture describes a genuine emotion. In *Play Strindberg*, Alice and Kurt firstly repeat the accompaniment to the dance, then: Stage-direction: "Kurt turns round, sees Edgar unconscious on the floor. Alice turns round. *Alice*: Jesus! Gong". (p.30). All three characters then leave the stage. Strindberg uses the scene to demonstrate a development in the relationship between the characters; Dürrenmatt seeks laughter by parodying this development which he finds "soul-searching". The scene becomes a comic one.

In the rarely-played Part II of *Dance of Death*, Edgar suffers a stroke which renders him speechless: "Blu-blu-blu . . ." is all that he can stammer. Alice triumphs: "At last this tongue is silenced . . . You, Kurt, you believe in God! Thank Him in my name! Thank Him for freeing us from this town, from the wolf, from the vampire!" (*TT*, p.112). When Dürrenmatt's Edgar is paralysed, Alice feeds him with soup as if he were a child: "A little spoonful for little Judith . . . a spoonful for little Olaf . . ." and then for four others! Strindberg's Edgar summons up all his hatred and spits in Alice's face. She cries:

"You can still spit poison, you adder ..." and slaps him. Dürrenmatt's Alice sums up *her* feelings with: "Just die, then we'll take you seriously" (p.55). The demonic has been removed from these scenes by the incongruous elements of the comic and the Strindbergian love-hate motif replaced by a comic ridicule.

We can now see what has happened to the characterization of Edgar. This self-pitying "wolf" and "vampire" has been parodied into a comic type, the braggart impostor, by means of these comic elements in the situation. The character is therefore intended to be seen in terms of comedy; the critic of a provincial West German newspaper might be taken as an example of those reviewers and critics who wrote of Dürrenmatt's "cynicism", "nihilism", and so on: In a review entitled "Macabre gruesomeness and cold hatred", the Fuldaer Zeitung wrote:

> Again and again the glowing needle of hate is plunged with a smile into the partner's side. And that makes the play so sadistic: the joy of torturing, of wounding.

This might indeed have been written of *Play Strindberg* – but only if it had been produced as if it were *Dance of Death*. As Arnim Arnold rightly remarked: "Hell in Strindberg is a good deal deeper and hotter than in Dürrenmatt".

★   ★   ★

Dürrenmatt has removed the Strindbergian demonic from Alice. She embroiders while talking to her husband in the first scene (p.8); the scene is a domestic one in comparison with the tense atmosphere of hatred which engulfs Strindberg's couple: *Stage direction*: "(Edgar) looks tired and annoyed. Alice sits *idle* (my emphasis) in an armchair right. She looks tired and seems to be waiting for something ..." (*TT*, p.5). By the end of *Play Strindberg*, Alice has finished her domestic chore, and we see that she has been embroidering Edgar's "coat of arms" for their silver wedding! Could this Alice have struck her paralysed husband – and could this Edgar have spat in his wife's face?

Alice is certainly less automated than Edgar, but her embroidery, like her piano-playing and her "patience", is a "repetitive" activity. The last two activities symbolize the monotony of this hell on earth in Strindberg's play, the "banality of the daily round ... the chaining of people to one another ..." (*TT*, p.125). In the *Komödie*, they serve to increase the comic in the characterization, since they become "automatic" gestures as well.

Altogether, there is a much greater similarity to the technique of laconic bored non-communication of the Absurd Theatre here than in any other work of Dürrenmatt's to date. (I was indeed tempted for a time to see a parody of the Beckett theatre in this "arrangement", since I had just heard Dürrenmatt scoff at the cult of "the absurd": "It's an absurd concept, a very superficial label", he said to me).

The main sources of laughter in the character of Alice lie in her witty ripostes whose similarity to the ancient "stichomythia" was noted by Werner Ross. He added: "In a way, the sentences should be read like poetry, by stylizing the strong, the pathetic and the profound passages into automated chants".[52] For Alice herself is really only a comic riposte; there is no roundness or motivation in her character: she is called an actress *manqué*, yet she remains what Dürrenmatt asks her to be: a member of a "trio playing with precision" (*Report*). Edgar and Alice (like George and Martha in *Who's Afraid of Virginia Woolf?*) are a pair of cabaret comedians, a comic duo, who mock each other from the audience's laughs. They are both professional clowns, both pure "entertainers" (in John Osborne's use and sense of the word), and both distanced from the audience by their buffoonery.

There is (or should be) no tragic here — neither in Edgar, who becomes a comic type and whose clownishness distances him from our sympathy, nor in Alice who, by remaining with Edgar at the end when Kurt finally departs the island, leaves us with a touch of "compensating (if sentimental) hope". Some critics claim that Strindberg's Alice also confesses a love for Edgar. This is true. She says: "I must have loved that man", but when Kurt adds, "And hated him" — Alice adds emphatically: "and hated him . . . Let him rest in peace!" One is left there with a sense of tragedy, or at least of Steinerian waste. These are tragic characters in a comic situation: the play is a tragicomedy. Dürrenmatt's characters are potentially tragic characters in a comic situation, which, I believe, makes this play into a *Komödie*.[53]

*   *   *

In his own production in Basle, Dürrenmatt arranged the whole action as a "game": forty spotlights played down on an almost bare stage, a "theatre without props", but fashioned like a boxing ring. This was Huizinga's "comic play" *a fortiori*, albeit a "game with Death, true, macabre, on the thinnest dividing line between illusion and reality . . .", Melchinger suggested in *Theater Heute*.

The comic of the game is heralded by the title, itself a parody of *Play Bach*, Jacques Loussier's trio which "parodied" the classics. It is the warning also of the "play" on Strindberg.[54] There is an immediate comic contrast between the extrovert nature of the sport (much loved too by Brecht, of course) and the immensely introverted nature of the original theme, and between the Wilhelminian background to the action and the ultra-modernity of the set.

The laughter came, secondly, from the entrances and exits of the characters. The twelve scenes were described as "Rounds"; they were introduced by one of the cast "ad spectatores" and separated from each other by gong-strokes. At the end of each "round", the actors retired to their "corners" to await the call to the next "round". The actors thus appeared literally as "professional clowns", music-hall turns performing their comic numbers. Miss Rubinstein's comment: "The metaphor 'marital war' is as old as marriage. Therefore its derivative 'marital boxing-ring' is only half-funny", seems to me to be wide of the mark. This is a fine comic "Einfall" which makes my point — the work is a comic parody of, or a "play on" August Strindberg.

(iv) TITUS ANDRONICUS

Play Strindberg was the last work of the "Dü-Dü" era in Basle. I had visited Dürrenmatt in Neuchâtel in early 1969 and realize now how traumatic these years 1969-1970 must have been for the author. His illness of that year and his consequent absence from the theatre led to the final rupture of his relationship with Werner Düggelin in October 1969 (ostensibly over the latter's refusal to meet Dürrenmatt's wishes for a production of Lessing's *Minna von Barnhelm*) and Dürrenmatt's subsequent return to the Zürich Schauspielhaus.[55] In the same month, Dürrenmatt had been awarded the "Grand Prize for Literature of the Canton of Berne" and had scandalized his audience by presenting the 15,000 francs cheque to the three "subversive elements" (*Basler Zeitung*), Sergius Golowin, Paul Ignaz Vogel and Arthur Villard, declaring that this trio possessed the quality that contemporary Switzerland was in danger of losing: courage (or "valour").[56]

In November 1969, Dürrenmatt travelled to Philadelphia, where he received a Doctorate in Literature from Temple University. There he declared that his academic career was now completed since he had given

up work on his own dissertation on Kierkegaard some 25 years previously in order to wait for an honorary degree!

In 1970 Dürrenmatt suffered a heart-attack which did not prevent,
however, the appearance of, firstly, his *Sätze aus Amerika* (*Sentences
from America*) (Arche 1970), 91 short paragraphs of reminiscences
of his journey.

Comparisons are made with his 1964 journey to the other "supernova", the USSR, continuing the theme of the relationship between
"those in power" and the "victims". Where the USA is "Rome before
the age of the Emperors", the USSR is more "Eastern Rome", a "Marxist Byzantium" (p.67). These "comparative" thoughts then led to his
short Novelle, *Der Sturz* (*The Downfall*) (Arche 1971), the story of
the machinations behind a Politburo-like meeting which, he told Heinz
Ludwig Arnold in 1975, was "not an allegory, but a picture produced
by reality". The anti-Soviet tone of this work lent a critical balance to
the anti-USA sentiments of the *Sentences*.

There then followed a remarkably creative period between October
and December 1970. Dürrenmatt, now back in Zürich, produced three
more "reversions", *Titus Andronicus*, Goethe's *Urfaust* and Büchner's
Woyzeck, and one original work *Portrait eines Planeten* (*Portrait of a
planet*) which I shall consider in the next chapter.

★   ★   ★

Titus Andronicus had its première on 12 December, 1970 in the Düssel-
dorfer Schauspielhaus and was directed by Karl Heinz Stroux. Dürrenmatt was recovering from his heart attack and therefore did not witness
the "shocked reaction of the audience" (NZZ) to his play. For the first
time since *It is written* in 1947, he had a theatre scandal to his name.
Half the audience walked out, the others stayed to boo the absent
author.[57] The reasons are familiar to readers of this study: once again,
Dürrenmatt added to an established "classic" alienating comic elements which caused offence. As with *Play Strindberg*, he believed that
he could, if not "improve" a poor play, then at least give it something
to say to a contemporary audience.

Dürrenmatt had first seen *Titus* in Peter Brook's rehearsal in Paris
and had always wanted to present it, not as a *literary*, but as a *theatrical*
experience.[58] As in *King John*, his reversion concentrated on the
power of the "rulers" *vis-à-vis* the ruled. Like *King John*, too, it is
clearly a political play, political in the Dürrenmattian sense, that is,

"it concerns us all". "The only people who believe in patriotism are
those who profit from it, those in power, and justice only serves to legi-
timize their power" (*Notes to Titus Andronicus*, p.191), is the theme.

The method was a mixture of the old and the new: the old was
Dürrenmatt's familiar use of the elements of the comic with a "potentially tragic character in an actual comic situation". The original is a
(1594?) disputed Marlowe-like Shakespearean play well known in a
German version of circa 1600 and based on the tragic careers of Titus,
"a noble Roman", and Tamora, "Queen of the Goths". It is an unlovely
horror tragedy, unloved by Shakespeareans because of what Dr Johnson
called "the barbarity of the spectacles". So Dürrenmatt cannot really
be attacked for the crudities of the play – we hear of sixty deaths, of
numerous mutilations, of buggery, lasciviousness and, finally, before
Titus stabs Tamora (in Scene IX), of a "meat pasty" containing the
"kidney, liver, brains and ribs" of Tamora's sons, Demetrius and Chiron,
and served up to Saturninus, the Emperor of Rome. Practically all of
this is present in the original; Dürrenmatt sought to use these crudities
as a further proof of the corruption of "those in power", an ageless,
timeless theme. It could well be, as Hans Schwab-Felisch suggested in
the Frankfurter Allgemeine Zeitung, that it was the audience's ignorance of the original, linked to the poverty of invention of Stroux'
production, which provoked the scandal.[59] Dürrenmatt introduced
a mythical, destructive "Alaric the Goth" as a parallel to the "heroic",
brutal Theoderich in his *Romulus*, another metaphor for the destruction of the western world through the lust for power of its leaders.

Dürrenmatt claimed that he had turned a "play within an outmoded
social order" into "the last rites of an outmoded society", drawing a
parallel with his portrait of Rome in *Romulus* (*Notes*, p.192).

From the audience's and the critics' reaction, it is fair to assume that
the play was a failure on the stage. Lack of space precludes a detailed
study, but the text does show that we have here a typical Dürrenmattian *Komödie*. Titus, of whom his son, Mutius, says: "All your moves
are planned in advance" (p.15), is made to act as a "Fool" by the
inhumanities of war, while at the end of the work, Alarich, having
"disposed" of the last remaining Romans, proclaims that *he* has plun-
dered Rome; the "stupid course of Time" will bring "Huns, then
Turks, then Mongolians, all lusting for world domination" and "the
orb of the world rolling on in space / will die as senselessly as we shall
all die / What was, what is, what will be, must perish" (p.79).

Thus, this last printed reversion brings a familiar warning: only
"those in power" profit – the "victims" suffer as always. And now we
wondered: Would the "new" Dürrenmatt, sensed in the ascetism of
Play Strindberg, seek a new target?

NOTES TO CHAPTER NINE

(i) DIE WIEDERTÄUFER (THE ANABAPTISTS)

1. In *Dramaturgische Überlegungen zu den Wiedertäufern (Dramaturgical Considerations to The Anabaptists* in *Die Wiedertäufer (The Anabaptists)*: *Eine Komödie in zwei Teilen*, Arche 1967, here p.109 (= *DWT*). Also now in *KIII*, Arche 1972.
2. H.Loetscher: *Das Engagement im Welttheater*, Programme of the Schauspielhaus Zürich, 1966-1967, pp.1-3, here p.3.
3. Neue Zürcher Zeitung, 21.4.47. Kirchenbote, 16.4.67. See too H.Karasek in Stuttgarter Zeitung, 17.3.67 and Loetscher, op.cit., p.2. See too A. Dütsch for a very fruitful discussion on the point (Reformatio, 14.4.67). He compares both versions. Note U.Jenny in *Das kleinste Risiko mit dem grössten Effekt*, Theater Heute, April 1967: His Dürrenmattian "Law" of "the maximal theatrical effect" is posited with the question: Will a work ever come which will fulfil the *inner* necessity of Dürrenmattian dramaturgy?
4. Cf. P.Wyrsch; *Der reife Dürrenmatt ist dem jungen Dürrenmatt begegnet*, Schweizer Illustrierte, March 1967, pp.30-32, here p.32. Werner Düggelin had suggested the new version. See M.Biedermann: *Vom Drama zur Komödie, FD I*, pp.73-85. I found the argument disappointing.
5. cf. Dürrenmatt: "One doesn't do it in the hope of finding something definitive, it's more because of the pleasure of encountering an old adventure again". To Leber in the Tagesanzeiger, 18.3.67.
6. C.H.Whitman: *Aristophanes and the comic hero*, op.cit., p.30.
7. These can perhaps be taken as evidence of his rôle as an impostor, since it would appear that, but for one, the works attributed to (Lucius Annaeus) Seneca do not exist. The Hölderlin translation from *Oedipus Rex* (p.15) and from Seneca's *Hercules furens* (line 1228 f.) (p.40) are genuine. The other works are: Seneca's *Nero* (p.41), Seneca's *Prometheus* (p.41), Seneca (p.48 and p.73), his own *Judith and Holofernes* (p.73); he admits that *Kaiser Tiberius* (p.71) was a "pure forgery". Senecan tragedy (or melodrama), which was used as a model for much Renaissance drama, is a particularly good vehicle for the rumbustious Bockelson. Certainly, Seneca was ordered by Nero to commit suicide, but there is no record of a tragedy on Nero – a most appropriate "heroic" character for Dürrenmatt's braggart actor to portray. See C.W.Mendell: *Our Seneca*, Yale UP., 1941, particularly pp.189-200. For the Senecan canon, see Schanz-Hosius: *Geschichte der römischen Literatur*, München 1935 (4th edn.) VIII, 2, para. 368, p.456 ff. Strangely enough, Emperor Saturninus in *Titus Andronicus* would like to have become a poet or a singer (*TA*, p.23).
8. In FD, op.cit., p.162. Dürrenmatt relates how a German friend preferred the more "demonic" first version of Bockelson. He gives us to understand that *It is written* was penned in a state of despair (*GHLA*, p.67).
9. See *GHLA*: "I am a doubter and I doubt and doubt and doubt" (pp. 40-41). It is therefore rather surprising to find the suggestion that Dürrenmatt's plays are written by a convinced "Calvinist": E.Diller: *Friedrich Dürrenmatt's Chaos and Calvinism*, Monatshefte, Vol.63, No.1, Spring 1971, pp. 27-40.
10. cf. in *ESG*: "It is necessary above all that he (man) stumbles around on this earth" (*KII*, p.33). Peter Graves agrees that the Bishop's final question ("the courageous stance of the mutige Mensch") is a meaningful response on the restricted level of the individual, "though the problem of humanity at large remains unresolved". He finds this a typical Durrenmattian paradox. But paradoxes do contain truths. P.J.Graves: *Disclaimers and Paradoxes in Dürrenmatt*, GLL, Vol.XXVII, January 1974, No.2, pp.133-142.

11. The audience quickly recognized the reference to Emil Staiger's attack on modern dramatists during his acceptance of the Zürich Prize for Literature. The controversy is dealt with in my *The Zürcher Literaturstreit*, GLL, Vol.XXVII, January 1974, No.2. pp.142-150. See Dürrenmatt's "reply" to Staiger in his speech of acceptance of the Zürich Art Prize to his "way-out" painter friend, Varlin: *Varlin schweigt: Sprache im technischen Zeitalter*, Kohlhammer 1968, pp.88-93 and now in *TSR II*, pp.60-73.

12. The "mathematical monk", Hans Zicklein, represents the attack on Reason in the play. "My reason will conquer this irrational world", he says, but he goes to the gallows as a comic symbol of the intellectual who believes that the world's problems can be solved by logical reasoning. See G.Waldmann: *Requiem auf die Vernunft*, op.cit., pp.376-384.

13. Judith's "heroic" sacrifice is treated even less seriously than before: "That cursed female heroism", says the Bishop as he sends her to her death. Matthison is still the cuckolded Don Quixote figure and again earns the Bishop's posthumous praise − but he remains a comic vignette with traces of the *eiron*.

14. R.Stumm in the Basler Nachrichten, 20.3.67.

15. For antipathetic reviews, see Jacobi in Die Zeit, 20.3.67, Karasek in the Stuttgarter Zeitung, 17.3.67, Kaiser in the Süddeutsche Zeitung, 18/19.3.67. and Luft in Die Welt, 17.3.67.
    Dürrenmatt said that he was "gradually getting proud of being the most criticized dramatist. That keeps me up to the mark". See Brock-Sulzer, *FD*, op.cit., 171.

16. To Bienek in 1962. Note too: "That the concept of reality has replaced − if not totally, at least to a large degree − the concept of God, becomes clearer when one compares the effect of God in the earlier plays, and "reality" in the later, on the hero or the central character". M.Deschner: *Dürrenmatt's Die Wiedertäufer: What the dramatist has learned*", GQ, Vol.XLIV, No.2, March 1971, pp.227-234, here p.232. See too E.Pulver: *Literaturtheorie und Politik, FD I*, 1976, pp.41-52 for a sensible discussion of Dürrenmatt's relationship to Marxism.

17. cf Bockelson: "I still cannot see a way out, let me go / Wherever the action takes me / Surrounded by piety and terrible trash / *All string along. That's the miracle*" (p.70) (my emphasis). Friese admits to Krechting how they came to believe in the Anabaptists: "We just slithered into it" (p.80).

(ii) KÖNIG JOHANN (KING JOHN)

18. Possibly Bales' *Kyng Johan* (c.1545)? The "original" was "The Troublesome Raigne of John, King of England, with the Discoverie of King Richard Cordelions Base Sonne (vulgarly named the Bastard Fawconbridge"): also the Death of King John at Swinstead Abbey. As it was (sundry times) publikely acted by the Queenes Maiesties Players . . . 1591". It was reprinted in 1611 and 1622, the former year attributing the play on the title-page to "W.Sh". See A.L.Attwater: *Shakespeare's sources*, in *A Companion to Shakespeare Studies*, CUP 1941, pp.219-241, particularly pp.227-228. Also J.D.Wilson: (editor) *King John*, CUP 1954, p.xx.

19. H.R.Linder: Der *Autor als Leser*, Interview in the National-Zeitung, Basle, 16.9.68. E.Plumien makes the point that Dürrenmatt has improved a play which had "many flaws and inconsistencies, many careless passages and a plethora of scrappy plot lines . . ." *Shakespeare im Wendemantel*, Die Welt, 23.12.68.

20. C.H.Herford: *The Works of Shakespeare*, Macmillan 1899, here Vol.VI, p.6 and p.11.

21. *Prinzipien der Bearbeitung (Principles of the Revision)* in *König Johann*. *Nach Shakespeare von Friedrich Dürrenmatt*, Arche 1968, and in *KIII*, Arche 1972. The Principles (pp. 99-101) are also in *TSR II*, pp.179-184. The play was the ninth most performed work in German-speaking theatres in the 1969/70 season. It had 297 performances in 55 theatres (statistics culled from Inter nationes, (Cultural Review) January 1971, p.13.

22. *Zwei Dramaturgien*? in the Zeitung der Basler Theater, September 1968, p.2, and now in *TSR II*, pp. 128-131.

23. To Rainer Litten, *Dürrenmatts Team-Theater*, Christ und Welt, op.cit., Düggelin added that *he* wanted "no covering-up and glossing-over of political and social conditions" (See Jan Knopf, p.120). See too Dürrenmatt's "open letter" to the actress Maria Becker in the *EHM* programme of the Schauspielhaus Zürich in 1967/68: "An actor is more than a rôle-bearer, he is a human being on the stage . . . through him, the stage is more than literature".

24. "One cannot escape the impression that Dürrenmatt's accusation: that our age is losing its humanity, is becoming more urgent with each play." J.Scherer: *Der mutige Mensch*, op.cit., p.311. Ten days before the *King John* première, Dürrenmatt, Grass, Frisch and other leading authors had spoken out against the Soviet invasion of Czechoslovakia. (See the pamphlet *Tschechoslowakei 1968*, Arche 1968, and Dürrenmatt's speech in *TSR II* pp.117-127). His "accusation" evidenced itself later in his involvement in the anti-Britain week in Basle in 1970 (because of the events in Biafra), and earlier in his protests against the bomb in 1962 (see Chapter Six, p.133) and against the Vietnam and Middle East hostilities. His deep concern with the Arab-Israeli problem found expression in *Zusammenhänge (Connections)*, Arche 1976, the record of his journey to Israel to receive an honorary degree. The *locus classicus* for Dürrenmatt's anti-Marxism is on pp.52-56 of that essay.

25. The critics noted the relevance of *King John*. Bruno Scherer welcomed the third Dürrenmatt première in Basle and thought that the author had made the play into a "grotesque and fearful *Komödie*": Weltwoche, 27.9.68. p.25. The National-Zeitung, Basle wrote: "Thus one of Shakespeare's historico-mythological battle-epics, ending with England's glory, has become a cruel satire relevant to our times", while the NZZ saw Shakespeare's "baroque royal tragedy" turned into a "tragicomedy of a ruling system" and an "allegory-like play with a relevance to our own times". If Professor Subiotto's comment: "The *Monstervortrag* may put an end at last to the interminable discussions about Dürrenmatt's political standpoint and dispel the misconception that it is relevant to his drama", means that Dürrenmatt there shows that he is no communist, then I agree. If, on the other hand, it means that *King John* is in no wise related to the contemporary political scene and that it should be read solely as "a work of art", then I disagree. It is a political play. As Dürrenmatt said: "The question really is: Can anyone write *un*political plays? Can that be done at all?" (*GHLA*, p.72). See A.Subiotto: The *"comedy"* of *politics: Dürrenmatt's "King John"*: In *Affinities* (ed. R.W.Last), Oswald Wolff, 1971, pp.139-153, here p.146. In *TSR II*, p.191, Dürrenmatt writes that our age has made us all political animals and that we can read Shakespeare nowadays only "politically".

26. *Principles*, p.99. The two authors made their scene divisions as follows (Shakespeare first): *Act I*: One scene, two scenes; *Act II*: One, two; *Act III*: Four, four; *Act IV*: Three, two; *Act V*: Seven, three. Dürrenmatt thus adhered fairly closely to the Shakespearean structure.

27. *KJ*, Note 5, p.97. Frau Brock-Sulzer has pointed out: "The Bastard is the King's "Reason", but he cannot influence the political action precisely because he is a socially debased figure" *Dürrenmatt and Shakespeare*: Lecture in ACV Freiheit Centre, Basle; cf. Basler Nachrichten, 17.9.68.

28. Dürrenmatt obviously had comic intentions – he said: "We would have had
     all these little Bastards marching along together – and thus created high
     comedy!" (Brock-Sulzer: *FD*, p.187).

29. "The Bastard's retreat is not the renunciation of Reason, it is the querying
     of the possibility of reforms within the system . . ." in *Provokation zur
     Vernunft*, Zeitung der Basler Theater, 1968-1969. Hans Heinz Holz saw him
     as "half beatnik, half Dutschke" in the Frankfurter Rundschau of 21.9.68.

30. W.S.Churchill: *A History of the English-Speaking Peoples*, Cassell, 1956,
     Vol.I, p.190. A translation appeared in the programme of the première.

31. cf. *John*: "Thus have I yielded up into your hand / The circle of my / glory.
     Pandulph: Take again / From this my hand, as holding of the pope / Your
     sovereign greatness and authority": *King John*, V,i, 1-2. Nevertheless, the
     august Times saw this as a "brilliant piece of egregious fooling" (15.11.68).
     To say that "Of course, this is all only comic in a Dürrenmattian sense"
     seems a singularly uncritical criticism! See T.E.Reber: *Dürrenmatt und
     Shakespeare: Betrachtungen zu Friedrich Dürrenmatts König Johann (Nach
     Shakespeare)* in *Friedrich Dürrenmatt: Studien zu seinem Werk*, op.cit.,
     pp.80-89, here p.88.
     Schwab-Felisch in FAZ, 24.12.68. The Handelsblatt actually preferred
     Dürrenmatt's *König Johann* to Palitzsch's original in Stuttgart! (24.12.68).

32. H.Spiel: *Dämonen werden behäbig* in FAZ, 18.12.70, a review of Vaclav
     Hudećek's production in Vienna (significantly, perhaps, in the Volkstheater).

33. J.Dover Wilson: *King John*, op.cit., p.1x.

34. Urs Jenny felt unwell at "the explosive jokes". One wonders why. (Die
     Zeit, 27.9.68). The NZZ (op.cit.) felt that the play avoided "the pure
     grotesque and thus the dangerous neighbourhood of a cabaret-like lark" –
     with the exception of this scene. But there is nothing grotesque here. It is
     richly comical on the stage. What "grotesque" there is, is elsewhere.

35. The character is a compound of the Duke of Austria, in whose grounds
     Richard the Lionheart slew the lion, and the Viscount of Limoges. Richard
     died in the siege of the latter's castle. (Dover Wilson, op.cit., p.xxxviii).

36. In addition, Leopold is made to sound comically "Austrian" when, during
     the meal, he asks in pained tones: "Keine Knödel?" (Austrian-Bavarian
     "dumplings"). It is therefore (comically) fitting that his end should also be
     connected with food – the Bastard enters (Act III,2), bearing Austria's hand
     in a soup-tureen. The Times saw this as an "element of unbridled gruesome-
     ness" (15.11.68.) In his *Dramaturgy of the Audience* (1970), Dürrenmatt
     mentions how the laughter of the audience brought about the "necessary
     gruesomeness" of the scene. (*TSR II*, p.148).

37. Professor Subiotto sees John's entrance with the Magna Carta as "such a
     blatant inversion of the historical facts that it can only be meant ironically",
     but, surely, the author is trying to make a comic contrast between John's
     "conversion" to Reason (p.91) and his illogical "reversion" to stupidity
     (pp.92-93) when he is faced with the Bastard, the cause of his laughable
     death? It is the "paradoxical comic". See Subiotto, op.cit., p.143.

38. The three female characters offer us little: Like Arthur's, their fates are
     "comic", since they are all affected victims. They are all "playthings of
     politics", puppets manipulated by the rulers of their world.

39. I therefore disagree with Arnim Arnold who sees the Bastard as a "tragic
     figure". His justification is that "whatever he does, goes wrong" (op.cit.
     pp.87-88) – but that is just what makes him *un*tragic!

40. Günther Rühle recalled Dürrenmatt's essay *On the carpets of Angers*, in
     which he wrote of mankind today: "Incapable of shaping the world to his
     Reason, he shaped it to his greed and surrounded himself with the smould-
     ering fires of his actions which now redden his horizon, a prisoner of his
     own sins" (In *TSR I*, pp.40-41). Rühle suggested that *KJ* is "the scenic

image of that early insight" (FAZ, 20.9.68). Indeed, but as I have stressed, the play has a positive side as well.

(iii) PLAY STRINDBERG

41. In *DMMK*, Dürrenmatt wrote that *PS* was the first play in which the plot was placed in the actors *themselves*. Before that, he had believed that the plot alone was the important thing (p.285).
42. W.Kayser: *Das sprachliche Kunstwerk*, op.cit., p.196. Curiously enough, he was dealing with Strindberg's *A Dream Play*.
43. Melchinger's essay is in the Reclam edition of Willi Reich's translation. (pp.117-126, here p.122 of the 1963 edition). I have translated Reich's version. See August Strindberg: *Dramen in drei Bänden*, trans. W.Reich, Langen-Müller, Band II, München-Wien, 1964. Strindberg abandoned the Saint Saëns' melody because Ibsen had used it in *John Gabriel Borkman*. See F.L.Lucas: *Ibsen and Strindberg*, Cassell 1962, p.388.
44. See *Bericht (Report)* in the programmes of the première in the Basler Komödie, (No.9, 1968-1969), now in the book version *Play Strindberg. Totentanz nach August Strindberg. Arrangiert von Friedrich Dürrenmatt*, Arche 1969 (p.67). Now also in *KIII*, Arche 1972. James Kirkup's translation appeared in Cape, 1972.
45. W.Mittenzwei: *Gestaltung und Gestalten im modernen Drama*, op.cit., p.73.
46. FAZ, 13.5.61. The play received nearly 700 performances in 1969-1970. It was seen on 33 stages by nearly 220,000 people. (Cultural news, Inter nationes, Bonn, January 1971, p.13).
47. *Totentanz* (hereafter *TT*). P.V.Brady sees these devices as examples of "extreme ritualization": "ritual gestures, trivializing or deflating their verbal context. They inject a certain incongruity, even a touch of anarchy into the situation". Of course, but I think that he misses the *comic* significance for the stage performance – and for Dürrenmatt. P.V.Brady: *Captain Scott in the Cold-Store: Some ritual formalities in Friedrich Dürrenmatt*, FMLS, Vol.VIII, No.1, January 1972, pp.27-39, here p.32. Strindberg in *Okkultes Tagebuch. Die Ehe mit Harriet Bosse*, Hamburg 1964 (cf. Basler Theater No.9, op.cit.).
48. James Kirkup's translation "a barrowload of *shit*" perhaps indicates a lack of knowledge of a) Swiss mores and b) gardening!
49. E.Spriggs: *Twelve Plays by August Strindberg*, Constable 1955 (English edition 1963), p.341.
50. G.Highet: *Anatomy of Satire*, op.cit., p.69. The Swedes were not amused. The Stadsteater in Stockholm answered the parody with one of its own: "Dödsfighten: Arrangement des Arrangements. Der Totentanz von August Strindberg / arranged by Friedrich Dürrenmatt / arranged by Gosta Bredefeldt / arranged by Roger Fernström . . ."followed by six more "arrangers"! See H.Rubinstein: *Der Schauplatz von Friedrich Dürrenmatt*, Frankfurter Hefte, Vol.25, 1970, pp.202-206, here p.202.
51. S.Melchinger: *Was hat der bitterböse Friedrich mit Strindberg gemacht?* Theater Heute, March 1969, pp.36-39, here p.36.
52. W.Ross: *Zimmerschlachten*, Merkur, Jg.23, 1969, p.970. It was strange (comic!) that Jürgen Buschkiel in Die Welt (11.2.69) should misunderstand Dürrenmatt's dialogue as "stereotyped . . . clichés"!
53. Interestingly enough, Irving Wardle, in The Times review of the Newcastle University theatre "English première" in 1972, complained that "in place of hard-edged farce, the piece is softened into comedy".

54. Sister Corona Sharp shows how Dürrenmatt has all sorts of games in his
     version viz. music, dance, cards – and sex. See *Dürrenmatt's Play Strind-
     berg*, Modern Drama 14, 3, December 1970, p.277. It is extraordinary that
     Kirkup in the notes to his translation says that "the title *Play Strindberg*
     is very odd and seems to indicate an unfamiliarity on Dürrenmatt's part
     with English usage"! (p.9.)

(iv) TITUS ANDRONICUS

55. On Dürrenmatt's departure from Basle see particularly Basler Nachrichten
     15.10.69, National-Zeitung, Basle 15.10.69, 17.10.69 and 23.10.69, and the
     NZZ of 17.10.69. H.Karasek wrote sanely on it in Die Zeit (25.10.69) as did
     Melchinger in Theater Heute No.10 (12.12.69). Dürrenmatt then took over
     the former Zürcher Woche and made it the Sonntags Journal which he
     co-edited with Rolf Bigler, J.R. von Salis and Markus Kutter.
56. See his address *Über Kulturpolitik* now in *TSR II*, pp.21-40. Note too: "The
     modern rockers and hippies are the first group to free themselves (in their
     own way) from modern civilization. They no longer ask about the meaning
     of it all, civilization is no longer a prison for them, it is *nature*". (in *Gigantic
     Lecture on Justice and the Law* (1969) p.92). See too *Ds Vouk isch mit üs*
     in National-Zeitung, Basle, 31.10.69.
57. See FAZ (14.12.70) and Die Welt, and NZZ (15.12.70) for good reviews,
     although little enthusiasm for either the play or the production is revealed.
     The text is *Titus Andronicus. Eine Komödie nach Shakespeare*, Arche 1970,
     now in *KIII*, Arche 1972.
58. See *Notizen zu Titus Andronicus* in *TSR II*, pp.187-193, here p.189. In the
     Foreword to the Zürich production of *Portrait of a Planet* (see under), he
     wrote that he wanted the stage to be a "theatrical medium", not a "literary
     platform" (p.5.) Although he used Baudissin's translation as a basis, he made
     his own version of *Titus* – because he believed that the play was untranslate-
     able!
59. "For me as a dramatist, murders and killings are legitimate dramaturgical
     means, for me as a political human being, murders and killings are bestial".
     (Programme notes to *Portrait of a Planet*, Düsseldorf version, 1970). I
     suppose it was impossible for a sensation-drenched public to see the "human-
     ity" of Dürrenmatt's version beside the crudity of Shakespeare's?

Chapter Ten

THE "NEW" DÜRRENMATT?

(i) PORTRÄT EINES PLANETEN (*Portrait of a Planet*) (1970)
(ii) DER MITMACHER (*The Man Who Never Said: No!*) (1973)
(iii) DIE FRIST (*The Waiting Period*) (1977)

Michael Patterson in his *German Theatre Today* (Pitman, 1976) shows that Dürrenmatt was the most-produced German playwright during the period 1964-1974, with 213 productions. Peter Hacks followed with 111, Peter Handke, with 91, Max Frisch 87, down to Heinar Kipphardt with 49. Dürrenmatt's *Play Strindberg* led the list of most frequently produced plays with 62 productions, then came Hacks' *Amphitryon* (46) and Martin Walser's *Zimmerschlacht* with 41. *König Johann* was in tenth place with 27 productions.

Play Strindberg was an end and a beginning. It was an end to a particular chapter in Dürrenmatt's career as a *Dramaturg*, but, likewise, it heralded a new style, a quieter, more economical, perhaps more ascetic, style which took his oft-quoted desire to "write *with* the stage", as far as it could go. "I am trying to write more simply for the stage, to become more and more economical, to leave out more and more, just to give hints", he wrote. "My dramas take place between the lines, not in the lines", he continued.

I believe that Dürrenmatt has again grown suspicious of the "Word" and its temptations for the stage, and is striving to find his way back to the "Image". Again and again, he has remarked how painting was always his first love, how solving the technical problems of painting a picture gives him much greater pleasure than writing a play. In these later works, Dürrenmatt becomes much more clearly the Searle-like caricaturist, the satirical painter to which I have referred. Now the savage wit, the coruscating humour, is presented unvarnished, plain on the canvas, the prose stripped of colourful verbiage and rhetoric. And what is lost? Just the verbiage?

The programme note of the Zürich production of *Portrait of a Planet* quotes from Karl Stumpf's 1957 edition of the Fischer Lexikon on "Astronomy": ". . . there is a large number of working hypotheses (about novae and supernovae) which sometimes assume an *external* cause (collision or close encounter of two stars), but usually however an *internal* cause, an instability which somehow or other induces this enormous explosion within the star". These seem to me to be the ,"themes" of *Portrait*: firstly, the "collision" of two "stars", here the great powers, the USA and the USSR, and, secondly, the "instability" of our modern civilization, brought about by men's greed, lust, lack of care and caring for others, culminating in that loss that Dürrenmatt never ceases to deplore, man's loss of *freedom*. And once again, to present his themes, he has chosen the guise of *Komödiant*:

> One must reproduce the strict form of the work, nothing else. There *is* nothing else, which does not mean that my work is to be performed with deadly seriousness, on the contrary, only great comedy-actors will be able to play it properly".

he wrote at the end of the Zürich programme note.[1] Six years later, he was to close his own commentary on his play *Der Mitmacher* with the same injunction: "Well alright then, but how is it all to be acted? And I answer as the night swallows me up, as it swallowed them all up . . . with humour!" (*DMMK*, p.288).

The première of *Portrait of a Planet* took place under the Czech Erwin Axer's direction in the Düsseldorf Schauspielhaus on November 8th, 1970.[2] The play itself contains 21 short scenes ("Bilder"), seemingly unconnected, but, which when taken together, do form a damning indictment of modern civilization. An "octet" of actors, four men and four women, take on different rôles to show the interchangeability of rank, age, opinions and nationality. The men, Adam, Kain, Abel and Henoch, and the women, Eva, Ada, Zilla and Naema, incorporate the Bergsonian comic law of "the transposition of the ancient into the modern", since the characters (or their names) have Biblical sources, i.e. from Genesis IV. In verse i, we have Adam and Even, man and wife, and Cain, their first-born son; verse ii, Abel, Cain's brother; verse xvii, Enoch (Henoch), Cain's son; verse xix, Adah (Ada) and Zillah (Zilla) wives of Lamech, Henoch's great-great-grandson; verse xxii, Naamah (Naema), Zilla's daughter: a "team" of players. Their "functions", however, are of this century – they play "mankind" in all the various dispiriting rôles of the species. In the Prologue, Dürrenmatt specifically asks that it be made clear that these are actors playing rôles which do not obscure their identity. Adam must *remain* Adam etc. The distancing effect thus created was obviously intended to create laughter, Dürrenmattian laughter, of course, at the wasted lives and opportunities, presented and represented. Because that is what he is saying: Mankind is destroying itself and the Earth – the Earth which, as Adam says in the scene with Cain and Abel, ". . . is a chance" (p.51), an opportunity for future happiness which is vanishing day by day. Adam, who "has seen it all", finishes the play by throwing backstage an ammunition-belt in a gesture of hopelessness. "War is useless", as a solution to human conflict and stupidity. Mankind never learns, has never learned. . .and will never learn? To answer that question, Dürrenmatt returns to the words that he proclaimed 26 years previously in his *Finger exercises for the present-day*: "I am here to warn. The passengers, ladies and gentlemen, should not despise the pilot. It is true, he doesn't know much about navigation and he cannot finance the journey, but he does know the shallows and the tides. We are still on the open sea, but the cliffs will soon heave into sight — and *then* the pilots will be needed" (*TSR I*, p.45).

Dürrenmatt's warnings are the signs of non-human behaviour; he attempts to give us, in a series of "snapshots", a "portrait" of those areas of the world, geographical and moral, where stupidity, lust, greed, lack of respect for one's own humanity and for the freedom of others are to be found: in the Third World, in the polite surrounds of a World Aid organization, in a bourgeois family with a problem son, in the various ramifications of the Vietnam War, in a drug orgy scene, on the moon, and among Dürrenmatt's favourite butts, the doctors and the scientists.

His characters are comic caricatures, lightning sketches of comic types, all played by members of a modern repertory company, as it were. Adam, the major character and "director of the Rep.", begins as the "first god", then becomes a cannibal, then, in turn, the Secretary General of the World Aid organization — ("Unreason and selfishness seem unconquerable, but they too will have to yield and afford a sight of the liberated earth" (p.25)) — a wounded prayer-reciting soldier, a passionate black man making love to a white girl, a member of a drug orgy, a tortured political prisoner, a director of a moon-landing project, the 40-year old father of a 17-year old girl-hippy, an 87-year old ex-revolutionary, then a neurotic scientific assistant to a President — and finally, the leader of the last group on earth before its end! Since the characters are all playing rôles all the time, and since there are no "props", we have a truly alienated, distanced theatre, presenting a "conflict" in our modern age. The four men and four women are meant to represent the whole spectrum of human effort and destiny, photographed "eschatologically", as Dürrenmatt says, in the last dying moments of a dying planet. That the actions and the dialogue may appear "banal" needs no excuse from Dürrenmatt who has always maintained (as far back as *Problems of the Theatre*) that our age only deserves banalities. Now he writes: "The older I become, the more I

detest literariness and rhetoric in the theatre, the beautiful aphorisms
and the beautiful phrases" (*Foreword to Portrait of a Planet*, p.9).

It was plain that the Düsseldorf public at least did not find his argument unpalatable. The *Gazette de Lausanne* reported that "author
and cast received protracted applause" (28/29.11.70). The critics
could not understand this: Schwab-Felisch in Theater Heute wanted
to know just whom they were applauding? For him, the jokes fell flat,
the scenes were superficial, everything was "too short of breath". Yet
when he wrote: "It is just so vexatious how cheaply Dürrenmatt gives
away that great theme of the tragic and the inevitable that lies within
him", we realize that some critics *still* misunderstand Dürrenmatt's
intentions. The "tragic" has *still* to be gleaned from the "comic". He
is still working with Bergsonian means: the clown-like characters speak
in chorus (p.79, when they all recite Psalm 104), or as automata:

> *All*: We are
> *Eve*: Eva
> *All*: We are
> *Ada*: Ada
> *All*: We are
> *Zilla*: Zilla

and so on through the cast (p.16), or in anachronistic modern junkies'
jargon: "Shall we have a fix?"; "Have you had a trip?" (p.46), or in the
linguistic non-sense of the "modern" theatre: "The two-cornered face
of the three-cornered earth eats the round hole of the one-cornered
child", repeated with the numbers in changed positions (p.46), remind-
ing us of the contemporary Peter Handke's device of "Sprechfolterung"
("speech-torture").

The critics were just as cool when the "revised" Zürich version had
its première on three successive evenings in March 1971. Again, they
had to admit that the performance brought laughs and applause, but
Gerda Benesch in the Wiener Zeitung (1.4.71) felt that this only proved
that Dürrenmatt's self-distancing from "true" theatre was only a
temporary solution, while Hans Heinz Holz in the National-Zeitung,
Basle, was among the more savage cities: "*The Portrait of a Planet*
remains vaguely flat and therefore without hope".

Portrait of a Planet showed us the "new" Dürrenmatt – one who
was perhaps too close to the modern political scene, so close and so
concerned that he feels that he has to "go along" with all contemporary
manifestations. As a step in his development as an artist, however, and
that is what this play must mean to us, it shows that my suspicions,
mentioned in earlier chapters, have all along been well founded.

Dürrenmatt is now, more than ever, a man of the theatre — he writes solely for actors, can do without props or scenery, and is concerned as ever with the presentation of a conflict. The play is written with the stage, his theme is political, his ends are obtained by means of the use of traditional comic elements.[3]

*   *   *

From 1970-1975, Dürrenmatt worked as *Dramaturg* at the Schauspielhaus Zürich, staging either his own adaptations (Goethe's *Urfaust*, which had its première on 22 October, 1970, or Georg Büchner's *Woyzeck*, with a première on 17 February, 1972, as well as *Titus Andronicus* and *Portrait*), or helping the company with the normal repertoire. Staging a Dürrenmattian *Urfaust* in the town where some years before Dürrenmatt had charged the venerable Germanist, Professor Emil Staiger, with speaking "Goethe-Deutsch" was a risky venture, and indeed the critics took exception mainly to Dürrenmatt's simplification of the Goethean plot. "Urfaust for Beginners" was the headline in *Die Welt* (27.10.70). The passionate love scenes between a very old Faust (played by the famous 80-year-old Viennese actor, Attila Hörbiger, of "Third Man" fame), and a very young Gretchen were also bound to disturb.

Woyzeck was more straightforwardly produced. Dürrenmatt remained fairly faithful to the original, re-arranging rather than rewriting the lines. Woyzeck had always attracted him as a powerful character study, and we know how relevant Büchner's (and Alban Berg's) monosyllabic character had become to the "linguistic" theatre of the 60's. Three years previously, Dürrenmatt had pointed out that "Woyzeck. . . says very little, he is almost incapable of speech. . .The actor on the stage doesn't need to say much, he only needs to hint at things", which clearly was in keeping with his own newly-discovered theatrical philosphy.[4]

Although both of these adaptations were reasonably successful, in retrospect it was the lack of support which Dürrenmatt received for his work in Zürich at this time that led to a feeling of resentment which he later put into words to Heinz Ludwig Arnold: "No one supported these productions. Brecht always had people behind him. I never had people behind me", which might sound rather childish.

However, one last effort to make a success of the post was in the offing.

★   ★   ★

To understand fully Dürrenmatt's *Der Mitmacher* (which, for reasons which will be explained, I should like to translate as *The Man who never said: No*! in preference to versions like *The Conformist*)[5] — the première was in Zürich on 8 March 1973 — one has to look forward — and backwards: forward to the appearance, in 1976, of the 288-page "explanatory" book, *Der Mitmacher: Ein Komplex* which contained the text, an "Epilogue" and then, in typical Dürrenmatt fashion, an "Epilogue to the Epilogue"! There were also several interesting essays, relevant to the *Komödie*.

But to look back first to the notes which Dürrenmatt supplied to *An Angel comes to Babylon* in 1957: he told us that he had been thinking for years about the theme of the Tower of Babel, mankind's most senseless undertaking. His first attempt at a play on the theme (in 1948) had failed, and then came *Angel* in 1953: "I don't know yet whether the plot will be continued. According to plans, the building of the tower was to be the next play: *Die Mitmacher*. All are against the Tower, yet it is *still* built. . ." (KI, p.248). *Angel* was supposed to depict the "causes" of the building of the tower and we saw how Man's greed and stupidity had led him to reject Heaven's angelic gift. I have been trying to demonstrate that Dürrenmatt's subsequent plays have continued to attack these human shortcomings. He makes clear in the *Komplex* that the Watergate scandal in the USA only served to underline the truth of his warnings over many years. The dust-jacket of *Komplex*, indeed, calls the play a "*Komödie* on corruption", and Dürrenmatt tells us that it was the introduction of Cop's *maquama* in Act V, the Persian verse-form that Akki uses in *Angel*, which turned the work into a *Komödie*, "as I understand, and have always understood the term" (*DMMK*, p.186). Tragedy, he reminds us, is played out against a "fixed background, against that of the Gods of Fate". The *Komödie*, on the other hand, has to invent its background, and the truth of "comedy" is the tension between its invented world and the real world, between illusion and reality, in other words. Watergate was not the first or only proof that the world is in part corrupt, "yet it is the prerogative of the *Komödie* to represent the world as one great

Watergate, to make of its aspects an absolute". This exaggeration makes the world "comical" — and Dürrenmatt cites Gogol's *Revisor* as another "comedy of corruption". One cannot take "seriously" a political world in which corruption plays such a major rôle.[6]

Later in the *Komplex*, Dürrenmatt relates a story which was never written, but which served as the drawing-board for *Der Mitmacher: Smithy* (pp.202-206) was conceived on a hot steaming 3 May, 1959 on Manhattan Island during Dürrenmatt's visit to New York. That was the year of the conception of both *The Physicists* and *The Meteor*. Smithy is a fantastic, Kojak-like story of corruption in the Police Department, a typical soap-opera example of the banalities in contemporary living which Dürrenmatt notices all around us. J.G. Smith, alias Smithy, the last of many names, and finally "Doc" in the *Komödie*, aided by a medical assistant named Leibnitz (!), disposes of corpses passed on to him by a homosexual police chief ("der Bulle", the fuzz) in the pay, firstly, of a homosexual gangster (Holy) disguised as a priest who is then "disposed of" by a Jew (van der Seelen) ("who said he was a Russian or a Pole, was probably an Italian or a Greek, though some said he really was a Dutchman") who takes over the operation. After dissection, Leibnitz dissolves the bodies in acid in a bath and flushes them away from their room on the fourth floor of a decrepit warehouse. After a few minutes passionate intercourse with an expensively-dressed woman who has appeared as from nowhere, Smithy is driven to a luxury hotel to meet Jacob Friedli (= Jack) who takes him to the new police chief (= Nick). There is a big job in the offing ("worth 500,000"), and Smithy is led to a bedroom where the woman with whom he had just slept lies strangled. The "customer" was an English-speaking man whom "he had often seen on TV", "enormously famous" — the corpse to be disposed of is the woman next door — his wife — because she had slept with other men. Smithy is offered a million to do the job, but, disgusted, he insults the man and offers to do the job gratis, since a 'wild tenderness' had arisen in him because "he had loved her". At the end, van der Seelen has Smithy killed for having fouled up their operation.[7]

Out of this "labyrinthine" story, as Dürrenmatt called it, arose, albeit vaguely, *The Man who never said: No!* (*Der Mitmacher*): Doc, a failed doctor, the "unbeliever", is in the employ of Boss, the gangster, while the go-between is the police chief, Cop. Doc does the dirty work himself now — by means of his "necrodialyser" (literally "corpse dissolver"), he disposes of the Boss' victims. The plot is then complicated by an addition to the cast of, firstly, Bill, Doc's son, an idealist Marxist who "believes", who has "faith" in his cause and who

222   The Theatre of Friedrich Dürrenmatt

is killed for it by his father, and Ann, who "goes along with it all", who says "Yes" to corruption as Boss' mistress, but who is also loved by Doc and for the sake of whom Doc is eventually beaten up, while Cop, the police chief, tries to break out of the system and is murdered, by Boss' men.

The audience, and the critics who castigated the play, could not, of course, guess, even faintly, what was in Dürrenmatt's mind as they watched the play on the stage. It seemed to them – as it must to any casual spectator or reader – a fantastic grotesque, founded on a banal idea and couched in banal language – and yet, as the 286-pages of commentary try to make it clear, we are dealing with Dürrenmatt's philosophical *credo* – his theory of the comic as a *Weltanschauung* made flesh. We can see from this *Prologue to the Epilogue* (pp.81-84) and so on, that Dürrenmatt (perhaps even because of his American and Israeli academic distinctions) has returned to those philosophical studies of which I wrote earlier (see p.15 above). The key to the story, the play, to the "new" Dürrenmatt, lies, I believe, in these lines from the *Epilogue to the Epilogue* where Doc relates Cop to Smithy: "This dirty little business man is quite obviously not an ironic hero" – *ironic* derives, it will be realized, from the Greek *eiron* – "he lacks the consciousness, but unwittingly he becomes proud that he is some-thing more than a rat gnawing its way through Life in dubious affairs; instinctively, he becomes an individual confronting a world, not out of megalomania, but out of the self-respect that he has found vis-à-vis a dead woman and vis-à-vis one of the great men of the world. He has stumbled on something worth dying for, has stumbled on himself, on this last insoluble secret which is applicable to the self as it is to the 'objective world'" (pp.231-232). As Archilochos the Greek said: "The world is terrifying and senseless. To keep the hope alive that there is some sense behind all the non-sense, behind all the terrors, can only be achieved by those that *love*" (*Once a Greek*, p.137).

These words show that Dürrenmatt had much more important considerations in mind than a "mere play" when he wrote *Der Mitmacher*. The *Komplex* shows that he was deeply hurt by the criticism of his stage-works produced since *Play Strindberg* in 1969. His bravado remark to Heinz Ludwig Arnold in March 1975 (with reference to Rischbieter in Theater Heute) does not ring quite true somehow: "Contemporary theatre criticism takes place on a level that has no importance for me – even when it sometimes annoys me. You can see that I live well, I drink good wines. . .criticism doesn't bother me. My work is my interest" (*GHLA*, p.46).

But the prose works which have appeared since 1973 all bear the sign of a "retreat from the stage", as if to lick wounds and think back on past successes.[8]

*   *   *

The Gigantic Lecture on Justice and the Law (sub-titled a *Mini-dramaturgy of politics*) with "An Helvetic Intermezzo" added (1969), returned to the theme worked out in *The Physicists*. Reality, that is, the world, is not changed by an individual, but by all — and we are all individuals (p.103). All must "stand up and say: No!" like Romulus, like Mobius, like Cop, which is why I translated *Der Mitmacher* as I did. Dürrenmatt's theatre and his politics are inextricably linked and my study has been attempting to show this from the outset. True justice, for Dürrenmatt, means *freedom for the individual* — and in neither Super State is Man free, neither where man sees his neighbour as an intelligent *wolf (homo homini lupus*, in capitalist countries), or as an intelligent *lamb (homo homini agnus*, in socialist countries). The theme is underlined in his two polemics: against the USA in his *Sentences from America*, that "unstable entity", like an unstable star which may one day turn into an all-destroying supernova (p.18), and then later against the USSR in *The Downfall*, a picture of a country where only one thing was lacking — security. "To be powerful was dangerous" (p.99). The characters, lettered "A-P" and thus as inter-changeable as the political power-system depicted, represent "those in power" against whom Dürrenmatt inveighed in his *Thoughts on the Theatre*, originally published in his own Sonntags Journal in 1970 and again as *Sentences on the Theatre* in 1976. Their petty internecine squabbles for further power are played out against the innocent hopes of the victims of a better world.

These essays and other writings now to be found in *TSR II*, have been continually referred to throughout my study, since much of the material was reprinted from other sources. For this part of the study, however, perhaps the long essay *Aspekte des dramaturgischen Denkens* (*Aspects of dramaturgical thinking*) in (*TSR II* pp.206-231) is worth another look, since, in it, Dürrenmatt once again touches on the importance of the clown for his drama. "Here (as a clown), the actor has only one function: to present a man that everyone can laugh at, the original "unlucky man" who does everything in a clumsy way and on whom inanimate objects take their revenge". These clowns are "end-people in end-games...", "bereft of any social function, seen from inside, he is the internal man *a fortiori* and thus the objectified self..." (pp.222-224) — a thought to which I shall shortly return.

Zusammenhänge (*Connections*) (1976) again confirms Dürrenmatt's interest in matters political: it is an account of his visit to Israel to receive an honorary degree from the Ben-Gurion University in Beersheba. Dürrenmatt had already supported the Israeli cause in *Israel's right to existence* (in *TSR II*, pp.109-116) calling Brecht's famous closing lines in *The Caucasian Chalk Circle* as his final witness. ("That what is there should belong to those for whom it is good...). Here, too, is the *locus classicus* for Dürrenmatt's anti-Marxist opinions and indeed for his attitude to institutionalized Christianity as well. "Just as the Church prevents Christianity from becoming Christian, so the Party prevents Communists from being "communistic" (p.56). We are reminded — and not for the first time — of that Lessing-like streak in Dürrenmatt's intellectual make-up. The true religion lies in our own hearts. Dürrenmatt describes here too the death of his 89-year-old mother — "the sword of her belief still lay between her and me, her victory and my defeat" (p.188) — and the understanding that all struggles on earth are about "beliefs", confirms to him that Israel's struggle is to remain *free*.

*   *   *

To return to *The man who never said: No!*: The seeming banality of the text conceals Dürrenmatt's return to philosophy. We can see from the *Komplex* that, as he wrote in the Foreword to *Portrait*, his theatre is now being played "between the lines". The *Komödie*, however, remains — although Dürrenmatt did stress that "the text does not set out to be comical" (p.189). Yet I would claim that Cop is one of our spiritual clowns; he is the "non-conformer", the one who tries to be an individual. But his plan is scotched when, having duped Boss, he himself is duped by those "who are even more unjust than Boss". And it is the senselessness of his chance death which robs the scene and the play of tragedy. Unlike the tragic death, his serves nobody but himself, it is not a representative death. "He who dies, no longer needs to say: Yes!" ("Wer stirbt, macht nicht mehr mit") (p.167). Dürrenmatt then goes out of his way to relate Cop to those other characters, Romulus, Bodo, Akki, even Titus, whom I have called "valiant men".

Why? Because all of them dared to stand up and say No, they all dared to be free. Dürrenmatt wrote: "The characters I wrote about, conceived in wilder days, are returning. They are my dreams, in which one theme, one simple theme, stubbornly recurs — again and again: the possibility in which I believe, to which I cling, the possibility of becoming wholly an individual, the possibility of freedom" (*DMMK*, p.178).

But Doc, the failed scientist, the intellectual who "never said No!" is "unfree". He, like the other "alazon-figures", hamstrung by an ideology, an *idée fixe*, or, as in Doc's case, by "absolute indifference", only deserves our scornful laughter. For that, Dürrenmatt has always claimed, is the only thing that will move the "tyrants of our planet". His latest play *Die Frist* (*The Waiting Period*) (1977), a typical Dürrenmattian gallimaufry about the "waiting-period" before a tyrannical Generalissimo's death, reiterates the point: The themes of the play, he writes, "arise from the unreality in which reality loses itself". Far from moving away from reality, as Tino Tiusanen sums up the work of the later Dürrenmatt, it has actually been more "aktuell" than ever. As Dürrenmatt would claim, critics need imagination to *discover* reality in these plays (See *The Waiting Period*, pp.11-16).[9]

In *The Waiting Period*, Dürrenmatt brings out many of his old favourite ploys: there is "the inability-to-die" theme from *The Meteor*; there is the "interchangeability-of-power" theme from the *Angel*; there is the "TV-cameramen" theme from *The Visit of the Old Lady*; there is the "world-collapse" theme from *Portrait* and the "operation-by-an-ex-Nazi-doctor-without-anaesthetic" theme from *Der Verdacht* (*The Suspicion*). New, however, is the strong (and strongly-criticized) Women's Lib theme which is represented by the "comic repetition" *a fortiori*: nine aged women, all named "Rosa. . .", Rosa, Rosarosa, Rosablanca, Rosanegra, Rosabella, Rosalaura, Rosaflora, Rosaberta, Rosagrande. The ambience is a Ruritanian-like State (Saltovenia) once left-wing, now on the Fascist right; the action, the fall of this right-wing party and its corrupt support, the Church. (Dürrenmatt, the ardent soccer fan, allows a European Cup game against Leeds United to run through the play, as the Bergsonian "running gag").

Again, the result of Man's planning is nought — but brought about this time by the intervention not only of Chance, but also of Woman: Rosagrande's last grotesque "chorus" vilifies Man *and* his God for their interference in omitting Woman from their reckoning. The "Immortal Women" end the play, Faust-like, with: "What no longer is, was only a happening/What no more will be, was just a simile/The Feminine has as its goal/Eternity and Sterility" (p.120).

Bibliography

A. Bibliographies of Dürrenmatt-Literature

J. Hansel: *Friedrich-Dürrenmatt-Bibliographie*: Verlag Gehlen 1968.
W. Hönes: *Bibliographie zu Friedrich Dürrenmatt*, in: *Friedrich Dürrenmatt I*,
   Vols. 50/51, Text + Kritik, München, Mai 1976, pp.93-108. (To 1975).
K.W. Jones: *Die Dürrenmatt-Literatur*: Börsenblatt für den deutschen Buchhandel,
   Frankfurter Ausgabe, 24 Jg., 23.7.68, pp.1725-1736.
G.P. Knapp: *Bibliographie der wissenschaftlichen Sekundärliteratur*, in *Friedrich
   Dürrenmatt. Studien zu seinem Werk*, Lother Stiehm, Verlag, Heidelberg,
   1976. (To 31.12.74).
E. Wilbert-Collins: *Bibliography of four contemporary Swiss-German authors:
   Friedrich Dürrenmatt, Max Frisch, Robert Walser, Albin Zollinger*: Francke,
   Bern, 1967. (For Dürrenmatt, see pp.13-32) (Only up to 1965).

B. Primary Literature (All published by Verlag der Arche, Zürich, except where stated)

1. PLAYS

Komödien, I, 1957, (7th edition, 1965) containing:
   Romulus der Grosse (1964 version) (first published separately 1958)
   Die Ehe des Herrn Mississippi (3rd version) (1966)
   Ein Engel kommt nach Babylon (2nd version, 1957) (1954)
   Der Besuch der alten Dame (1956)
Komödien II and frühe Stücke, 1964, containing:
   Es steht geschrieben (1959)
   Der Blinde (1960)
   Frank der Fünfte (Bochumer version, 1964) (1960)
   Die Physiker (1962)
   Herkules und der Stall des Augias (1963)
Komödien III, 1972, containing:
   König Johann (1968)
   Der Meteor (1966)
   Play Strindberg (1969)
   Titus Andronicus (1970)
   Die Wiedertäufer (1968)
Porträt eines Planeten, Zürich 1970. (Düsseldorf version, 1970; Zürich version, 1971).
Der Mitmacher: Ein Komplex, 1976. (1973)
Die Frist, 1977. (*Lesebuch*, 1978, contains a revised version of *Die Frist*, as well
   as some unpublished stories and essays).

a) IN ENGLISH TRANSLATION
The Visit, Cape 1962 and 1973. (By Patrick Bowles). (By Maurice Valency, New
   York, 1958).
Four Plays 1957-1962 (comprising *Romulus the Great, The Marriage of Mr
   Mississippi, An Angel comes to Babylon, The Physicists*) by various hands:
   Cape 1964.
The Meteor (by James Kirkup), Cape 1973.
Play Strindberg (by James Kirkup), Cape 1973.

b) SCHOOL EDITIONS

Der Besuch der alten Dame (ed. P.K. Ackermann), Methuen 1961.
Romulus der Grosse (ed. H.F. Garten), Methuen 1962.
Die Physiker (ed. A. Taylor), Methuen 1966.

2. THEORETICAL WRITINGS

Theater-Schriften und Reden, 1966, (= *TSR I*).
Theater-Schriften und Reden, 1972, (= *TSR II*), sub-titled *Dramaturgisches und Kritisches*.
Tschechoslowakei 1968 (speeches held by Dürrenmatt, Frisch, Grass, Bichsel and Marti against the invasion of Czechoslovakia by the USSR). Held in the Stadttheater Basel.
Monstervortrag über Gerechtigkeit und Recht nebst einem helvetischen Zwischenspiel: (Eine kleine Dramaturgie der Politik), 1969.
Sätze aus Amerika, 1970.
Zusammenhänge. Essay über Israel, 1976.
56 Sätze über des Theater, in *Friedrich Dürrenmatt I* (op.cit., Text + Kritik 1976). (pp.1-18).

a) IN ENGLISH TRANSLATION

Problems of the Theatre in Tulane Drama Review, III, i (October 1958), pp.3-26. (Also in *Four Plays 1957-1962* (see above).
Writings on the Theatre (translated by H.M. Waidson) contains a translation of *Problems of the theatre* on pp.59-91, as well as essays from *TSR I* and *II*, Cape 1976.

3. NOVELS AND NOVELLEN

Der Richter und sein Henker Benziger, Einsiedeln 1952 and Rowohlt 1955 (rororo No. 150).
Der Verdacht Benziger Einsiedeln, 1953, and Rowohlt 1961 (rororo No.448).
Grieche sucht Griechin, Arche 1955. (Ullstein Bücher (No.199), 1958.)
Das Versprechen, 1958.
Der Sturz, 1971.

a) IN ENGLISH TRANSLATION

The Judge and his Hangman: (trans. C. Brooks), Jenkins 1954, Penguin 1969 (*Der Richter und sein Henker*).
The Pledge: (trans. R. and C. Winston), Cape 1959, Penguin 1964 (*Das Versprechen*)
The Quarry, (trans. E.R. Morreale), Cape 1962 (*Der Verdacht*)
Once a Greek: (trans. R. and C. Winston), Cape 1966 (*Grieche sucht Griechin*).

b) SCHOOL EDITIONS

Der Richter und sein Henker (ed. L.W. Forster), Harrap, 1962.
Der Verdacht (ed. L.W. Forster), Harrap, 1965.
Das Versprechen (ed. L.W. Forster), Harrap, 1967.

4. RADIO PLAYS

Gesammelte Hörspiele, 1961 contains: *Abendstunde im Spätherbst, Der Doppelgänger, Herkules und der Stall des Augias, Nächtliches Gespräch mit einem verachteten Menschen, Die Panne, Der Prozess um des Esels Schatten, Stranitzky und der Nationalheld, Das Unternehmen der Wega.*

a) IN ENGLISH TRANSLATION
Incident at Twilight, in *Postwar German Theatre* (eds. M. Benedikt and G.E. Wellwarth), Macmillan 1968. (*Abendstunde im Spätherbst*).

5. SHORT STORIES

Die Stadt: Prosa I-IV (1952) contains: *Weihnacht, Der Folterknecht, Der Hund, Das Bild des Sisyphus, Der Theaterdirektor, Die Falle, Die Stadt, Der Tunnel, Pilatus.*

a) IN ENGLISH TRANSLATION
A Dangerous Game, (trans. R. and C. Winston), Cape 1960. (*Die Panne*).
The Tunnel in *Modern German Stories* (ed. H.M. Waidson), Faber 1961. (*Der Tunnel*).
The Tunnel in *Deutsche Reihe für Ausländer*, Reihe F., Vol.III, Hueber 1964.

b) SCHOOL EDITIONS
Die Panne and *Der Tunnel* (ed. F.J. Alexander), Oxford U.P., 1967.

C. A Selection of Secondary Literature

a) BOOKS IN GERMAN
Allemann, B: *Friedrich Dürrenmatts Es steht geschrieben* in *Das deutsche Drama*, Band II (ed. B. von Wiese), Bagel, Düsseldorf, 3rd edn. 1964, pp.420-438.
Allemann, B: *Die Struktur der Komödie bei Frisch und Dürrenmatt* in *Das deutsche Lustspiel*, Band II (ed. H. Steffen), Kleine Vandenhoeck-Reihe, Göttingen, 1969. (Vol.I, 1968).
Angermeyer H.C: *Zuschauer im Drama: Brecht-Dürrenmatt-Handke*: Athenäum, Frankfurt, 1971.
Arnold, A: *Friedrich Dürrenmatt*: Colloquium Verlag, Berlin, Band 57, 1969.
Bänziger H: *Frisch und Dürrenmatt*: Francke, Bern, 1960 (7th edn. 1976).
Bergson, H: *Le Rire: Essai sur la signification du comique*: Presses universitaires de France: (233rd edn., 1967). (Original edn. 1901).
Bienek H: *Werkstattgespräche mit Schriftstellern:* Hanser, München, 1962.
Bräutigam K (ed.): *Europäische Komödien*: Frankfurt 1964.
Brock-Sulzer E: *Friedrich Dürrenmatt*, Arche 1960 (4th edn. 1973).
Brock-Sulzer E: *Dürrenmatt in unserer Zeit*: Reinhardt, Basel, 1968.
Calgari G: *Die vier Literaturen der Schweiz*: (trans. E. Tobler), Walter-Verlag AG, Olten, 1966.
Cases C: *Stichworte zur deutschen Literatur* (trans. F. Kollmann), Europa Verlag, Wien, 1968.
Daiber H: *Deutsches Theater seit 1945*: Reclam, 1976.
Dietrich M: *Das moderne Drama*: Kröner, Stuttgart, 1963.
Durzak, M: *Dürrenmatt, Frisch*, Weiss: Reclam, Stuttgart, 1972 (2nd edn. 1973).
Duwe, W: *Deutsche Dichtung des XX. Jahrhunderts*: 2 vols. Orell Füssli, Zürich, 1962.
Duwe, W: *Ausdrucksformen deutscher Dichtung*, E. Schmidt, Berlin, 1965.
Ernst F: *Helvetia mediatrix*: Fretz und Wasmuth, Zürich 1931 (1945 edn.)
Franzen E: *Formen des modernen Theaters*: Beck, München, 1961. (2nd edn (1970).
Freud S: *Der Witz und seine Beziehung zum Unbewussten*: Gesammelte Werke: Vol. VI, Imago, London, 1940.
Frisch M: *Tagebuch 1946-1949* (1950), Droemer Knaur, 1965.
Geissler R (ed.): *Zur Interpretation des modernen Dramas*, 4th edn. Frankfurt, 1961.

Giese P.C.: *Das "Gesellschaftlich-Komische": Zu Komik und Komödie am Beispiel der Stücke und Bearbeitungen Brechts*: Metzler Studienausgabe, 1974.

Grimm R, Jäggi W and Oesch H (eds.): *Der unbequeme Dürrenmatt*, Band 4: Theater unserer Zeit, Basel-Stuttgart, 1962.

Grimm R, Jäggi W and Oesch H (eds.): *Sinn oder Unsinn: Das Groteske im modernen Drama*, Band 3, Theater unserer Zeit, Basel-Stuttgart, 1962.

Guggenheim K: *Heimat oder Domizil*: Schriften zur Zeit, Heft 25, Artemis, Zürich, 1961.

Guthke K.S.: *Geschichte und Poetik der deutschen Tragikomödie*: Göttingen 1961.

Guthke K.S.: *Die moderne Tragikomödie*: (trans. G. Raabe) Kleine Vandenhoeck-Reihe, Göttingen, 1968.

Heidsieck A: *Das Groteske und das Absurde im modernen Drama*: Kohlhammer, Stuttgart, 1969.

Hinck W: *Das moderne Drama in Deutschland*: Sammlung Vandenhoeck, Göttingen, 1973.

Hinck W (ed): *Die deutsche Komödie*: Bagel, Düsseldorf, 1977.

Howald J: *Ulrich Dürrenmatt und seine Gedichte*: Loepthien Verlag, Meiringen, 1927 (2 Vols).

Huizinga J: *Homo ludens: Versuch einer Bestimmung des Spielelements der Kultur*: Pantheon, Akademische Verlagsanstalt, Amsterdam, 1939.

Jaeckle E: *Der Zürcher Literaturschock*: Langen-Müller, München-Wien, 1968.

Jauslin C: *Friedrich Dürrenmatt: Zur Struktur seiner Dramen*: Juris-Verlag, Zürich, 1964.

Jenny U: *Durrenmatt:* Friedrichs Dramatiker des Welttheaters, Band 6: Velber, Hannover, 1965 (5th edn., 1973).

Jens W: *Statt einer Literaturgeschichte*: Neske Pfullingen 1957 (5th edn. 1962).

Jens W: *Deutsche Literatur der Gegenwart*: Piper, München 1961 (4th edn., 1962).

Kayser W: *Das Groteske: Seine Gestaltung in Malerei und Dichtung*: G. Stalling Verlag 1957 (2nd edn. 1961).

Kayser W: *Das sprachliche Kunstwerk*: Francke, Bern, 1948. (12th edn. 1967).

Kesting M: *Das epische Theater*: Kohlhammer, Stuttgart, 1959.

Kesting, M: *Panorama des zeitgenössischen Theaters*: Piper, München, 1962.

Knapp G.P. (ed.): *Friedrich Dürrenmatt. Studien zu seinem Werk*: Lothar Stiehm Verlag, Heidelberg, 1976.

Klotz V: *Geschlossene und offene Form im Drama*: Hanser, München, 1960 (3rd edn. 1968).

Knopf J: *Friedrich Dürrenmatt*: Autorenbücher, Beck, München, 1976.

Lengborn T: *Schriftsteller und Gesellschaft in der Schweiz*: Athenäum, Frankfurt, 1972.

Mann, O: *Poetik der Tragödie*: Francke, Bern, 1958.

Mann, O: *Geschichte des deutschen Dramas*: Kröner, Stuttgart, 1963.

Marti, K: *Die Schweiz und ihre Schriftsteller – Die Schriftsteller und ihre Schweiz*: Polis 28, EVZ Verlag, Zürich, 1966.

Mayer H: *Zur deutschen Literatur der Zeit*: Rowohlt 1967.

Mayer H: *Dürrenmatt und Frisch*: Neske, Pfullingen, 1963.

Mayer H: *Über Friedrich Dürrenmatt und Max Frisch*: Neske, Pfullingen, 1977.

Melchinger S: *Theater der Gegenwart*: Frankfurt, 1956.

Melchinger S: *Drama zwischen Shaw und Brecht*: Schünemann, Bremen, 1957 (5th edn. 1963).

Mittenzwei W: *Gestaltung und Gestalten im modernen Drama*: Aufbau Verlag, Berlin, 1965. (2nd edn. 1969).

Neumann G. Schröder J and Karnick M: *Dürrenmatt, Frisch, Weiss*: Fink, München, 1969.

Profitlich U: *Friedrich Dürrenmatt*: Kohlhammer, Stuttgart, 1973.

Reich-Ranicki M: *Literatur der kleinen Schritte*: Piper, München, 1967.
Reich, H: *Der Mimus*: Vol. 1, Berlin 1903.
Rischbieter H: *Theater im Umbruch*: Dtv, 1970.
Rommel O: *Die Alt-Wiener Volkskomödie*: Wien, 1952.
Schmid K: *Aufsätze und Reden*: Artemis, Zürich, 1957.
Schmid K: *Unbehagen im Kleinstaat*: Artemis, Zürich, 1963.
Schneider P: *Die Fragwürdigkeit des Rechts im Werk von Friedrich Dürrenmatt*:
    Müller, Karlsruhe, 1967.
Seel O: *Friedrich Dürrenmatt: Das erzählerische Werk*: Huber, Frauenfeld und
    Stuttgart, 1972.
Staiger E: *Grundbegriffe der Poetik*: Atlantis, Zürich, 1946.
Steffen H: *Das deutsche Lustspiel*: Kleine Vandenhoeck-Reihe, Göttingen: Vol.1,
    1968, Vol.2, 1969.
Strelka J: *Brecht, Horváth, Dürrenmatt*: Forum-Verlag, Wien-Hannover-Bern,
    1962.
Strindberg A: *Dramen in drei Bänden* (trans. W. Reich), Langen-Müller, München,
    1964.
Strindberg A: *Totentanz* (trans. W. Reich), Reclam 1963.
Syberberg H-J: *Interpretationen zum Drama Friedrich Dürrenmatts*: D.Phil,
    München, Verlag Uni-Druck, München 1963 (2nd. edn. 1965).
Szondi P: *Theorie des modernen Dramas*: Suhrkamp 1956 (1966).
Szondi P: *Versuch über das Tragische*: Insel, Frankfurt, 1961.
Taëni R: *Drama nach Brecht*: Basilius, Basel, 1968.
Text + Kritik (publ. H.L. Arnold): *Friedrich Dürrenmatt I*: Vols. 50/51,
    München, Mai 1976.
Text + Kritik (publ. H.L. Arnold): *Friedrich Dürrenmatt II*: Vol. 56, München,
    Oktober, 1977.
Vietta E (ed): *5. Darmstädter Gespräch − Theater 1955*: Neue Darmstädter
    Verlagsanstalt GmbH, 1955.
Von Salis J.R: *Schwierige Schweiz*: Büchergilde Gutenberg, Frankfurt, 1968.
    (Orell Füssli, Zürich, 1968).
von Wiese B (ed): *Das deutsche Drama*, Vol.II: Bagel, Düsseldorf, 1958 (1968
    edn.).
Zielinski S: *Die Gliederung der altattischen Komödie*: Leipzig 1885.

b) BOOKS IN ENGLISH
Abel L: *Metatheater*: Hill and Wang, New York, 1963.
Arnold A: *Friedrich Dürrenmatt*, New York, 1972.
Benedikt M and Wellwarth G.E: *Postwar German Theatre*: Macmillan 1968.
Bentley E.R: *The Life of the Drama*: Methuen, 1965.
Brustein R: *The Theatre of Revolt*: Methuen, 1965.
Butler M: *The Novels of Max Frisch*: Oswald Wolff, 1976.
Chiari J: *Landmarks of Contemporary Drama*: Herbert Jenkins, 1965.
Clayborough A: *The Grotesque in English Literature*: Ph.D., Leeds, 1963.
Cornford F.M: *The Origin of Attic Comedy*: Arnold, 1914.
Ellis-Fermor U: *The Frontiers of Drama*: Methuen 1945 (2nd edn. 1964).
Esslin M: *Brecht, a choice of evils*: Eyre and Spottiswoode, 1959.
Esslin M: *The Theatre of the Absurd*: Eyre and Spottiswoode, 1962.
Esslin M: *Brief Chronicles*: Temple Smith, 1970.
Frye N: *Anatomy of Criticism*: Princeton UP, 1957.
Garten H.F: *Modern German Drama*: Methuen 1959 (1964 edn.).
Hayman R: *The German Theatre*: Oswald Wolff, 1975.
Highet G: *The Anatomy of Satire*: Oxford U.P., 1962.
Hinchliffe A.P: *The Absurd*, Methuen, 1969.
Hodgart M: *Satire*: Weidenfeld and Nicholson, 1969.

Jennings L.B: *The Ludicrous Demon*: University of California Press, 1963. .
Jenny U (trans. K. Hamnett and H. Rorrison): *Dürrenmatt: A study of his plays*, Methuen, 1978.
Kerr W: *Tragedy and Comedy*: Bodley Head 1967: 1968.
Kierkegaard S: *The Concept of Irony* (trans. L.M. Capel), Collins, 1966.
Knight G.W: *The Wheel of Fire*: Methuen 1930 (4th edn. 1960).
Kott J: *Theatre Notebook 1947-1967*: Methuen, 1968.
Lane Cooper: *An Aristotelian Theory of Comedy*: Blackwell, Oxford, 1924.
Last R.W. (ed.): *Affinities*: Oswald Wolff, 1971.
Nathan A. (ed.): *Swiss Men of Letters*: Oswald Wolff, 1970.
Nathan A. (ed.): *German Men of Letters* (Vol.III), Oswald Wolff, 1964.
Patterson M: *German Theatre Today*: Pitman, 1976.
Peppard M: *Friedrich Dürrenmatt*: Twayne, New York, 1969.
Potts L.J: *Comedy*: Hutchinson U.P., 1949 (4th edn. 1963).
Richards I.A: *Principles of Literary Criticism*: Routledge and Kegan Paul 1926 (1960 edn.)
Steiner G: *The Death of Tragedy*: Faber, 1961 (1963 edn.).
Steiner G: *Language and Silence*: Faber 1967.
Steiner G: *After Babel*: Oxford U.P., 1975.
Styan J.L: *The Dark Comedy*: CUP 1967 (2nd edn. 1968).
Thompson J.A.K: *Irony*: London 1926.
Thomson P: *The Grotesque*: Methuen, 1972.
Tiusanen T: *Dürrenmatt: A study in plays, prose, theory*: Princeton U.P., 1977.
Tynan K: *Curtains*: Athenaum, New York, 1961.
Walsford E: *The Fool: His social and literary history*: Faber, 1935 (1968 edn.).
Whitman C.H: *Aristophanes and the Comic Hero*: Harvard U.P., 1964.
Williams R: *Modern Tragedy*: Chatto and Windus, 1966.

c) ARTICLES IN GERMAN (purely journalistic reviews are omitted)

Benn G: *Die Ehe des Herrn Mississippi* in *Der unbequeme Dürrenmatt*, op.cit., pp.32-33.
Berghahn W: *Friedrich Dürrenmatts Spiel mit den Ideologien*: Frankfurter Hefte, 11 Jg., Heft 2, 1956, pp.100-106.
Blum R: *Ist Friedrich Dürrenmatt ein christlicher Schriftsteller?* Reformatio, 8, 1959, pp.535-539.
Brock-Sulzer E: *Das deutsch-schweizerische Theater der Gegenwart*: German Life and Letters, Vol.XII, October 1958, pp.12-23.
Brock-Sulzer E: *Dürrenmatt und die Quellen* in *Der unbequeme Dürrenmatt*, op. cit., pp.118-136.
Buri F: *Der "Einfall" der Gnade in Dürrenmatts dramatischem Werk:* In *Der unbequeme Dürrenmatt*, op.cit., pp.36-69.
Dick E.S: *Dürrenmatts Der Besuch der alten Dame –Welttheater und Ritualspiel*: ZfdPh 87, 1968, pp.498-509.
Gignoux H (in French): *Dürrenmatt et le comique contemporain*: Esprit des Lettres, 1963, Vol.31, 1, pp.264-277.
Grimm R: *Parodie und Groteske im Werk Friedrich Dürrenmatts*: In *Der unbequeme Dürrenmatt*, op.cit., pp.431-451.
Haller H: *Friedrich Dürrenmatts ungeschichtliche Komödie Romulus der Grosse*: Germanistische Studien I, Braunschweig, 1966, pp.77-106.
Horst K.A: *Notizen zu Max Frisch und Friedrich Dürrenmatt*: Merkur, VIII, Jg., Heft 6, 1954, pp.100-106.
Jonas, W: *Friedrich Dürrenmatt und die abstrakte Bühne*: Zürcher Woche, 30.6.61, p.17.
Immoos, T: *Dürrenmatts protestantische Komödie*: Schweizer Rundschau 72, 1973, pp.271-280.
Knörrich O: *Tragödie und Komödie heute*: Welt und Wort IX, 1954, pp.335-336.

Kuczynski J: *Friedrich Dürrenmatt – Humanist*: Neue deutsche Literatur, Band 12, Nr.8, 1964, pp.59-89.

Kühne E: *Satire und groteske Dramatik*: Weimarer Beiträge, 12, 1966, pp.539-565.

Lehnert H: *Fiktionale Struktur und physikalische Realität in Dürrenmatts Die Physiker*: Rice University Studies, Vol.55, No.3, 1969, pp.115-130.

Madler H.P: *Dürrenmatts mutiger Mensch*: Hochland, Band 62, 1970, pp.36-49.

Massberg U: *Der gespaltene Mensch*: Der Deutschunterricht, Band 17, nr.6, 1965, pp.56-74.

Mayer, H: *Dürrenmatt und Brecht oder die Zurücknahme*: In *Der unbequeme Dürrenmatt*, op.cit., pp.98-116.

Mayer, H: *Friedrich Dürrenmatt*: ZfdPh, 87, 1968, pp.482-498.

Müller J: *Max Frisch und Friedrich Dürrenmatt als Dramatiker der Gegenwart*: Universitas, Band 17, Nr.7, 1962, pp.725-738.

Müller J: *Verantwortung des Dramas für unsere Zeit: Bertolt Brecht und Friedrich Dürrenmatt*: Universitas 20. 1965, pp.1247-1258.

Oberle W: *Grundsätzliches zum Werk Friedrich Dürrenmatts*: In *Der unbequeme Dürrenmatt*, op.cit., pp.9-29.

Pawlowa N: *Theater und Wirklichkeit: Über das Schaffen von Friedrich Dürrenmatt*: Kunst und Literatur, Sowjetwissenschaft 14, 1966, pp.76-86.

Pestalozzi K: *Friedrich Dürrenmatt*: In *Deutsche Literatur im 20. Jahrhundert*: (ed. Mann und Rothe), Band II, Bern 1967, pp.385-402 and 415-416.

Petersen K-D: *Friedrich Dürrenmatts "Physiker"-Komödie*: Pädagogische Provinz, Nr.5, 1967, pp.289-302.

Poser T: *Friedrich Dürrenmatt*: In *Zur Interpretation des modernen Dramas*, (ed. R. Beissler), op cit., pp.69-96.

Rommel O: *Die wissenschaftlichen Bemühungen um die Analyse des Komischen*: DVJS, XXI, Band 1, 1943, pp.161-195.

Rommel O: *Komik und Lustspieltheorie*: DVJS, XXI, Band 2, 1943, pp.252-286.

Scheible K: *Max Frisch und Friedrich Dürrenmatt*: Rice University Studies, Vol. 55, No.3, Summer 1969, pp.197-235.

Scherer J: *Der mutige Mensch*: Stimmen der Zeit, Band 169, 1961/62, pp.307-312.

Schumacher E: *Dramatik aus der Schweiz*: Theater der Zeit, Band 17, Nr.5, 1962, pp.63-71.

Steiner J: *Die Komödien Dürrenmatts*: Der Deutschunterricht, 15, Heft 6, 1963, pp.81-98.

Völker K: *Das Phänomen des Grotesken im neueren deutschen Drama*: In *Sinn und Unsinn* (ed. Grimm R et al.) op.cit., pp.9-46.

Waldmann G: *Requiem auf die Vernunft*: Pädagogische Provinz 15, Hefte 7/8, 1961, pp.376-384.

Weber J-P (in French): *Friedrich Dürrenmatt ou la quête de l'absurde*: Le figero littéraire, 10.9.60, p.3.

Werner H-G: *Friedrich Dürrenmatt – Der Moralist und die Komödie (I)*: Wiss. Z.U. Halle, Band XVIII, Heft 4, 1969, pp.143-156.

Wyrsch P: *Die Dürrenmatt-Story*: Schweizer Illustrierte, 18.3.63, 25.3.63, 1.4.63, 7.4.63, 15.4.63, 22.4.63 (all on pp.23-25, except 15.4.63 on pp.37-39, and 22.4.63 on pp.37-39).

Züfle M: *Friedrich Dürrenmatt – Der Christ auf der Bühne*: Schweizer Rundschau, LXVI, 2, 1967, pp.29-39.

Züfle M: *Zu den Bühnengestalten Friedrich Dürrenmatts*: Schweizer Rundschau, LXVI, 2, 1967, pp.98-110.

d) ARTICLES IN ENGLISH

Askew M: *Dürrenmatt's The Visit of the Old Lady*: Tulane Drama Review, Vol.V, No.4, June 1961, pp.89-105.

Carew R: *The Plays of Friedrich Dürrenmatt*: Dublin Magazine IV, 1965, pp.57-68.

Daviau D: *The Role of Zufall in the Writings of Friedrich Dürrenmatt*: The Germanic Review, 47, 1972, pp.281-293.

Deschner M: *Dürrenmatt's Die Wiedertäufer*: German Quarterly, Vol. XLIV, No.2, 1971, pp.227-234.

Diller E: *Aesthetics and the Grotesque*: Friedrich Dürrenmatt: Wisconsin Studies in Contemporary Literature, No.7, 1966, pp.328-335.

Diller E: *Despair and the Paradox*: Friedrich Dürrenmatt: Drama Survey V, 1966, pp.131-136.

Diller E: *Dürrenmatt's Use of the Stage as a Dramatic Element*: Symposium 22, 1966, pp.197-206.

Diller E: *Friedrich Dürrenmatt's Theological Concept of History*: The German Quarterly, Vol.XL, 1967, No.3, pp.363-371.

Diller E: *Friedrich Dürrenmatt's Chaos and Calvinism*: Monatshefte, Vol.63, No.1, 1971, pp.28-40.

Esslin M: *Dürrenmatt — Merciless Observer*: Plays and Players, 1963, pp.15-16.

Fickert K: *Dürrenmatt's The Visit and Job*: Books abroad, XLI, 1968, pp.30-33.

Graves P.B: *Disclaimers and Paradoxes in Dürrenmatt*: German Life and Letters 27, 1973/1974, pp.133-142.

Guth H: *Dürrenmatt's Visit: The Play behind the Play*: Symposium 16, 1962, pp.94-102.

Heilmann R: *The Lure of the Demonic*: Comparative Literature, XIII, 1961, pp.353-356.

Heilmann R: *Tragic Elements in a Dürrenmatt Comedy*: Modern Drama, 1967, No.XX., pp.11-16.

Helbling R.E: *The Function of the Grotesque in Dürrenmatt*: Satire Newsletter No.IV, 1966, pp.11-19.

Holzapfel R: *The Divine Plan behind the Plays of Friedrich Dürrenmatt*: Modern Drama VIII, Lawrence, Kansas, 1965, pp.237-246.

Hortenbach J: *Biblical Echoes in Der Besuch der alten Dame*: Monatshefte, Vol.LVII, 1965, No.4, pp.145-161.

Jennings L.B: *Klein Zaches and his Kin — The Grotesque Revisited*: DVJS, 44 Jg., Heft 4, 1970, pp.687-703.

Klarmann A.D.: *Friedrich Dürrenmatt and the Tragic Sense of Comedy*: Tulane Drama Review, Vol.4, No.4, 1960, pp.77-104.

Loram J.C: *Der Besuch der alten Dame and The Visit*: Monatshefte, January 1961, (Vol.LIII), pp.15-21.

Morley, M: *Dürrenmatt's Dialogue with Brecht*: Modern Drama 14, 1971/72, pp.232-242.

Murdoch B.O: *Dürrenmatt's Physicists and the Tragic Tradition*: Modern Drama, Vol.XIII, 1970, pp.270-275.

Reed, E.C: *Friedrich Dürrenmatt's Besuch der alten Dame*: A Study in the Grotesque: Monatshefte, Vol.LIII, Heft 1, 1961, pp.9-14.

Reed, E.C: *The Image of the Unimaginable*: Revue des langues vivantes, No.2, 1961, pp.117-123.

Siefkin H: *Dürrenmatt and Comedy: Der Meteor*: Trivium 17, 1977, pp.1-16.

Subiotto A.V: *The "comedy of politics": Dürrenmatt's King John*: in *Affinities* (ed. R.W. Last) op.cit., pp.139-153.

Subiotto A.V: *The Swiss Contribution*: in The German Theatre (ed. R. Hayman) op.cit., pp.171-188.

Speidel E: *"Aristotelian" and "Non-Aristotelian" Elements in Dürrenmatt's Der Besuch der alten Dame*: German Life and Letters, Vol.28, 1974, pp.14-24.

Usmiani R: *Friedrich Dürrenmatt as Wolfgang Schwitter*: Modern Drama, Vol.11, No.2, 1968, pp.143-150.

Waidson H.M: *Friedrich Dürrenmatt*: In German Men of Letters, op.cit.,pp.323-343 and in Swiss Men of Letters (both ed. A. Natan), op.cit., pp.259-286.

Weimar K.S: *The Scientist and Society*: Modern Language Quarterly, No.27, 1966, pp.431-438.
Weiser E.L: *Dürrenmatt's Dialogue with Schiller*: German Quarterly Vol.XLVIII, 1975, pp.332-338.
Whitton K.S: *The Zürcher Literaturstreit*: German Life and Letters, Vol.XXVII, No.2, January 1974, pp.142-150.
Whitton K.S: *Friedrich Dürrenmatt and the Legacy of Bertolt Brecht*, Forum for Modern Language Studies, Vol.XII, No.1, January 1976, pp.65-81.

e) SOME INTERESTING INTERVIEWS AND CONVERSATIONS WITH DÜRRENMATT
Arnold H.L: *Gespräch mit Heinz Ludwig Arnold*: Arche 1976.
Bienek H: *Werkstattgespräch mit Friedrich Dürrenmatt*; Neue Zürcher Zeitung, 11.3.62.
Fringeli D: *Nachdenken mit und über Friedrich Dürrenmatt*: Jeger-Moll, Breiten-bach-Schweiz, n.d. (Conversation in May 1977).
Joseph A: *Gespräch mit Friedrich Dürrenmatt*: Süddeutsche Zeitung, 8/9.2.69, p.123.
Ketels V: *Friedrich Dürrenmatt at Temple University*: Journal of Modern Liter-ature, Vol.1, 1971, pp.88-108 (The interview is translated).
Litten R: *Gespräch mit Dürrenmatt*: Christ und Welt, Band 19, Nr.4, 28.1.66.
Mayer H: *Interview mit Dürrenmatt*: Programmheft des Schauspielhauses Zürich, 1965/66.
Sauter, R: *Gespräch mit Dürrenmatt*: Sinn und Form, 18 Jahr, Heft IV, 1966, pp.1218-1232.
Whitton K.S: *Afternoon Conversation with an Uncomfortable Person*: New German Studies, Vol.II, No.1, Spring 1974, pp.14-30. (The text is in English, the conversation in German).

Index of Names

Adorno, Theodor, 98
Allemann, Beda, 29, 30, 39, 40, 43, 44, 50, 98, 175
Aristophanes, 15, 16, 17, 21, 24, 26, 27, 31, 38, 79, 124, 151
Aristotle, 35, 38, 44, 50, 118
Arnold, Arnim, 52, 93, 120, 158, 159, 204, 212
Arnold, Heinz Ludwig, 10, 18, 50, 148,172,174,207,219,222,226
Arp, Hans, 14
Arrowsmith, William, 98
Askew, M.W., 101, 111, 120
Atkinson, Brook, 94
Axer, Erwin, 216

Ball, Hugo, 14
Baensch, N., 94
Bänziger, Hans, 12, 13, 18, 76, 93, 94, 101, 120, 147, 174, 175
Beckett, Samuel, 131, 205
Beethoven, Ludwig van, 95
Benesch, Gerda, 218
Benn, Gottfried, 76, 95, 97
Bentley, E., 99
Berghahn, W., 51, 85, 99
Bergmann, Ingrid, 120
Bergson, Henri, 22, 23, 31, 35, 37, 38, 41, 69, 74, 99, 187, 193
Bienek, Horst, 38, 97, 122, 124, 126 133, 210
Bird, L.J., 40
Bloch, Ernst, 144
Blum, Ruth, 97
Bowles, Patrick, 101, 121
Boyd, U.D., 42, 50
Brady, P.V., 213
Brahms, Johannes, 118
Brecht, Bertolt, 9, 14, 17, 25, 26 29, 30, 31, 35, 36, 40, 41, 54, 71, 75, 76, 77, 84, 88, 93, 99, 101, 103, 118, 123, *Contra-Brecht*, **124-143**, 219
Breuer, P.J., 121, 123
Brien, Alan, 120
Brock-Sulzer, Elisabeth, 12, 13, 18, 25, 38, 47, 50, 57, 66, 91, 92, 94, 99, 129, 132, 146, 147, 148, 158, 162, 173, 175, 179, 184, 186, 187, 198, 210, 211
Brook, Peter, 120, 147, 207
Bruford, Walter, 20, 37

Büchner, Georg, 41, 71, 219
Bunyan, John, 39
Buri, F., 101, 120
Burkhard, Paul, 145, 146
Buschkiel, Jürgen, 213

Camus, Albert, 28, 32, 39, 41
Carew, R., 94
Carlyle, 30
Cases, C., 12
Cervantes, Miguel de, 22
Chiari, J., 148
Churchill, Winston, 54, 212
Cicero, 23
Collier, Patience, 173
Cornford, F.M., 23, 38, 44
Curtius, E.R., 148
Cusack, Cyril, 147

Dante, 39
Daviau, Donald, 100, 131, 146, 149
Dejmek, Kasimierz, 227
Deschner, M., 210
Dick, E.S., 109, 122
Dickinson, P., 147
Dietrich, Margret, 96
Diller, E., 145, 209
Dittberner, Hugo, 101, 120, 122
Düggelin, Werner, 188, 206
Dürrenmatt, Hulda, 10
Dürrenmatt, Reinhold, 10
Dürrenmatt, Ulrich, 11
Durzak, Manfred, 99, 147
Dütsch, A., 209
Duwe, W., 57, 92
Dyrenforth, H., 54, 92

Einem, Gottfried von, 121
Einstein, Albert, 133
Eliot, T.S., 31, 40
Ellis-Fermor, Una, 27, 39
Erhard, Ludwig, 53
Ernst, Fritz, 12
Esslin, Martin, 14, 31, 40, 64, 93, 131, 146
Everding, August, 100

Feller, C.M., 98
Fickert, K.H., 122
Field, F., 40
Fontanne, Lynne, 120
Forster, L.W., 95, 121
Franz, H. & E., 173

Index of Dürrenmatt's Works